HUMANISM AND POETRY IN
THE EARLY TUDOR PERIOD
An Essay

HUMANISM AND POETRY IN THE EARLY TUDOR PERIOD

An Essay

by

H. A. MASON

ROUTLEDGE & KEGAN PAUL

London, Boston and Henley

First published in 1959
by Routledge & Kegan Paul Ltd
39 Store Street, London WC1E 7DD,
9 Park Street, Boston, Mass. 02108, USA and
Broadway House, Newtown Road,
Henley-on-Thames, Oxon RG9 1EN
Reprinted 1966, 1980
Printed in Great Britain by
Redwood Burn Ltd
Trowbridge & Esher

ISBN 0 7100 1804 5

CONTENTS

HUMANISM AND POETRY IN THE
EARLY TUDOR PERIOD

Nec dubito, quin ipse sim in his quae attuli, saepenumero falsus, uidelicet, qui lapsos esse illos contendo, cum quibus ego nec ingenio, nec studio, neque usu & cognitione rerum ulla ex parte sum comparandus. Sed quemadmodum Aristoteles pro inuentis a se reposcebat gratiam, ueniam uero pro omissis: ita ego uoluntatem meam oro, consulatis boni, erratis autem in nouo dumtaxat inuento faciles benignique ignoscatis. Nulla ars simul & inuenta est, & absoluta. Si quis haec mea et expolire dignabitur rudia, et explere defecta, fortasse efficietur id, quod cum fructu aliquo iuuet cognosci.

PROLOGUE

'A Central, A Truly Human Point of View'

. . . itaque quoties ad studium accedimus, ab oratione auspicandum est, quod fecisse Thomam Aquinatem, et alios permultos sanctos uiros, memoriae est proditum: idque est orandum, ut sana sint nostra studia, ut nemini noxia, ut nobis et omnibus in commune salutifera: ceterum si omnibus uitae actionibus propositus esse debet finis aliquis, quanto magis studiis, ut constitutum sit nobis, quo pertineat labor noster; neque enim studendum est semper ut studeamus solum, nec ut se animus inani quadam contemplatione, ac cognitione rerum exlex et immunis oblectet . . .

THE reader is not normally interested in what an author claims to have been doing, but in what has been done. He may, however, on looking back, wonder why other things he had expected to be done were not attempted, or he may, on opening the book, wish to be told in a general way what expectations he can count on being met, and perhaps satisfied. A critical essay should always indicate its point of entry, and show precisely in the field of discourse where the main heading lies under which it properly falls. This, however, is just what I am unable to do; for, as Pirandello once thought of characters in search of an author, so the topics I have handled in this essay are still in search of the right head under which they should be classified. My difficulty is that, in offering an approach to a chronological stretch of writing -- roughly, the first fifty years of the sixteenth century—I feel it would be equally misleading to the reader to label this enquiry critical or historical. If it did not sound too pretentious, I should be inclined to say that the object of the essay is to question the propriety of this dichotomy.

At any rate my point of entry may be roughly described as joining in the debate that has been going on for the last twenty-five years on the aims and methods of literary study by questioning the aims and methods of the current literary historians and literary critics who have written on the authors and their times in the period from the birth of Sir Thomas More to the death of Sir Thomas Wyatt. It is my hope that the comments I have made on these authors and their times will at least serve to sharpen the reader's sense that the issues in the modern debate are perplexing and the consequences of choosing sides in the debate are far-reaching. What I am more confident of having done is to show that it is an illusion to think that these authors and their times can be studied in isolation from the contemporary debate. This confidence emboldens me to sketch for the reader's convenience what I take to be the inevitable context of perplexities both for this essay and any similar enquiry into the literature of the past.

An instance of the questionable dichotomy may be found in the current distinction between fact and opinion. The reasons why this distinction is often invidious are obvious. Every reader has had the experience of looking for help from a work of literary criticism and finding instead of insight into facts, a welter of fiction. In reaction, the reader is apt to long, not for true opinions, but for something the opposite (he feels) of opinion. In a similar mood, Mr Eliot once wrote: 'it is fairly certain that 'interpretation' is only legitimate when it is not interpretation at all, but merely putting the reader in possession of facts which he would otherwise have missed.' So strong was his dislike of what passes for literary criticism that he added, 'any book, any essay, any note in *Notes and Queries*, which produces a fact even of the lowest order about a work of art is a better piece of work than nine-tenths of the most pretentious critical journalism, in journals or in books.' And under the *afflatus* of this mood, he went so far as to say: '*fact* cannot corrupt taste; it can at worst gratify one taste—a taste for history, let us say, or antiquities or biography—under the illusion that it is assisting another. The real corrupters are those who supply opinion or fancy.'

The satisfaction with which we read these lines derives in great measure from the gratification of a longing that, I suppose, every reader has: to remove literary discussions from the realm of the personal or merely personal. At one time this longing and loathing were expressed in another distinction, between 'objective' and 'subjective'. People longed to make the study of our literature an objective study and to banish from it what was thought to be an undesirable subjective element. Above all, people in *academies* tried to distinguish their literary pursuits from those of people styled by the university

2

professors of literature, journalists or fabricators of *belles-lettres*. At the other extreme we have those who regard these English professors as themselves literary *dilettanti*, more interested in empty 'appreciation' than in establishing the facts. This extreme view, however, that the study of literature is a science—*Literaturwissenschaft*—dealing with facts such as those handled by the sciences related to mathematics, is not popular to-day. Nevertheless traces of the shame felt by professors of our literature at not being able to make this claim for their profession and their endeavour to make the study of literature appear as 'scientific' as possible can still be found, as, for instance, in the use of the word 'research' to characterise intensive literary studies. If we confine our view for the moment to professional studies, I think a world survey would show that a misplaced respect for 'fact' and a misplaced distrust of 'opinion' still characterise the universities' share in the recreation of the masterpieces of our literature.

For if this is what we study literature for, if literature exists as *experience*, something we take in and in a sense recreate, it can never be properly described or handled at all with tools that do not belong to this order of reality. Literature, that is, cannot be thought of as something *totally* outside us, if, to side-step metaphysics, we are allowed to use the word 'outside' for the 'objects' we see with our eyes. If so, we must abandon the ideal implied in the word 'objective' as illusory. Our objects are unattainable without mixing ourselves with them. On the other hand, our objects when we study literature are not merely private moods. I shall not labour to *prove* that literature is sufficiently non-subjective for two people to be able to argue about it, that a given work is the same for two minds: I simply assume that the experience of ages that great poems are in a real sense the common property of mankind is not an illusion.

A more difficult claim to refute is that, in studying literature, there are two separate roads, or two separate acts to perform: the descriptive and the evaluative; that there is a real distinction in our experience of literature; that in one act we possess it in a neutral, public way as it lies inertly before us, and in this act we describe the facts of literature, and in a separate act we add on to this experience something private, our considered opinion of what we have possessed. This view can be expressed with great metaphysical refinement in a form I am quite unable to follow. Where, however, it descends to my level, and forms one of the perplexities this essay hopes to grapple with, is in the consequence often drawn from this distinction, that there are two distinct branches of study, one, that of the literary scholar, concerned with fact, the other, that of the literary critic, confined to expression of opinion. This distinction has indeed dogged me at every step and forced me to the attempt to demonstrate that it is a distraction from the true pursuit of literary studies. The formulation of the distinction I have most often returned to is that made long ago by Mr F. W. Bateson. It may not be the most brilliant, but I have found it more provocative of thought than many longer and more pretentious discussions of the differences between the literary historian and the literary critic. What gives weight to Mr Bateson's remarks is that they arose out of a concern for practice. He himself composed an experimental literary history embodying his ideas and was thereupon challenged to a sharper formulation of his beliefs. The exchange of ideas between himself and Mr Leavis is still after all these days a model which I, at least, am grateful to be able to fall back upon here.

The arguments that concern us now are those used to support the view that literary history consists of facts that can be *proved* to be true, whereas literary criticism can never rise beyond opinions whose truth cannot be brought to a public test. As I am not about to engage in controversy over the exact ground covered by Mr Bateson and Mr Leavis, the reader is referred to the pages of *Scrutiny* (vol. iv, pp. 181–7). For my purpose a few quotations from Mr Bateson will suffice.

'A critical judgement . . . is the expression of an immediate intuition. In its entirety it is necessarily inexplicable and incommunicable. . . . An element of faith, on the reader's part, and of impressiveness or persuasiveness on the writer's, must always enter into the effective propagation of every form of literary criticism. For a literary historian, on the other hand, and for the readers of literary historians, life is much simpler. Here there are no difficulties of communication at all. A historical thesis . . . either proves or disproves itself. The historian has simply to present his reader with the evidence upon which he has himself based his conclusion, and if the evidence proves to be trustworthy and adequate his reader can have no alternative except to concur in it.'

And to reinforce the point, Mr Bateson adds:

'The qualifications of a good critic and a good historian are . . . very different. The intuitions of the critic emerge from a temperament worlds away from the sober evidence-weighing of the historian. Taste, literary skill, a certain self-confidence, and finally an imperious urge to impose order upon the chaos of contemporary opinion— these are perhaps the *desiderata* of criticism. Literary history, on the

4

other hand, demands the more prosaic virtues only of curiosity, learning, patience and accuracy.'

These remarks prompted me to ask myself a question I owe it to the reader to answer in these prefatory remarks: what is the ordering principle in virtue of which I may claim to have a subject or a theme? For when this principle is grasped and we hold firmly to what it is the essential business of literary study to be, then we see that the distinction Mr Bateson sets up falls away, that the true facts of literature are not opposed to opinions in the way he would suggest, and consequently, that the methods by which facts are found and established cannot be divided, as he would wish, into the scholarly and the critical. My reaction, then, to Mr Bateson was to remind myself as vigorously as I could of the tradition by virtue of which we claim to be civilised people and in the framework of which all our literary studies find their place and their justification.

The embarrassing thing, however, is that this tradition no longer seems to speak with one voice, and the words of Heracleitos, as Mr Eliot saw, have come to have a new and poignant meaning for us:

τοῦ λόγου δ' ἐόντος ξυνοῦ, ζώουσιν οἱ πολλοί ὡς ἰδίαν ἔχοντες φρόνησιν.

Consequently, in setting out the guiding principle in literary studies which I certainly did not invent and could not dare to deviate from without the self-charge of eccentricity, I must seem to be challenging the fundamental beliefs of other champions of tradition, such as Professor C. S. Lewis. Modesty alone, therefore, would counsel me to shift my ground and say, whether I am recalling eminent opponents to the common ground from which they have strayed, or whether I am wrenching tradition to suit views alien to the great tradition in which I mistakenly believe I stand, my starting points lie within the following mosaic of key formulations by what I take to be eminent spokesmen of that tradition.

In searching, then, for what I was to look for in considering the literature of the first fifty years of the sixteenth century, I took Matthew Arnold's essay *The Study of Poetry* as my guide. This essay is not generally found satisfactory; indeed, it is commonly used—in excerpts—to ridicule Arnold. Many of its key phrases, taken out of context, or without regard to the meaning Arnold gave them, have a bizarre look and an odd ring in our ears. It would be useless, for example, to say without qualification that literature deserves study because of its *high seriousness*. Even when we make out what Arnold meant by this phrase and even when we find an apt modern translation, it would be awkward to begin the justification of any literary

5

studies *there*. Perhaps a less notorious passage will prove more immediately acceptable:

'Sainte-Beuve relates that Napoleon one day said, when somebody was spoken of in his presence as a charlatan: "Charlatan as much as you please; but where is there *not* charlatanism?"—"Yes," answers Sainte-Beuve, "in politics, in the art of governing mankind, that is perhaps true. But in the order of thought, in art, the glory, the eternal honour is that charlatanism shall find no entrance; herein lies the inviolableness of that noble portion of man's being." It is admirably said, and let us hold fast to it. In poetry, which is thought and art in one, it is the glory, the eternal honour, that charlatanism shall find no entrance; that this noble sphere be kept inviolate and inviolable. Charlatanism is for confusing or obliterating the distinctions between excellent and inferior, sound and unsound or only half-sound, true and untrue or only half-true. It is charlatanism, conscious or unconscious, whenever we confuse or obliterate these. And in poetry, more than anywhere else, it is unpermissible to confuse or obliterate them. For in poetry the distinction between excellent and inferior, sound and unsound or only half-sound, true and untrue or only half-true, is of paramount importance.'

To this passage on charlatanism I should like to add, as it were, a dash of bitter from a *nouvelle* by Henry James, written in 1884, and reprinted in *Stories Revived: First Series*, entitled *The Author of 'Beltraffio'*. There the hero, a distinguished novelist, gives the following warning to a younger practitioner:

'If you're going into this kind of thing there's a fact you should know beforehand; it may save you some disappointment. There's a hatred of art, there's a hatred of literature—I mean of the genuine kinds. Oh the shams—*those* they'll swallow by the bucket!'
(quoted from the New York edition)

But to set out the theme of my essay I need a document which goes outside literature and brings out the distinction between the genuine and the sham in human terms.

'Somewhere inside there is a great chagrin and a gnawing discontent. The body is, in its spontaneous natural self, dead or paralysed. It has only the secondary life of a circus dog, acting up and showing off: and then collapsing.
'What life could it have, of itself? The body's life is the life of sensations and emotions. The body feels real hunger, real thirst, real

6

joy in the sun or the snow, real pleasure in the smell of roses or the look of a lilac bush; real anger, real sorrow, real love, real tenderness, real warmth, real passion, real hate, real grief. All the emotions belong to the body, and are only recognised by the mind. We may hear the most sorrowful piece of news, and only feel a mental excitement. Then, hours after, perhaps in sleep, the awareness may reach the bodily centres, and true grief wrings the heart.

'How different they are, mental feelings and real feelings. To-day, many people live and die without having had any real feelings— though they have had a "rich emotional life" apparently, having showed strong mental feeling. But it is all counterfeit.'

This is taken from a pamphlet by D. H. Lawrence *A Propos of Lady Chatterley's Lover*. To-day, Lawrence argues, we are

'creatures whose active emotional self has no real existence, but is all reflected downwards from the mind. Our education from the start has *taught* us a certain range of emotions, what to feel and what not to feel, and how to feel the feelings we allow ourselves to feel. All the rest is just non-existent. The vulgar criticism of any new good book is: Of course nobody ever felt like that!—People allow themselves to feel a certain number of finished feelings. So it was in the last century. This feeling only what you allow yourselves to feel at last kills all capacity for feeling, and in the higher emotional range you feel nothing at all. This has come to pass in our present century. The higher emotions are strictly dead. They have to be faked.

'And by higher emotions we mean love in all its manifestations, from genuine desire to tender love, love of our fellowmen, and love of God: we mean love, joy, delight, hope, true indignant anger, passionate sense of justice and injustice, truth and untruth, honour and dishonour, and real belief in *anything*: for belief is a profound emotion that has the mind's connivance. All these things, to-day, are more or less dead. We have in their place the loud and sentimental counterfeit of all such emotion.'

The trouble with quotations from Lawrence, and especially from a pamphlet connected with *Lady Chatterley's Lover*, is that we are too inclined to treat the author as a specialist or a crank. Hence we overlook the fact that, like all great and original artists, Lawrence was reaffirming and recreating the most orthodox of our traditions. For, as he says in this pamphlet, he was concerned, on the side of the Pope, to draw attention to the *essential nature of the human being*.

7

To bring out the orthodoxy of Lawrence's 'line', let me adduce Samuel Johnson, who makes what is in essence the same plea on the same subject: the difference between real and counterfeit feelings, especially feelings of love. The following comes from the *Life of Dryden*:

'Upon all occasions that were presented he studied rather than felt, and produced sentiments not such as Nature enforces, but meditation supplies. With the simple and elemental passions, as they spring separate in the mind, he seems not much acquainted, and seldom describes them but as they are complicated by the various relations of society and confused in the tumults and agitations of life. . . .

'Love, as it subsists in itself, with no tendency but to the person loved, and wishing only for correspondent kindness, such love as shuts out all other interest, the Love of the Golden Age, was too soft and subtle to put his faculties in motion. He hardly conceived it but in its turbulent effervescence with some other desires. . . .

'He is therefore, with all his variety of excellence, not often pathetick; and had so little sensibility of the power of effusions purely natural that he did not esteem them in others. Simplicity gave him no pleasure. . . .

'We do not always know our own motives. I am not certain whether it was not rather the difficulty which he found in exhibiting the genuine operations of the heart than a servile submission to an injudicious audience that filled his plays with false magnificence. It was necessary to fix attention; and the mind can be captivated only by recollection or by curiosity; by reviving natural sentiments or impressing new appearances of things; sentences were readier at his call than images: he could more easily fill the ear with some splendid novelty than awaken those ideas that slumber in the heart.'

'Those ideas that slumber in the heart'—there, in Arnold's phrase, is something to hold fast to, since it describes what weds us to the great work of art. Because of this, the study of literature can never be an external relation, an approximation of two things that make only external contact.

I hope that the variety of examples chosen—and I could add many more—will allow me to return to the argument of Arnold's essay without being charged with advocating a specifically nineteenth-century point of view. The two starting-points I derive from it are that literature matters to us because its essence is bound up with our essential human nature, and, secondly, that the literature that so matters is made up of the great works. What is salutary, what is formative, in the ways I have hinted at by quoting from Lawrence and Johnson, is the best. I therefore begin from this remark:

'So high is that benefit, the benefit of clearly feeling and of deeply enjoying the really excellent, the truly classic in poetry, that we do well . . . to set it fixedly before our minds as our object in studying poets and poetry, and to make the desire of attaining it the one principle to which, as the *Imitation* says, whatever we may read or come to know, we always return. *Cum multa legeris et cognoveris, ad unum semper oportet redire principium.*'

So far I may seem to have been trifling with the reader's patience, for who doubts or questions these generalities? The first outcry arises when we press the word 'study'. Clearly feeling and deeply enjoying sound like dilettante activities and make no special call on the general reader to become a student. At the risk of giving pain, I must brand as a vice the form of enjoyment, even of deep enjoyment, that characterises the dilettante and differentiates him from the student. The dilettante, first of all, only bothers with authors who please him: he reads, as we say, purely for pleasure. In defence of this practice, we might say that no other sort of reading is likely to yield much profit, for the access of a work of literature to our minds is solely through the channel of pleasure: the work of literature cannot be recreated unless it pleases. There is no vice here. Yet it is characteristic of the dilettante as distinct from the student to seek his own pleasure rather than the pleasure proper to the work of art. Characteristic, too, of the dilettante is the remark: 'Ah, I have my own Shakespeare, leave me to enjoy Shakespeare in my own way. My enjoyment is genuine, my reading is not tainted by ulterior motives or the suggestions of other minds.' The objection to this is, at bottom, that the dilettante has made an inferior choice. He has certainly found enjoyment, he has been pleased, but he might have had a different enjoyment. The strength of the case against the dilettante lies in the fact that all great works of literature demand of us a sort of self-sacrifice, a disposition to lose ourselves and our personality before we can recover them. We must be lost and found in the great work. The dilettante is never lost and he tends to find only himself. And this happens because of the deliberate set of his mind. His pleasure comes first and foremost, he tends to ignore or slide over what appear as difficulties in the great work. In a word, the 'otherness' of the masterpiece eludes him.

When we are thinking of masterpieces of the past, as most of them

9

are, the argument can be put positively. To feel clearly and enjoy deeply what is really there involves labour. There is no great author of the past who can be fully enjoyed by us without taking pains to equip ourselves with necessary knowledge other than what presents itself at a first reading. The question is: how much knowledge and of what sort? Here I must give pain to another class of reader, the advocate of 'wide reading' and the loaded university syllabus. A comparison of the indexes of this essay and those of the two current standard treatments of my period, *Early Tudor Poetry* by Professor J. M. Berdan and *English Literature in the Sixteenth Century excluding Drama* by Professor C. S. Lewis, will show how scandalously little reading I advocate, or how monstrous and unnecessary an amount of attention to the unimportant these eminent scholars recommend.

Yet that study involves some width of reading is clear if we put an extreme case, and ask what would be deficient as study in devoting oneself to the works of a single great author? The answer comes if we ask a counter-question: why not one single work of a great author? It is, clearly, that, great as is the understanding of our essential human nature that may be obtained from a single master-piece, we need something to measure it by, there must be something to compare it with. We know this from our private history. There was a time when, say, *Lorna Doone* was our standard of epic narrative. Clearly, then, our minimum equipment for clearly feeling and deeply enjoying must be the study of a sufficient number of masterpieces. But how many? Here we must distinguish the ideal from a respectable and valuable practical possibility. Ideally, we cannot advance our judgements about great works with any confidence, we cannot claim authority for them, if the great works we know are very few. Yet when we consider what a sound taste was often acquired by men who based their standards of judgement almost exclusively on the Bible, Shakespeare and Milton, we should not underestimate what we might do by devoting ourselves seriously to very few masterpieces. This was well said by Coleridge in his *Biographia Literaria*:

'It is noticeable, how limited an acquaintance with the master-pieces of art will suffice to form a correct and even a sensitive taste, where none but master-pieces have been seen and admired: while on the other hand, the most correct notions, and the widest acquaintance with works of excellence of all ages and countries, will not perfectly secure us against the contagious familiarity with the far more numerous offspring of tastelessness or of a perverted taste.'

This will not meet the arguments of those in favour of wide reading, for they could plausibly continue: 'Besides comparing one masterpiece with another, must we not for the same reason compare the work of the master with that of his contemporaries and predecessors? How else can we appreciate the master's superior use of the resources open to him unless we can point to an inferior use of the same resources?' I do not find this a very strong argument when by master we mean one of the very great, whose greatness is not in dispute. We have always our own inferior minds to compare with his. Comparison with inferior contemporaries is useful when we wish to show that in a poor period one author is very much superior to others. And in fact those who advocate wide reading among minor authors do not use this as their main argument, since very few comparisons of minor and major are needed even in a borderline case where we do not on first reading recognise a good work as major.

A much stronger argument is that our proper study is not individual masterpieces but a literature, a vast stream of writing in which the masterpieces are borne along. This is true, and yet I do not think it justifies the reading of many minor works. For this argument misrepresents the relation of the great work to the literary tradition. In the metaphor of the stream the great writer is improperly merged with the mass. At best he emerges as the crest of a wave and the argument runs, would it not be natural to make our study of the whole wave? We can see that this argument will not work by asking ourselves whether we should have an object of study if there were no supreme authors. There would still be a stream of writing—but why should we bother with it? The stream is only worth study because there are masters: the masters in fact make the stream. Literature begins to be interesting when a master first produces a masterpiece. The great work kills the possibility of similar great work until the language changes with changes in sensibility and the possibility of another masterpiece emerges. The study of literature is thus essentially the study of the relations between masterpieces: and all the masterpieces. For it is perfectly true that full understanding of any one masterpiece involves relating it to all the others. This thought is taken from Mr Eliot:

'No poet, no artist of any art, has his complete meaning alone. His significance, his appreciation is the appreciation of his relation to the dead poets and artists. You cannot value him alone; you must set him, for contrast and comparison, among the dead. I mean this as a principle of aesthetic, not merely historical, criticism. The necessity that he shall conform, that he shall cohere, is not one-sided; what happens when a new work of art is created is something that happens

11

simultaneously to all the works of art which preceded it. The existing monuments form an ideal order among themselves, which is modified by the introduction of the new (the really new) work of art among them. The existing order is complete before the new work arrives; for order to persist after the supervention of novelty, the *whole* existing order must be, if ever so slightly, altered; and so the relations, proportions, values of each work of art toward the whole are readjusted. . . .'

When I ask myself what makes me resist the popular notion that a great work is the product of inferior works or is essentially continuous with inferior works, I find myself going back to the passage where Arnold contrasts the romance-poetry of France with the poetry of Chaucer:

'If we ask ourselves wherein consists the immense superiority of Chaucer's poetry over the romance-poetry—why it is that in passing from this to Chaucer we suddenly feel ourselves to be in another world, we shall find that his superiority is both in the substance of his poetry and in the style of his poetry. His superiority in substance is given by his larger, free, simple, clear yet kindly view of human life,—so unlike the total want, in the romance-poets, of all intelligent command of it. Chaucer has not their helplessness; he has gained the power to survey the world from a central, a truly human point of view.'

Here Arnold gives us the traditional account of what authors we should study and the spirit in which we should study them. I like the phrase 'the power to survey the world from a central, a truly human point of view'—as long as we do not regard as the criterion of greatness the explicit judgements the poet draws from his observations. Arnold lends himself to this perversion by using the phrase 'criticism of life', but his selected touchstones show that, though he included explicit judgements, he also regarded as supreme examples of the great the dramatic expression in which the wisdom is implicit.

Lastly, it has always been part of the traditional account that the authors we should study are those who strike us as living to-day. For a contemporary formulation of this view, I turn to Mr Leavis, who when reviewing the *Oxford Book of Seventeenth Century Verse* wrote:[1]

'After ninety pages of (with some minor representation) Fulk

[1] *Scrutiny*, vol. iv, pp. 236–7.

Greville, Chapman and Drayton, respectable figures who, if one
works through their allotments, serve at any rate to set up a critically
useful background, we come to this:

> I wonder by my troth, what thou, and I
> Did, till we lov'd? were we not wean'd till then?
> But suck'd on country pleasures, childishly?
> Or snorted we in the seven sleepers den?
> 'Twas so; But this, all pleasures fancies bee.
> If ever any beauty I did see,
> Which I desir'd, and got, 'twas but a dreame of thee.

At this we cease reading as students, or as connoisseurs of anthology-
pieces, and read on as we read the living. The extraordinary force of
originality that made Donne so potent an influence in the seventeenth
century makes him now at once for us, without his being the less felt
as of his period, contemporary—obviously a living poet in the most
important sense. And it is not any eccentricity or defiant audacity
that makes the effect here so immediate, but rather an irresistible
rightness.'

The great writer is perpetually shocking, because he is perpetually
new—and this shocking new quality is not something we can define
in purely literary terms. Indeed by comparison the great writer makes
the inferior writers seem literary. True originality is, as it were, of
another dimension. Yet, for this essay and for the purpose of closing
the account of the traditional view of our business, in seeking to
define the quality that makes us say of a great writer that on reading
him after reading his predecessors or contemporaries 'we suddenly
feel ourselves to be in another world', I am content to mention
another classic formulation, Samuel Johnson's proclamation of the
reasons why Shakespeare is a classic.

If I have not achieved my purpose of setting out the ground
common to all students of literature, I cannot be accused of pervert-
ing the account to justify the undertaking of this essay, for at more
than one point the argument has seemed to cut away all possible
justification for giving any attention to my chosen stretch of writing.
For whatever I have to present for study cannot claim the indispensable interest that is obviously there when the study is of Chaucer or
of Shakespeare, or any 'living poets in the most important sense'.
There are no such names in the chosen period, nor can it be said that
any essential illumination comes from the Early Tudor writers in a

backward light upon Chaucer or in a forward light upon Shake-speare. Worse than this: not only have I been able to find no justifica-tion, I have passed over the reasons that would condemn such a study as I have undertaken as a dangerous distraction. Arnold plainly warned the student: 'this real estimate, the only true one, is liable to be superseded, if we are not watchful, by two other kinds of estimate, the historic estimate and the personal estimate, both of which are fallacious.' Of the former, which is the fallacy I seem to be guilty of, he wrote:

'Everything depends on the reality of a poet's classic character. If he is a dubious classic, let us sift him; if he is a false classic, let us explode him. But if he is a real classic, if his work belongs to the class of the very best (for this is the true and right meaning of the word *classic, classical*), then the great thing for us is to feel and enjoy his work as deeply as ever we can, and to appreciate the wide difference between it and all work which has not the same high character. This is what is salutary, this is what is formative; this is the great benefit to be got from the study of poetry. Everything which interferes with it, which hinders it, is injurious.'

An eminent warning for me can be found in a recent work, where the author was faced with the same perplexity: how to treat a period of literary history which does not contain any work of classic quality: *Chaucer and the Fifteenth Century* by H. S. Bennett. I draw attention to it here because of some comments on it in an anonymous review in the *Times Literary Supplement* (April 17th, 1948) which carry my argument a step forward and place before me a further requirement in the justification of my essay:

'(Mr Bennett) is concerned with "the fifteenth-century's contribu-tion to the body and continuity of our literature" rather than with literary value. Now it is obvious enough that any literary history must discuss a great deal of work possessing little intrinsic merit, and that much of the historian's activity will necessarily be cultural sociology rather than criticism. But unless the underlying purpose is critical, unless the primary concern is with that in literature which is alive for us to-day as part of the "mind of Europe" in Mr Eliot's useful phrase, the social and cultural history will lack point and significance. Unrelated to any clear system of value-judgements, it will tend to become a dull and academic recital of facts contributing nothing to the understanding of the relation between literary modes

14

and ways of thinking and feeling, between quality of writing and quality of living.

'It cannot be said that Mr Bennett has altogether succeeded in avoiding this danger.'

My gloss on this is that, as a result of experiencing great works of art, we not only heighten our sense of being alive, of the worth of human existence, but we gain direct insight into the life of the times when the work was written. Mr Bennett appears not to have appreciated what this insight is, for he seems to regret that Chaucer gives us no picture of everyday London: 'Chaucer, despite a lifetime of experience of London at one of its most interesting periods, tells us nothing.' The life mirrored in great literature is not everyday life, but what Johnson called *general nature*, the truth and reality *in* everyday life, a truth and reality we are blind to until the great writer shocks us into perceiving it. Properly used, great works give us insight into the quality of life, what made life significant to people capable of seizing its significance, people capable of surveying the world from a central, a truly human point of view. Consequently, to evoke the details, the furniture, as it were, of existence in Chaucer's day, is to pursue a will-o'-the-wisp which will take us further and further from the reality or true significance of Chaucer. If we submit ourselves to the great work as a whole and take it in the spirit in which it was written, then we can if we wish proceed to another kind of study, that of the comparative worth of civilization at various times. But the clues or keys to this study cannot be lifted from the work before we have experienced it fully. For this reason most of the books of social history I have read are to be condemned as superficial, since they attempt to lift from literature only the facts about life that can also be taken from non-literary writings; letters, diaries, state trials, etc.

There is thus a second study which flows naturally out of the study of literature. To the reader who has found Arnold restricting the proper range of healthy curiosity, I would point to the width and range of studies that flow from a proper concentration on the great works of literature. My own view is that it is impossible to stop flowing out in the way I have sketched. I do not see how anyone who has deeply enjoyed even a few of the classics can prevent himself from enquiring further into the essential life of the times which he has gained insight into by his enjoyment. By refusing to be distracted from the real in our study of literature, we equip ourselves for the general broad enquiry into what civilisation means.

The second problem for me, then, is that my period cannot have this kind of significance, for it does not contain works which rise above mere literature in the way Chaucer and Shakespeare transcend mere literature. The age between the two great poets did not succeed in knowing itself fully. Consequently, we cannot, by deeply enjoying the literature, provide ourselves with primary documents in this secondary study, an understanding of the quality of life in the period.

It is now clear that if the study of this period has a place in the general study of our literature it must be both subordinate and ancillary to the study of Chaucer and Shakespeare. Yet, by ruling out the possibility of illuminating the work of either poet by studying his successors or predecessors, I seem to have denied a place for the Early Tudors. It might, however, be argued that, by looking at a few works composed between Chaucer and Shakespeare, we can add to our understanding of these two poets by studying the consequences of the *absence* of certain features. We might be able to discover in what the essential greatness of the two masters rests by noting what is *missing* in the writers of the intervening time. We might test various hypotheses put forward to account for the success of these poets and note whether their absence in the lesser figures is the cause of their comparative insignificance. For instance, both Chaucer and Shakespeare appear to triumph by blending an element that we may roughly call 'popular' with an element that can be conveniently termed 'courtly'. Consequently we can praise them at the same time for 'simplicity' and 'sophistication' without falling into contradiction, and we can say that we could hardly call them civilised if they had not been able to blend the two elements. It might then be argued that in the intervening period we can see the consequences of presenting these two elements in separation. Similarly, we might say of the best parts of Chaucer and Shakespeare that matter and manner go hand in hand, while during the years between them we find authors who sacrifice everything to *what* they have to say and others who have practically nothing to say, but are chiefly interested in *how* they say it. Readers of Professor C. S. Lewis might find this a malicious account of his attempt to order these authors under the heads of 'golden' and 'drab'. Though I can see a certain interest in thus studying the elements of greatness in separation, and a possibility that it might make our sense of the mystery of greatness in literature more precise, yet it does not strike me as a claim on the interest of the general reader, who has only one life to live. The period must be shown to be one in which he is already much more deeply involved before he can be expected to take an active interest in it.

Fortunately, there is a topic which at the same time unites all that we need attend to in the period and requires of us a life-decision, which will be not only a verdict on the past but an evaluation of the present. My belief that there is such a topic will not be fully presented until the last word of the essay has been reached. Then and only then will the reader be able to judge whether anything significant has been put before him. But I can here, as it were, offer a programme, point in a certain direction and invite the reader to accompany me. Having thus cleared the way, I can at once proceed to sketch a point of view which I think gives significance to the study of the literature between Chaucer and Shakespeare.

The reader will have noted how often the word 'human' has occurred in this attempt to define literary studies. He may think I have relied too much on the word, and have tried to make the word do too much for me, since I have put nothing or very little into it and have left it essentially undefined. In particular I may be thought to have been moving very fast indeed in claiming that, because of the revelation of essential human nature in the great classics of our literature, we should make English the basic study in a humane education, in the attempt to attain a central, truly human view of life, in the attempt to enrich our lives and make them more worthy of the name human. Among the many objections that may be raised against these pretensions, one that is likely to occur is that this claim is made in one University in England, not for the study of English, but for the study of Latin and Greek literature, history and philosophy, the claim expressed in the title of the Oxford degree *Literae Humaniores*. I shall not proceed directly to a discussion of these rival claims, since the whole of the essay will be in essence a study of this rivality: it will be an enquiry into the meaning of 'truly human' and the ways in which literature can help us to distinguish the genuine from the sham uses of the word 'human'. In this sense it will be a challenge to examine what we do as students of literature, what ends we should have in view and what kinds of contemporary literature serve our ends and what tend to defeat them.

How can all this be at the same time the most significant way of studying a selected portion of the literature of the past? It is because we are still living in the same stretch of time which includes the sixteenth century. I say this, *pace* those who, like Professor C. S. Lewis, feel that a decisive break has occurred, and that in consequence when we use the word 'human' we mean something essentially different from what was meant by Dante in the famous passage where Ulysses stimulates his tired fellow-oarsmen to one last dedicated voyage beyond the range of familiar experience:

Considerate la vostra semenza:
Fatti non foste a viver come bruti
Ma per seguir virtute e canoscenza.
(Recall to mind of what stock you come: you were not born to live like
animals but to respond to the call of knowledge and power.)

No doubt we should differ in many ways from Dante if we could
discuss with him what distinguishes the truly human from animal
life and it would be foolish to overlook these differences. Yet are
not the points we have in common far more important and striking?
Surely Dante still lives in us, he is not a dead classic or an alien
figure? We do not have to deny in ourselves all we most value if we
wish to enter sympathetically into his 'crazy flight', as he more than
once calls it, through the three realms of his comedy. Surely Dante
belongs to *modern* literature?

The special bond of the sixteenth century, however, lies in the fact
that the immediate sources of our meanings for 'human' and 'civilised' come from the next attempt to see life from a central, a truly
human point of view after Chaucer's. Let me illustrate the bond by
an example: the career of the late J. M. Murry. When he was a
schoolboy, he passed through several forms, one called Little
Erasmus, followed by Great Erasmus, and in the highest form he was
styled a Grecian. From being a Grecian he passed to Oxford, where
he read for the degree already named. From there he went on to
found a literary review championing D. H. Lawrence and later he
wrote a study of Shakespeare. Now this whole programme of studies
was laid down and defended in the Europe of the sixteenth century
and some of the most memorable formulations of its principles and
ideals were composed in England during that century. One may reply
that this only goes to show how backward and old-fashioned the
whole public-school-and-University system is, and that a truly
modern human point of view would reject the whole foundation of
this method of forming an educated mind. Who now thinks, one
might further say, that Latin and Greek are the best foundations for
a man who wishes both to champion the young genius just springing
up in our midst and to recreate for us the access to our greatest
English classics? To this I would reply, granted, but the very arguments that must be used to repudiate the rôle of the classics of Greece
and Rome are derived from the champions of these classics in the
sixteenth century.

Our study is thus one in which we cannot distinguish subject and
object. The very tools we use are made of the matter we intend to
use them on. For what I am engaged on is at bottom an attempt to
define 'truly human' in such a way as to distinguish it from what was

18

thought 'truly human' in the sixteenth century. In all this I am imprisoned in the sixteenth century, or rather, in so far as the language the Humanists used and the categories they set up have proved inadequate and distorting, to be fully of our own time, we must change the language and burst the categories. But in so far as their language and categories were right, we have only to intensify our sense of what they meant. Essentially we are their children. Our revolt and our affirmation are still within the family tradition. That at least is my claim, but I am well aware that many able thinkers to-day reject the family tradition altogether and repudiate all that was meant by *human* and the importance given to the word in this essay and by the best minds of the sixteenth century. This I regard as one of the most sinister turns in our intellectual history.

To make a literary study of sixteenth-century Humanism is therefore at the same time to enter a contemporary debate. To deny that in such a study Mr Bateson's distinction between literary critic and literary historian has relevance is to question the whole present-day organisation of literary studies. In my opinion, the distinction could only have been set up because of a failure to see these studies from a central, a truly human point of view. As for the attempt to distinguish the historian of literature from the critic, in what respectable branch of studies where the facts are human values could a historian be distinguished from a critic? Here again it is only possible to erect an artificial distinction by abandoning centrality and so regarding as basic what is ancillary, and what is peripheral as if it were of the essence. There are no important facts about Humanism which can be had without a critical valuation. There is no neutral agreed position from which to assess these facts.

This essay, however, would fall short of its aim if its findings were thought to be mere opinions. It hopes to establish real relations and to show that the discovered values were really there; discovered, that is, not invented and put there by me. Having expatiated on the critical aspect of the work, it is time I turned to the historical. But one prior observation has still to be made. The critical enquiry, the attempt to see where the period 'comes in', also dictates the scale and proportion of the work. However great the claims made for the intrinsic interest of these fifty years, they clearly cannot justify more than a very limited demand on a student's time. This is not a concession to laziness, or passive acceptance of existing conditions inside or outside academies: this work *ought not* to claim more attention than the implied valuation of the subject demands. It therefore attempts to concentrate on the indispensable minimum, to discover

19

the basic texts, and to provide the just amount of commentary to make their significance plain.

The proportions, however, have been drawn with an eye to the convenience of readers far away from large or ancient libraries. Some strictly preliminary problems have taken up more space than they deserve because there was nowhere to direct the reader for their solution. For this reason alone, the essay cannot claim to be a definitive history; it merely hopes to suggest the lines on which such a history might be written. The contrary of this also holds: wherever possible, I have referred the reader to places where the essay is to be abandoned in favour of other secondary works. I have tried to show how such reading might be fitted together to make a unified study.

Without one such historical work, *The Waning of the Middle Ages* by J. Huizinga, this essay could neither have been planned nor executed. The limits of what literary criticism can do in this period have been indicated. Since there are no great works to criticise, we cannot expect by literary criticism alone to gain any deep insight into the relations between the literature and essential human nature. Since in this period word does not bear a sufficiently illuminating reference to thing, we are bound to consider what other approaches are open to us in an enquiry into the failure of great aspirations to produce commensurate works of art. Huizinga shows us how in such conditions we may conduct an investigation into the forms and spirit of the civilisation centring round the Tudor court. For though he deals with civilisation in the Netherlands and Burgundy in the fifteenth century, he penetrates through the local and temporal detail to the lasting forms of civilisation in such a way that what he points to and analyses applies to the very essence of civilisation in England in the early years of the sixteenth century. He provides us with a picture which tells us what to look for and how to interpret what we find in examining the quality of life in our period.

Not the least of the uses of this book is that it makes it easy to profit from a second almost equally indispensable aid: *The Civilization of the Renaissance in Italy*, an essay by Jacob Burckhardt. His essay is indispensable here, not because of its main thesis, which I think is mistaken, but because it calls up before us the essential aspects of a civilisation which provides us with the necessary *contrast* in studying the civilisation of England at this time. We can judge our civilisation better by understanding what it could not take over from Italy, what it tried to take over and what it refused to take over.

The starting point in this search for a significant point of view, for an approach that would give meaning to the study of the literature of these years, the basic idea of the whole, came to me from Huizinga. For thanks to him we can see the forms, the apparently static features of a civilisation as somehow dynamic. He teaches us to see these forms as more than accidents of history. He also teaches us to be dissatisfied with a view that would explain the forms as the sole product of economic forces. Marx has not lived in vain, and the contemporary reader is familiar with the general ways in which culture is linked to agriculture. Huizinga makes it plain that we cannot be content with a simple explanation such as that culture is a *reflection* of agriculture, or that culture is like a building constructed over a foundation of agriculture. He makes it seem plausible to look for the explanation of the forms of civilisation in the basic aspiration which gives rise to civilisation. There would be no civilisation if man did not wish to make more of his life on earth than could be made at any given time. Civilisation always represents an effort compared with what seems natural and customary at any time. Usually the effort is blind until it finds a form. Man cannot formulate what he wants very far ahead. The phrase 'a finer, fuller life' gets its meaning from whatever new form of life is brought about by the efforts of the will-to-civilisation.

When we come across a form, we should therefore ask: what aspiration was it created to fulfil? In what respects did it make life more worth living? The form is not explained until we discover the spirit which maintained it. Huizinga then illustrates how a form can come to have a life of its own. Once created, by one generation, it tends to dictate the choices of succeeding generations. Sooner or later it ceases to embody the purposes for which it was created: it ceases to be maintained by the original spirit. Huizinga analyses with great subtlety the animating spirit of many forms, such as chivalry, when the original motive for chivalric forms had disappeared. He thus provides us with a general framework for considering our period. For the England of the early years of the sixteenth century is characterised by the survival of mediaeval forms beyond their original intention. Huizinga invites us to look sharply at such forms and warns us, first, against supposing that, because the form persists, the original spirit must be maintaining it, and, second, against supposing that such a surviving form is utterly hollow, for something else must be maintaining it or it would disappear.

How are we, for instance, to interpret the accounts of the chroniclers who report that every year Henry VIII celebrated May Day as if it were still a sacred festival? He surely cannot have known the old, original, significance of the things he did. Yet we must not on that

21

account conclude that it was merely an excuse for dressing up. Here is Halle's account of a 'maiynge' in what we should call 1515:

'The kyng and the quene accompanied with many lordes and ladies roade to the high grounde of shoters hil to take the open ayre, and as they passed by the way, they espied a company of tall yomen, clothed all in grene with grene whodes and bowes and arrowes, to the number of ii.C. Then one of them, whiche called hym selfe Robyn hood, came to the kyng, desyryng hym to se his men shote, and the kyng was content. Then he whisteled, and all the ii.C. archers shot and losed at once, and then he whisteled again, and they likewyse shot agayne, their arrowes whisteled by crafte of the head, so that the noyes was straunge and great, and muche pleased the kyng the quene and all the company. All these archers were of the kynges garde and had thus appareled them selves to make solace to the kynge. Then Robyn hood desyred the kyng and Quene to come into the grene wood, and to se how the outlawes lyve. The kyng demaunded of the quene and her ladyes, if they durst adventure to go into the wood with so many outlawes. Then the quene said, that if it pleased hym, she was content, then the hornes blewe tyll they came to the wood under shoters hill, and there was an Arber made of bowes with a hal, and a great chamber and an inner chamber very well made and covered with floures and swete herbes, whiche the kyng muche praised. Then said Robyn hood, Sir, outlawes breke-fastes is venyson, and therefore you must be content with such fare as we use. Then the kyng and quene sate doune, and were served with venyson and vyne by Robyn hood and his men, to their great contentacion.'

Henry, of course, did not invent this festival, nor did his courtiers. At the same time they were clearly not merely following a tradition slavishly. The celebration of Robin Hood was adapted to fit the new aspirations of the young king and his young friends.

I have chosen this example to illustrate the spirit and form of this enquiry. For what we must look for in studying this period are the people capable of aspiring to give new life to the old forms. We must begin by finding *them* and trying to understand how they felt, to dis-cover through them which forms were felt to be dead and which were thought capable of embodying the new aspirations. What we must first grasp is the difference between genuine thinking and feeling and conventional or customary habits; the dead repetition of other people's thoughts and feelings. We must look first for those capable of weighing up the civilisation they were born into and of making innovations, the innovations necessary to permit the true values of the civilisation to be handed on. This is the sense in which we may say that our first task is to look for those capable of 'making it new'.

I start, then, by assuming, with Huizinga, that the times were such as to demand a great effort of innovation: that the civilisation men found themselves born into in the late fifteenth century was full of old forms which no longer fulfilled the aspirations of young people anxious to find and fulfil themselves. I shall not attempt to cover *all* the aspirations stirring in the young men born in the latter years of the fifteenth century. This is a literary study; but before entering on the study of the literature it may be as well to relate literary aspirations to the common aspirations of all the young people with a genuine hold on the real, and power, as we say, to realise it. I do not take for granted that all these aspirations tended the same way. There are always striking resemblances which tempt the historian to say that an age has a common stamp and that the same trends are visible in all the arts, in government, in dress, in farming, navigation, and in sports, religion, philosophy and love-making, in the arts of war, diplomacy, manufacture and trade. Yet the closer we come to appreciating the quiddity of any single branch, the clearer it becomes that each activity takes its new form in virtue of the special conditions it finds resisting and favouring the aspiration. Within the arts, it is impossible to equate music and poetry or poetry and painting or poetry and philosophy. There is no guarantee that by studying its literature we shall thereby come to understand all the other aspirations of the age.

Nevertheless, even though we renounce the ambition to sum up the aspirations of the age in one word; by confining ourselves to literature, we may perhaps venture to throw out a description that will cover all that is vital, all that is therefore significant for us in the age. The word I have chosen will cause surprise, surprise which may not be dissipated by all that is to follow. I hope, however, by the end of this essay to have enriched it with a sufficient number of applications to make it wide and flexible enough to perform the unifying function in this study. I introduce it now, naked of all the significance I hope to clothe it in,—for what I propose to study, what I consider the significant activity of the age is *translation*. I must, however, at once hasten to get rid of misapprehensions. It is well-known that this is the age of translation in the ordinary sense of the word. The great monuments of translation are still alive in the Bible and our Psalter, which owe most to the versions composed in these fifty years. Yet I do not in the first place think of translation in this sense. A hint of my meaning may be found in the praise of Chaucer as *grant translateur* if we apply it not merely to the translations of the *Roman de la Rose* and Boethius' *De Consolatione*, but to the whole of his work. For I mean a critical-creative activity, a process of assimilation in which the native digestive system is as important as the foreign matter assimilated. And if the activity may be described as selecting from foreign authors what could be incorporated into our own literature, I mean equally discovering what it was to be truly native.

The enquiry will therefore culminate in a discussion of poetry. But I propose first to examine the pretensions of the people who in the late fifteenth and early sixteenth centuries supposed they were the very people I have described in general terms as the first we should seek: people who were always proclaiming that they were making it new; people who were loud in their attacks on mediaeval forms; people, too, whose slogan might be said to be to teach their contemporaries *quam sit humaniter vivendum*, what it means to be a human being; people, that is, who claimed to have rediscovered what essential human nature was. The form of the early part of my argument will be, first, to give reasons for not taking these people at their word, for rejecting their pretensions to be the *élite* who should be our primary study. I shall then take an instance of an eminent genius to show what these pretensions amount to when they are genuine, and, by comparison between what was merely fashionable and what was genuinely new, I shall attempt to set up a critical attitude to the aspiration these people may be said to embody.

PART ONE

Humanism in the Early Tudor Period

BONAE LITERAE AND BELLES-LETTRES

The Relation of More
to the Humanists

NOTHING has proved more harmful to the cause I have at heart, the vindication of Humanism as a valuable and permanent moment in our intellectual life, than the indiscriminate admiration of all those who may rightly be termed Humanists. Yet how are we to discriminate? Here we are faced with the characteristic difficulty of all literary enquiries, the impossibility of distinguishing subject and object. The verdict we pass on the self-styled *élite* of English scholars who in the fifteenth century travelled to Italy to learn Greek and returned to England with manuscripts of Greek and Latin authors, recently restored to the modern world after lying neglected for centuries in German monasteries and elsewhere, or manuscripts copied from those brought into Italy from Constantinople, depends on our views of what constitutes good literature to-day.

If we turn to the two standard works which treat these scholars' activities in detail, *Der englische Frühhumanismus* by Professor Schirmer and *Humanism in England during the Fifteenth Century* by Professor Weiss, we find these professors taking it for granted that the travelling scholars mark an important turn in the history of our civilisation. They are not singular in doing so, for these fifteenth-century Humanists were asserting what almost all university people down to the end of the last century believed, namely that the study of the Latin and Greek classics is the primary, basic study if you wish to understand the essential nature of man and if you wish to know what civilisation is. Even to-day it is something of a paradox to make it a charge against these Humanists that in their cultivation of the Classics they confused *belles-lettres* with culture. To go further and equate the cult of *belles-lettres* with barbarism would in many circles lay me open to the charge of Philistinism. I must therefore find arguments to show that in attacking the cult of *belles-lettres* I am evoking the true spirit of Humanism to reprehend the fifteenth and sixteenth-century scholars' failure to embody that spirit.

It is, however, possible, before indulging in an orgy of what may be considered mere opinion, to establish one fact; that these scholars constituted a *vast mutual-admiration society*, and that one of their principal activities was self-praise. These scholars were conscious of belonging to a clique and they industriously puffed themselves as a body. In fact we may say with very little exaggeration that the conception of their rôle as we find it, for instance, in Professor Weiss's book, is an uncritical acceptance of the propaganda these scholars surrounded themselves with. I should therefore like to support these assertions with a document of our literary history and by a critical discussion attempt to bring out its full significance. It is evidence of the critical tone and temper in intellectual circles in the early years of the sixteenth century. It will serve at the same time to introduce the first of the criticisms of our current methods of study that I hope to bring home. For it is a serious deficiency in our literary histories that they neglect the evidence about the intellectual climate that can be obtained by bringing in contemporary writings in Latin. Since almost every English author was soaked in Latin, a historical and critical reconstruction and appraisal of the intellectual climate would have to consider the mass of writings in Latin that constitute, as it were, the true context of every work in English composed in these years. But here again, as with the English texts, we must select, we must try to discover which of the Latin writings are significant. A definitive history would make play, for example, with all the poems and comments of *Leland*—whose spare time was devoted to puffing the clique, while in his professional hours he was the king's antiquary—to show what it felt like to be a contemporary, a participant in the literary life of the period.

I have chosen one of his poems[1] to bring out the distinction between *belles-lettres* and true culture. The phrase *bonae literae* used by Leland in his title was the key phrase of the Humanists. In their eyes it denoted real and modern literature as distinct from the mediaeval nonsense, as they considered it, they had been brought up on, whether in English or Latin.

[1] 'Principum, ac illustrium aliquot & eruditorum in Anglia virorum, Encomia . . . etc.,' 1589, p. 74: *Instauratio bonarum literarum.*

The Revival of Belles-Lettres:

'The Renaissance is in full glory now that the Greek, Latin and Hebrew tongues are being studied and cultivated. The wealth of Greek learning and literature has migrated to Italy and shows every promise of being able to restore the liberal arts in that country. Spain has turned to the original source of eloquence, France is wholly dedicated to the study of the Classics, Germany is paying good salaries to Professors, whose reputations are rightly spreading over the civilised world. Our own country has a shining galaxy of talent to display. There is Free, Tiptoft, Widow and Flemming in the first generation. Later came Grocyn, Selling, Linacre, Latimer and Tunstall and (someone I have not been able to identify, called Phoenix by Leland), Stokesly and Colet, Lily and Pace. They all made successful visits to Italian universities, and shone in Italian seminars. When they had mastered the art of ready speaking and writing in Classical Latin, they all returned to England bringing their treasures with them. What do I mean by treasures? Why, the numerous copies of Greek manuscripts, fit to be kept on permanent exhibition in our university libraries. I wish long life to the manuscript import business. May it roll back the clouds and restore the bright sunshine of the ancient world to our cities.'

It would not be very helpful to supply short biographies of Free, Tiptoft & Co. It is more to the point to catch the *tone* of the poem: its complacency and the preference for an external sign of glory—the purchased manuscripts—rather than an exhibited sense of what true literary greatness consists in. Here we have the clique spirit at its inhibiting worst.

But if Leland's poem strikes the reader as childish, it is no sillier than the poem of Cecil Day Lewis beginning,

Wystan, Rex, all of you that have not fled[1]

and Leland's salute to his renascence is sober compared with the same author's effusion:

Beckon o beacon, and O sun be soon!
Hollo, bells, over a melting earth!
Let man be many and his sons all sane,
Fearless with fellows, handsome by the hearth.
Break from your trance: start dancing now in town,

[1] *The Magnetic Mountain*, p. 44.

And, fences down, the ploughing match with mate.
This is your day: so turn, my comrades, turn
Like infants' eyes like sunflowers to the light. [1]

Of course, to draw attention to the Humanists' self-praise would be pointless if the group in fact deserved praise. But if we look at the first generation of Humanists, who flourished towards the end of the fifteenth century, and ask what they did to deserve praise, it is hard to find anything, save the fact that they imported copies of manuscripts. This activity might have been more praiseworthy if the import of manuscripts had not overlapped with the import of printed texts of the classics. In fact I cannot discover what use was made of these manuscripts. Apart from this import work, the first generation of travellers to Italy were not essentially different from those who stayed at home. They contributed about as much to the enriching of life in England as the rich Americans of the late nineteenth century did for their country, who bought up European paintings and rare books to stock American museums and libraries.

There is something childish in the approach of these scholars to what they called *bonae literae*; in particular, in their approach to Greek. Greek for them was often like a new toy; they found no serious use for the so-called treasure. For example, one of the first northerners to acquire a great reputation as a Humanist, was the German, Rudolph Agricola. He became a legend during his life-time, though he does not seem to have published anything to justify this fame. He went on the inevitable pilgrimage to Italy, learned Greek there, and returned across the Alps. In January 1485, he wrote the following words in a letter to a friend:

'In addition to this, I am trying to keep up my Latin and Greek (though they are fast slipping from me) and am beginning Hebrew, which I find very difficult: indeed, to my surprise, it costs me more effort than Greek did. However, I shall go on with it as I have begun: also because I like to have something new on hand, and much as I like Greek, its novelty has somewhat worn off.' [2]

This play-attitude to Greek is characteristic of all the Humanists of the century. It is indeed a remarkable fact that Greek could not be assimilated into the Europe of the sixteenth century. The Greek texts worked on the Humanists only in so far as they could be re-thought in Latin. Greek becomes an essential part of English culture in the nineteenth century, not before. It had a very short innings and was quickly dropped in this present century. Even in the nineteenth

[1] *Op. cit.*, p. 55.   [2] Taken from *The Age of Erasmus*, p. 29, by P. S. Allen.

century the taste for Greek was an odd taste. How odd we may divine without a knowledge of Greek by looking at Mr Eliot's essay on *Euripides and Professor Murray*:

'The Classics have, during the latter part of the nineteenth century and up to the present moment, lost their place as a pillar of the social and political system—such as the Established Church still is. If they are to survive, to justify themselves as literature, as an element in the European mind, as the foundation for the literature we hope to create, they are very badly in need of persons capable of expounding them.' [1]

We need, says Mr Eliot, poets capable of translating the Greek into our world:

'We need a digestion which can assimilate both Homer and Flaubert. We need a careful study of Renaissance Humanists and Translators. . . . We need an eye which can see the past in its place with its definite differences from the present, and yet so lively that it shall be as present to us as the present. This is the creative eye. . . .' [2]

The next generation of scholars—roughly from 1490 on—is not essentially different from the first, save in one point. They could now write 'classical' Latin and could conduct diplomatic business in that pseudo-language. The abandonment of 'natural' Latin as hitherto written and spoken for 'imitation-Cicero' might be thought a harmless enough change. But it was accompanied by an immense propaganda drive to teach people to despise their working *lingua franca* and to raise 'imitation-Cicero' to the status of literature. This exaggerated claim proved a first-class disaster, for it strengthened an already strong mediaeval tendency to believe that 'fine writing' was the essence of literature. We might sum up this tendency in a phrase by saying that these Humanists merely replaced the mediaeval *florida verborum venustas* by *esse videatur* and the hundred-odd tricks of Classical prose style.

The first task is therefore to sift and distinguish among the Humanists. We must not confound those having genuine perceptions of the real and what must be done to realise it with those who merely occupy the stage of literary history. To grasp the nature of this distinction it may be helpful to refer once again to modern parallels. Self-advertisement does not constitute real achievement, yet at the time it passes for such. Indeed, as has happened with

---

[1] From *The Sacred Wood* (1928), p. 73.   [2] *Ibid.*, p. 77.

these very Humanists, the bluff may succeed for ages; but our business is not to be taken in by it. So when, for example, people tell us that the literature of the nineteen-thirties and the mental climate of the thirties were essentially what Cecil Day Lewis thought they were, we must salute the enterprise of the group that was able to impose its view of things on those too weak or too vacant to resist, but we must also apply another test; that of reality and real achievement. This is in fact one of the main tasks whatever the period we are studying: to distinguish what may be called the *Zeitgeist* or spirit of the times from the true spirit of those really 'making it new'. Literary histories in general fail in this essential task and are thus a harmful distraction. For to study the *Zeitgeist* alone is to engage in merely historical study, and to go in for what Matthew Arnold called the historical estimate. Life is too short to permit distraction from the real estimate, which deals with the genuine makers.

I shall therefore briefly characterise and dismiss the *Zeitgeist* in the late fifteenth and early sixteenth century, and shall do so by mentioning and recommending to notice a short work which concentrates on itself all I have to say about this self-styled *élite*. We can usually tell what work is original and what merely of the time by the following general rule. Since innovation is painful to those satisfied with the old ways, the original work usually arouses hostility or at least suspicion when it first appears. It is, however, greeted with enthusiasm by the kindred spirits, and when these kindred spirits are able to define sincerely what they genuinely admire, the genuinely new work has a smooth passage to its second and permanent rôle. For the genuinely new work is first a challenge to contemporaries to see their world in a new way. It has a special meaning for them which it never has again for later generations. We cannot experience the shock made by Mr Eliot's poem *The Waste Land*, for example, on the few first capable of registering it. The poem was not at once seen as the truly representative poem of the early part of the century. The age had other ideas of what was representative. Yet after this shock had registered itself, it was possible for later critics to say: this was the genuine original thing, the rest was merely fashion. But what later readers enjoy is not the specific shock to the normal ways of thinking and feeling in the years 1911–22, but whatever truth to things as they are and always will be is contained in the poem.

The typical product of the *Zeitgeist*, on the other hand, can be known by a similar rule of thumb. It, too, passes, when it appears, for something new. It is felt by the majority to express what is peculiar in the present. It is described in the very terms which later critics use to characterise the genuinely new. And it is never so described again once the fashion changes. It dies for ever when the next fashionable new thing is taken up. The poems of Humbert Wolfe are an instance. During the years when Mr Eliot was writing his early poems, Humbert Wolfe was thought to be the daring new thing. He shocked people and delighted them by printing the first letter of verse lines without capitals. I think it is true to say that he was dropped for ever by the very people who acclaimed him as soon as the news of his death was announced.

The typical Humanist, the representative of what was thought to be daring and new in the early years of the sixteenth century, was *Richard Pace*, the Paceus of Leland's poem.

His career is typical: he went to Italy to acquire the new learning and he secured a good post in the diplomatic service on his return. The book that calls out and justifies all I have said about his class is entitled *De Fructu*. It has never been reprinted since the moment of its success, and, of course, it does not deserve to be reprinted, since it is exclusively a product of the *Zeitgeist*, it would not have been written but for the *Zeitgeist*. The prestige of literature, the honours to be won through literature, cause many people to write who were not intended by Nature for literature. In our day this has been said of Mr Stephen Spender, but it is common in all ages to find books which, like *De Fructu*, have no other *raison d'être* than the author's desire to be in the literary swim. Secondly, it is a book with no substance whatever save as propaganda on the theme: the advantages of going to Italy and there acquiring Greek and the ability to write 'imitation-Cicero'. Thirdly, it is a piece of literary snobbery. On every other page Pace goes out of his way to refer to his intimacy with the great names in the literary world of his day. He talks continually of *Erasmus meus*, *Morus meus*, etc., just like modern authors who refer to Mr Eliot as 'Tom', to show their intimacy with the Great. Fourthly, though apparently an example of the latest thing, it is at bottom as unsophisticated and old-fashioned as the work of the benighted contemporaries Pace despised. (The sceptical reader may put this observation to the test by comparing what Pace writes of the advantages of learning geometry with what Stephen Hawes says on the subject in *The Pastime of Pleasure*.)

Yet this *is* after all an unfair summing up and makes it incredible that *De Fructu* could have been highly thought of in Pace's lifetime. If Pace could speak, he might rightly reproach us with missing the obvious animating purpose behind the book. For *De Fructu* is above all an exercise in Style, and it was valued for this quality and this alone. Pace's book is exactly what I mean by *belles-lettres*, and to bring home what I mean, I should like to take a group with similar

ideals to those held by the men who admired *De Fructu*, to compare
the Humanist *élite* with an *élite* of well-to-do *dilettanti* who flourished
and maintained Pace's ideal almost exactly four hundred years later.
There is a book to be written on the *milieu* constituted by the ex-
patriate Americans, Berenson, Edith Wharton, Santayana, Henry
James, L. P. Smith and others, who associated a rootless way of life
with a cult of fine writing derived from an admiration of Pater and
Flaubert. It would certainly help us in the effort to enter imaginatively
into the admiration of the Humanists who read *De Fructu* to note
how Henry James managed to admire Pierre Loti's book *Matelot*:

'I have read *Matelot* more or less over again; for the extreme
penury of the *idea* in Loti, and the almost puerile thinness of this
particular *donnée*, wean me not a jot from the irresistible charm the
rascal's very limitations have for me. I drink him down as he *is*—
like a philtre or a *baiser*, and the coloration of his *moindre mots* has
a peculiar magic for me. Read *aloud* to yourself the passage ending
section XXXV . . . and perhaps you will find in it something of the
same strange *eloquence* of suggestion and rhythm as I do: which is
what literature gives when it is most exquisite and which constitutes
its sovereign value and its resistance to devouring time. And yet what
niaiseries! [1]

But we can come closer to the Humanists' admiration and to
Pace's book, for there is an almost exact parallel to *De Fructu* in
L. P. Smith's *Trivia* and an equally close parallel in the admiration
it aroused. For Smith enjoyed a great vogue in his lifetime, and when
he died, the late Sir Desmond MacCarthy—thought to be England's
best critic and the living representative of Horace in the England of
the nineteen-forties—wrote:

'I agree with those reviewers of *All Trivia* who have predicted for
it a life beyond the grave of contemporary reputation. It is the sort of
bibelot that Father Time often keeps on his mantelpiece when he
changes the furniture in his house. For style is the best preservative
of thought when we mean by style a manner of writing both traditional and personal, and excellently adapted to the matter in hand.' [2]

At the moment the eminent critic appears to have been a false
prophet, for I know of nobody under thirty who has opened these
books. It may therefore be as well to give a sample of the creed that
makes Pace and Smith devotees of the same religion:

[1] Letter to Edmund Gosse, May 31st, 1893.
[2] For an expanded version, see *Memories* (1953), pp. 145–8.

PHRASES

'Is there, after all, any solace like the solace and consolation of Language? When I am disconcerted by the unpleasing aspects of existence, when to me, as to Hamlet, this earth seems a sterile promontory, it is not in Metaphysics nor in Religion that I seek for reassurance, but in fine phrases. The thought of gazing on life's Evening Star makes of ugly old age a pleasing prospect; if I call Death mighty and unpersuaded, it has no terrors; I am perfectly content to be cut down as a flower, to flee as a shadow, to be swallowed as a snowflake on the sea. These similes soothe and effectually console me. I am sad only at the thought that Words must perish like all things mortal; that the most perfect Metaphors must be forgotten when the human race is dust.

' "But the iniquity of Oblivion blindly scattereth her poppy." ' [1]

What is the relation of this passage to the classics but that of a parasite, and what is the activity of the parasite? It is to show that all that makes literature great and classical has existed in vain for the late Mr L. P. Smith. Just so with Pace and his contemporary Humanists. They battened on the classics and thought as did L. P. Smith that one could become great by slavish imitation of their styles. That these fifteenth- and sixteenth-century Humanists did not really appreciate the classics we know by the most certain evidence: they preferred their own imitations to the originals. Not only were they chiefly interested in the least interesting of the classics, not only did they prefer second-hand imitators of the great Greek writers to the Greek masters, they confess to preferring modern imitations of these second-hand imitations to everything else. They genuinely preferred the products of the *Zeitgeist*. There is, for instance, among Leland's poems one on his poetic contemporaries in which he places Pontanus first of modern poets, and in another poem he places Pontanus above Catullus. Sir Desmond MacCarthy was doubtless sincere when he called L. P. Smith 'a Saint of the Life of Letters': Leland's sincerity need not be questioned when he writes of Pace as

> Aonidum decus
> et secum in patriam lumina rettulit
> aut (uerum ut fatear) numina rectius.[2]

To begin with Pace—or rather with what Pace stands for—is, however, to make a false start. For our business is not, as I have

---

[1] *All Trivia* (1933), p. 111.
[2] *Encomia*, p. 25: 'In reditum Richardi Pacaei, vtriusque linguae ornamenti clariss.'

explained, with the *Zeitgeist* itself. To inform the reader that there are many thousands of books composed by the Humanists which are not worth reviving to-day is hardly to tell him anything new. Even to define what makes them, so readable once, unreadable now, is pointless, since no one is going to read them. The definition has a certain use when we wish to contrast the merely fashionable book with the book that still lives, but it is hardly necessary even then. Definition of the *Zeitgeist*, however, can become part of a serious enquiry, when the writer of permanently interesting work had himself to struggle with the merely fashionable; when the struggle leaves its mark on the work and qualifies its claim to be of the very best. To revert for a moment to the group of American expatriates, it would hardly be worth our labour to study L. P. Smith and what he stood for. The interesting theme would be to measure the influence of what he shared with Smith on Henry James or George Santayana. And in such a study, after pointing to what Smith stood for, it would still be necessary to examine just how the cult of fine writing was formative and deformative in the writings of James or Santayana.

This is the procedure I propose to adopt with the Humanists. Having denied to this *élite* the right to their claim that they were really 'making it new', it remains for me to search within the *élite* for the true makers, and the discrimination that matters is that within the work of the Humanists in the best sense—a sense still to be discovered. What we need for a real start, then, is a figure of pre-eminence, with a clear claim to have been a moulding force on the nascent society that was taking shape under the mouldering façade of mediaeval England, a man of genius and a literary artist. Such a man, fortunately, is not far to seek, for I have named, as the French say, *Thomas More*. But it is one thing to name him; to characterise him truly, to seize on his real significance, is quite another matter, and I shall have to postpone the discrimination between *bonae literae* in the best sense and *belles-lettres* in the bad sense I have indicated until the preliminary difficulties which arise when More is brought into the argument have been stated and clarified. For More is as controversial a figure to-day as he was both in his life-time and in the extended life he has enjoyed through his acts and words. He enjoys, for instance, the peculiar distinction of being a Saint in two rival religions. He is revered in Moscow and Rome, though not, of course, for the same qualities. As such, he is a figure of some power in one of the great spiritual wars of our times.

To claim that More's significance for our civilisation is missed by these spiritual warriors savours of impertinence. Indeed these powerful ideologies can only be faced by evoking the even more powerful 'central, truly human point of view' discussed in the prologue. To handle More effectively we need the support of an ideal figure—the Humanist judge of all values. We must posit such a figure as our ideal if we are to be true to literature. By putting it in this way, I hope I can rob of arrogance the claim that More is commonly misunderstood because he is not seen as this ideal figure would see him. More specifically, I need the reader's indulgence because I am about to argue that the More presented to us by the late R. W. Chambers is a radically false portrait.

The first critical wedge required to bring down the beloved image and substitute a juster one can be found in a curious passage from Henry Peacham's *Compleat Gentleman*, first printed in 1622. The passage is curious in that all readers of this delightful oddity have been puzzled to account for the presence of these lines:

'. . . Sir *Thomas Moore*, sometime Lord Chancellor of *England*: a man of most rich and pleasant invention: his verse fluent, nothing harsh, constrained or obscure, wholly composed of conceipt, and inoffensive mirth, that he seemeth *ad lepôres fuisse natum*. How wittily doth he play upon the Arch-cuckold *Sabinus*, scoffe at Frenchified *Lalus*, and *Hervey* a French cowardly Captaine, beaten at the Sea by our English, and his shippe burned, yet his victory and valor, to the English disgrace, proclaimed by *Brixius* a Germane *Poet-aster*? What can be more loftie than his gratulatory verse to King *Henry* upon his Coronation day, more wittie than that Epigramme upon the name of *Nicolaus* an ignorant Physitian, that had beene the death of thousands, and *Abyngdon's* Epitaph? more sweete than that nectar Epistle of his, to his daughters *Margaret, Elizabeth,* and *Cicely*? But as these ingenious exercises bewrayed in him an extraordinary quicknesse of wit and learning, so his *Vtopia* his depth of judgement in State affaires, than which, in the opinion of the most learned *Budaeus* in a Preface, before it our age hath not seene a thing more deepe and accurate. In his yonger yeeres, there was ever a friendly and vertuous emulation, for the palme of invention and poesie, betweene *William Lillie* the Author of our Grammar, and him, as appeareth by their severall translations of many Greeke Epigrammes, and their invention tried upon one subject; notwithstanding they lou'd and liu'd together as dearest friends. *Lillie* also was, beside an excellent Latine Poet, a singular Graecian; who after he travelled all Greece over, and many parts of *Europe* beside, and lived some foure or five yeeres in the Ile of the *Rhodes*: he returned home,

and by *Iohn Collet* Deane of *Paules*, was elected Master of *Pauls*
Schoole, which he had newly founded.'

What, readers have asked, is this doing in a book printed in 1622?
Some critics have tried to explain it as a piece of local pride, for
Peacham was born near St Albans, the place, as he tells us, where
'merrie John Heywood' wrote his epigrams and Sir Thomas More
his *Utopia*. The true answer is that Peacham is here testifying to the
fact that the continuing impact of More down to the seventeenth
century was due almost entirely to the selection of his Latin works
published at Basle in 1563, under the title of *Lucubrationes*.[1] For
Peacham is here reproducing directly or indirectly part of the preface
by Beatus Rhenanus to More's Epigrams, first published in 1518, and
reprinted in *Lucubrationes*. Peacham has selected for praise most of
the epigrams praised by Beatus Rhenanus a hundred years before
him and has transcribed the passage on *Utopia*, which reads so
oddly in a seventeenth-century book, and from the same source he
has taken the information about William Lily.

In the light of this I would argue that in the search for the living
More, the More who counts in our literary history, we should pay
more attention to his writings in Latin than Chambers was prepared
to give. In trying to find out what Humanism was and what is the
relation of Humanism to a valid literature, it is far more important
to know the contents of the small volume of *Lucubrationes* than the
vast tome of More's *English Works*. The little book contains all that
is inspiring and still alive in More: the massive volume was still-born.
In the course of this essay I shall have to qualify this remark in
details, pointing to what is merely of the time in the Latin volume
and referring to the parts of the English works which are still worth
reading, but the spirit of the remark will hold unchanged.

The second argument I hope to substantiate is that the More who
counts is not only a Latin author, it is Erasmus's More: the author
of *Lucubrationes*, not of the misnamed *Omnia Opera*. I mentioned
above that More was a controversial figure in his life-time. There
were even rival versions of his collected works after his death. That
Lucubrationes presents the More of Erasmus and the Protestants is
clear. Not only is the name of Erasmus the first word in the book,
but the volume contains all the praise More lavished on the works of
Erasmus and More's attacks on the vices of the monks and the clergy.
Two years after this piece of propaganda was issued from Basle, the
Catholic press issued an expurgated edition from Louvain in which
all mention of Erasmus is omitted—for Erasmus was in part on the

[1] This is not to say that the *Omnia Opera* went unread in England.

index—and More's attacks on religious institutions have disappeared. This they misnamed his *Omnia Opera*.

More, however, is the author of all his works, and in preferring *Lucubrationes* my grounds are literary and have nothing to do with the religious differences between Catholics and Protestants. I cling to the title of the book, for I should like to see this work restored to its rightful place in our studies as the basic text from which we can get our bearings. The affinity between More and Erasmus goes far deeper than reciprocal praise, as the patient reader will discover in the course of this argument. If the case for this affinity can be made out, the portrait of More we find in Chambers will have to be so changed as almost to become a new figure.

After this unfortunately necessary *détour*, I return to the argument. What I hope to do is to discuss the relation of a genuine writer to a mass of fashionable writers by showing in the work of the genuine writer where and how he became merged with the mass, and the consequence for the quality of his work. By this preliminary study I hope to make the contrast striking between what is merely of the time and what is still living in More and to clear the valuable aspect of Humanism from that which I regard as still capable of doing harm.

For these reasons I think it right to begin the argument by discussing More as a mere cultivator of *belles-lettres*. I consider it a fault in most of the attempts to assess More's greatness that they pass over the *Epigrams* so lightly. For not only do these Epigrams help us by contrast to seize on what is significant in More, they are a large and damning fact both in More and in the educated world of the early sixteenth century. They are not More's *juvenilia*: the most elementary research shows that many of them must belong to the years 1509–1519, the years of More's prime. Furthermore, these Epigrams were saluted with praise when they appeared, and they continued to be praised, as we have seen, down to the seventeenth century.

If we open *Lucubrationes* at page 171, we might start with the observation that it would seem very odd if a modern poet included in his first notable collection of verse a set of prize-winning entries to the *New Statesman's* or the *Spectator's* week-end competitions—for that is what the first poems in More's book, the *Progymnasmata*, seem to be. There we find More and Lily competing to make the neatest translation of a few trivial epigrams chosen from the Greek Anthology. And even if we reflect that to translate a poem for the

New Statesman to-day is a quite different matter from translating the same poem when it was comparatively unknown in the original, it is still hard to meet the further challenge: what are we to make of an age that praised More so very highly for so very little?

In answer, it would, perhaps, be more accurate to narrow the word 'age' down to the circle of More's literary friends, for, although these competition-poems were well thought of in their day, the small number of editions of the *Epigrammata* suggests that the circle of admirers was not . . . vast. Yet, narrow as the circle may have been, the praise it yielded made up in pitch for its lack of volume. As an instance, I offer Leland, once again, since, as we shall see, he provides an external link between the Humanists who wrote in Latin, and the poets who wrote in English. But I have no reason to suspect that the best critics of the day would have disagreed with Leland when he wrote:

'The modern age praises More for his sharp wit. Posterity will show itself even more appreciative of these qualities.'

Before we express our contempt for Leland and his sublime confidence that Englishmen for generations would go on writing verse in Latin, we might pause to recall that Samuel Johnson put More first of epigrammatists and Erasmus second.

Nevertheless, what we seem to have before us is further evidence of what I have called the Humanists' play-attitude to Greek. Yet the natural enquiry here would be, since these competition-poems are so frivolous, why, as it were, are they not more frivolous? Why select *these* epigrams? What were More's admirers looking for in epigrams that they found these rival translations so satisfactory?

To answer the latter question first: it is plain that More's admirers cannot have separated in their pleasure what we might call the pure pleasure of epigram from the pleasure of solving a puzzle. This second, puzzle-solving pleasure is so small for us to-day that we are cut off from sympathy with Johnson and from sharing the taste of the thousands and thousands of gifted people for whom that pleasure was very great. This verse was written and read very much in the spirit in which schoolboy prize verse compositions are written and read to-day in a few public schools. Only, in More's case, there was the added interest that some of the devices of word order and expression he tried out in his verses were later to be applied in the writing of English verse.

Another difficulty of approach for us comes out in the remark, 'They don't read like epigrams to me', which is the normal comment on the poems translated by More and Lily, and is often the final comment on the whole book of More's *Epigrammata*. When this remark is made, the stock retort is, 'By epigrams, I suppose you mean *Martial*. Read the Greek Anthology, and you will find that epigrams are something quite different.' There is a point in thus directing our interest, but it misses the real point of the normal reaction to More's epigrams. For More was writing in Latin, not in Greek. He 'knew' Martial—but the inverted commas round the word mean in the sense

All this the world well knows yet none knows well

—since More did not see what effects Martial was aiming at. Yet none of the Humanists was aware of this, for the ignorance was general, as we can see once again from Leland, who wrote:

'Many distinguished poets have written epigrams which have earned a chorus of praise from learned Humanists throughout the world. In my view, however, you, Martial, lead the field. But if More had handled your subject-matter, it would have been a neck-and-neck affair. More, however, was content merely to give a sample of his ability without stretching himself, whereas you, Martial, burst into a vast ocean. But let honours be easy; both your reputations will benefit if you are placed equal first.' [1]

If we reply, then, that More's epigrams are more Greek than Roman, we must go on, in Irish fashion, to deny that they are Greek. By this I mean that the taste that selected and translated them did not come to More from reading the Greek Anthology. They were chosen by the taste of the age, the taste we find notably exemplified in the commonplace books of the period. Since these books will figure in a later stage of the argument, and since without a rough idea of them we cannot understand what More was doing, I should like to remind the reader of a modern analogy: *The Weekend Book*, if this document of a previous generation is still familiar. Our fathers, when released from business at the weekends, would go some way into the country far from libraries, and after exhausting exercises in the open air, would gather together of an evening for entertainment in some cottage of Outer London or the Home Counties. The authors of *The Weekend Book* provided these hikers *avant la lettre* with the means of spending a cultured evening: some poems, some recipes, some jokes, some songs.

But the chief ingredient in More's epigrams and in the commonplace books of the sixteenth century and later is not represented in

[1] *Op. cit.*, p. 54.

the modern analogy: the pithy aphorism, such as we find George Herbert collected under the heading 'Outlandish Proverbs' or 'Jacula Prudentum', many of which were familiar to More:

> All is not gold that glisters
> A curst Cow hath short hornes
> The blind eate many a flie, etc. etc.

Everybody made these collections in the sixteenth century, not merely to garnish their speech and writings, but because they thought them of direct profit in promoting wisdom. They wrote them up on the walls, they wove them into their tapestries. Much of More's taste and matter would thus be immediately acceptable to his public, since this taste and matter were well-established at least by the middle of the fifteenth century. We may even say that both were a little old-fashioned.

This is not the whole story. Another comment often made is, 'I don't think a respectable man would nowadays publish some of the poems printed in these *Epigrammata*. He might write them, but they would not be allowed in print.' Now, although it is true that some Humanists thought that they were doing the Latin thing in making their epigrams as lewd and indecent as possible, and defended their practice by the bold defence made by Martial

> Lasciua est nobis pagina, uita proba
> (My poems are smutty but my life is clean),

yet, as we see from the introduction to More's epigrams, though this practice was understood, More is expressly, and rightly, differentiated from them:

'. . . dum Io. Pontanus ueterum nobis epigrammatistarum nequitias refert, quibus nihil sit frigidius, et boni uiri lectione magis indignum, ne dicam Christiani: scilicet usque adeo uetustatem istis aemulari, cordi fuit . . .'

But if More and all Christians could not abide Pontanus, there were Christians who found More hard to swallow. We can see this from the preface John Parkhurst wrote to defend the epigrams of his youth (1537–58) against the charge of indecency in the eyes of his later contemporaries; for part of his defence consisted in invoking the example of More:

'Although More wrote trifles similar to mine, some of which were rather *risqué*, and a few downright bawdy, this did not prevent him afterwards from being raised to the level of the gods and being paid divine honours by those of his faith.' [1]

We are somehow able to discover where decency lies in codes quite different from our own. I think these comments guide us sufficiently: More was not doing anything of which he need have been ashamed. But those who wish to offer us a plaster, instead of a wonderful, real Saint, have tried to explain away something in these epigrams that makes More's hair shirt more heroic: his palpable and human sensuality. I steer in these matters by a document dated 1519, the most precious of all the lives of More, and one specially written for people who could read More but not meet him in the flesh. It is a model of careful writing and its words are weighed. I refer to a long letter written by Erasmus to Hutten describing More in his life and habits as Erasmus had observed him from living with him. More himself, like the rest of Europe, read this letter, and, as far as we know, never challenged a syllable of it. He does not guarantee a syllable either, yet if the following quotation had been grossly untrue, he could not have remained silent. For Erasmus wrote:

'When he was of an age for it, he indulged in *amours*, but not at the expense of his good name. He preferred to accept what came his way rather than to chase after women. If he enjoyed physical possession, he enjoyed mutual affection more.' [2]

In thus apparently digressing from literary criticism, I have been responding to a second, but not secondary interest: that in More as a man. For I hope to show that in our attempt to assess the worth of the civilisation of the period, the evidence of More's life is indispensable. And in More's life, there is a further interest, for he was a pioneer in the attempt to establish a form of living not unlike that tried by the Little Gidding community. Even if he had not died in such a way as to deserve canonisation, he would still be a strong candidate for the honour of being a Saint of the Domestic Hearth. More's household and its immense influence as a focus for stimulating literature in others is a study in its own right. (Here the reader may feel insulted by the recommendation of the all-too-pretty account of *The Household of Sir Thomas More* by Anne Manning. Yet Victorian—mid-Victorian—as it is, it can serve as a start for a stricter enquiry.) For in the enquiry into the factors which made for a better civilisation and better literature, a more truly human way of

---

[1] Iohannis Parkhursti Ludicra, siue Epigrammata Iuuenilia 1573 A iiij.
[2] Opus Epistolarum Des. Erasmi Roterodami, Tom. IV, p. 17.

life, in the sixteenth century, the question of the ideals governing home life cannot be ignored.

The Epigrams, at any rate, offer us many opportunities to estimate the strength and delicacy of More's feelings in human relations. The book as a whole is not designed to produce a rounded self-portrait, but it does permit the inclusion of what we call occasional verse. Some of the pieces are clearly written to commemorate a fact. This is certainly true of his verse letter to his children[1] and of the poem I propose to consider first, which describes his meeting in later life what we might vulgarly call an old flame—though More here is as concerned to make pointed verse out of the incident as to record its details with precision.

Looking at this poem in the broadest way, two observations strike me as obvious: on the one hand, how genuinely human the situation is compared with the typical situation in a Roman love poem—so much so that we gladly call the latter 'erotic' to emphasise the less-than-human element in the love situation. On the other hand, how poor in human significance is the rendering of life compared with the English love poems with which we are familiar. After this a third observation comes: how poorly *set* are the 'conventional' elements. Contrast, for example:

> Ergo ita disiunctos diuersaque fata secutos

with Marvell's

> Therefore the Love which us doth bind
> But Fate so enviously debarrs
> Is the Conjunction of the Mind
> And Opposition of the Stars.

In short, whether we look for Wit or Manners, More's poem is primitive, it is not refined.

I hesitate, however, to decide how far its coarseness is due to the man, the manners of the day, or to the medium. I should like to stress the last possibility: that nobody knew how to express in Latin verse what the coarsest of contemporary Englishmen could say in English. Latin verse had not been used to express the delicacy of sentiment that had been evolved in English verse. At least I cannot conceive of a sixteenth-century Latin rendering of the following lines, taken from 'beastly Skelton':

> *To maystres Margaret Hussey.*
> Mirry Margaret,
> As mydsomer flowre,

---

[1] See, for a prose translation, 'The Latin Epigrams of Thomas More', by Leicester Bradner and Charles Arthur Lynch, University of Chicago Press, 1953.

Ientill as fawcoun
Or hawke of the towre:
    With solace and gladnes,
Moche mirthe and no madnes,
All good and no badnes,
So ioyously,
So maydenly,
So womanly
Her demenyng
In euery thynge,
Far, far passynge
That I can endyght,
Or suffyce to wryght
Of mirry Margarete,
As mydsomer flowre,
Ientyll as fawcoun
Or hawke of the towre:
    As pacient and as styll,
And as full of good wyll,
As fayre Isaphill:
Colyaunder,
Swete pomaunder,
Good cassaunder:
Stedfast of thought,
Wele made, wele wrought:
Far may be sought
Ere than ye can fynde
So corteise, so kynde
As mirry Margarete,
This midsomer flowre,
Ientyll as fawcoun
Or hawke of the towre.

How could the 'beast' Skelton write anything so refined as this? Not because he possessed native refinement, we may be sure. Nor because he had penetrated behind Lydgate to Chaucer, for he hadn't. The reason, I think, is that delicate modes of addressing women were enshrined in old singing forms connected with old processions, to and from sacred wells, to and from the greenwood, round the may-pole: processions to greet the arrival of noble persons newly married, processions to announce departures for a time or for eternity. In all these songs, dialogue occurs, women speak and are addressed, word patterns were tied to fixed patterns of the feet—but all had become so natural after so many centuries that Skelton could throw off this artless artfulness in extreme old age.

The so-called Humanist usually ignored all this material as beneath contempt or merely obscene. He had no real grasp of what made his civilisation what it was. I was going to say that More was no exception when I remembered that two of his epigrams are attempts to match in Latin the love songs that were set to music by court composers. We can thus see how unfit More's Latin was to render the love songs of the day.

> Benedicite! what dremyd I this nyʒt?
> Methought the worlde was turnyd vp so downe
> The son the moone had lost ther force and lyʒt
> The see also drownyd both towre and towne.
> Yett more meruell how that I hard the sownde
> Of onys voice sayyng: bere in thy mynd
> Thi lady hath forgoten to be kynd.[1]

This may strike the modern reader as too restrained, too cold. He may prefer one of Heine's poems

Ich hab' im Traum geweinet

where Heine has a somewhat similar dream, but instead of exclaiming Benedicite! weeps bitterly. Heine even weeps when he has a good dream. In his poems the emphasis is on the dreamer's feelings on waking and on his expression of those feelings. This English poem is not so simple as it looks; the composer's imaginary experience is more complex than the dramatic expression allowed it. It is also an effect of art to remove the person speaking as far away as possible from the foreground. The poignancy of the poem depends on our taking as admissible the formal terminology of courtly love.

More's touch seems to me so heavy as to deserve the epithet 'flat-footed'. More suggests rather the effect of a heavy night of drinking than of the disturbance of a mistrusting or jealous lover. The play on Phoebus and Phoebe strikes me as frigid. Very little is left of 'drownyd both towre and towne'. More has none of the mystery of the last line: we lose the uncertainty in the English poem whether the line was the refrain of a song overheard before falling asleep, or whether it was the voice of the speaker's own nagging worry, or a message from a clairvoyant spirit.

Now More's young fourteen-year-old Elizabeth would be no simpleton either. She would know hundreds of such songs. We must remember that youth was at a premium at court. Fourteen was, we might say, the *normal* age for the first sexual peccadillo or serious crime. A woman might find herself 'on the shelf' not long after she was twenty. We have no detailed *chronique scandaleuse*, but we have

---

[1] B. M. Add. M.S. 5465, ff. 13v.–14r.

enough evidence to show that serious court was paid to what we think of as children or adolescents. We should not therefore feel it unpleasant that More harps so much on the fact that *this* love affair was chaste. The implied norm that most such relations were *not* seems to be justified.

Though More conveys to us that his was a courtly affair and far from artless, yet, as he looks back on it from the age of forty-one, he sees that it could have been conducted with more art. But how ungallant he is to the lady all round, how thick-skinned and coarse; not really refined. Nor does he squeeze the situation to a very fine point. The poem thus provokes a stream of semi-sociological queries: was the possibility of a truly human way of life being hindered by deficiencies in the relations between the sexes? by want of breeding? does it look as though a school of well-mannered love poets was a *necessity* not a luxury for the coming century? would the central problem then become: how to combine politeness with sincerity?

Turning now to the other 'autobiographical' poem mentioned above, his verse epistle to his children, my first remark is: how much better he does this sort of thing in prose! Which is a reminder that the study of More cannot be carried on without *The Correspondence of Sir Thomas More* edited by Elizabeth Frances Rogers. This distinguished piece of editing has only one fault from our point of view: it presupposes that we already possess the monumental edition of the letters to and from Erasmus, edited by P. S. Allen, and, because of this, does not include that important part of More's Correspondence, the part made much of in *Lucubrationes*. Nevertheless it is a wonderful guide, as it contains the last exchanges between More and his daughter just before his execution, which throw a steadying light back on this poem about their earlier relations. Other letters enable us to determine how little mere literature there is in this verse epistle, which, apart from the element of joke bound up with the sending his children a letter in *verse*, is almost entirely a 'true-life' document.

To set the letter historically, we need to know that Margaret was about fourteen, Elizabeth thirteen, Cecily twelve, and John, about eleven. (The boy was not as gifted as his sisters and in the family portrait by Holbein looks rather foolish.) We also need to know that More was carrying out a new educational experiment: he founded a small university for men and women, to which the greatest professors of the day were invited. The university was situated in his home, and run on the lines of a mastercraftsman with his apprentices. The parallel extends to one of the consequences of such relations: the marriages between teachers and pupils and assistants. Various branches of research were carried on, with a strong leaning to the practical, especially medicine. More turned his grounds into a museum of natural curiosities and of curious scientific instruments. He himself was Head of the Drama Department and saw to it that the students had time for play.

To appreciate one of the lines in this epistle we also need to know that the normal seat of learning, the place where learning was usually inculcated, was the very human seat on which the learners sat. It was a mark of the true Humanist to revolt from this method of teaching and to insist that real education proceeds from love by awakening interest. But what is most Humanist about the poem comes in these lines:

'More than the bond of nature, what makes me love you, children, is that, though children in years, you have the manners of grown-ups, that your heads and hearts have been cultivated by reading the best books, that your tongues have learnt to pronounce and articulate words clearly and put them together with grace, that you know how to weigh exactly the meaning of every word you use.'

More was not advocating the acquisition of letters for the sake of *belles-lettres*. His ideal was the fully human being, and, for More, to be fully human was to be able to think, feel and express thoughts worthy of the best authors of the past. With such fervour—as the very naivety of the poem betrays—it was not surprising that More got the most out of his daughters that it was in them to give, and sent out many young men on fruitful careers.

More is here representative of the best side of the Humanists: their belief in the power of good schools to raise a country up towards civilisation. If Henry VIII had taken their advice and used the plunder of the monasteries for founding good schools, we might to-day have more than their ideals to be grateful for. But this is a topic outside the scope of my argument.

The next 'autobiographical' topic arising out of the epigrams is one that struck Erasmus at the time and strikes everyone to-day: the extraordinary number of poems against the arbitrary powers of kings. Erasmus reports that it was in fact a passion of More's—this hatred of the New Power which returned to the king with the accession of Henry VII. An American[1] has collected all the evidence suggesting that More's roots were in the City of London. One of More's first acts in Parliament, his opposition to the crown over taxes, puts him in a great tradition. This would not be so significant if More had been, as it were, born to opposition, but he was the

[1] Russell Ames: *Citizen Thomas More and His Utopia*, Princeton, 1949.

reverse. He accepted to the full the current doctrine that the King's service was God's service. More's greatness as a martyr depends in part on this deep loyalty to his king.

The question of More's political sense is a central one, for he is more than a man of letters, his ideal is more than a schoolmaster's; he is great just in proportion as he saw where the man of letters came in, where the schoolmaster came in, in a total picture of our civilisation. The Humanists are tiresome when they praise themselves and their *bonae literae*: they begin to matter when they turn themselves to the question: what can our studies do for the welfare of the civilisation as a whole? That is why the Humanist books worth study are those that deal with politics. But not quâ political theory. I should like to salute here another aid to our study: *A History of Political Thought in the Sixteenth Century* by J. W. Allen, but in doing so I must add that it is rather the underlying notion of man in his dealings with men that should concern us in reading *The Prince*, *The Courtier*, and *Utopia*. The Humanists must stand or fall, not by their cultivation of Style, but by the quality of their thought when applied to real things, real life.

I do not think it would be unduly cynical to remark that More cannot have taken these attacks on kings *very* seriously, since he puts at the head of his epigrams a long poem in praise of his actual king. It is certainly a point to be noted that More wished Europe to see him as the King's Servant. On the other hand, we should not be too quick to decide that it was *all* trifling in More when he denounced tyrants. For there is one historical fact which must never be forgotten in reading the poems of courtiers: the absolute power of life and death in Henry's hands. The proverb on everyone's lips in Henry's reign was

> Indignatio regis, nuntij mortis.
> (The kynges displeasure is a messaunger of
> death, but a wyse man wyl pacifie him.)

Writers were driven to wit, irony, or any masking device to avoid that messenger.

Nevertheless it is surprising to find More making an almost blasphemous application of the Bible in order to praise the king:

> Regem qui cunctis lachrymas detergat ocellis.
> (Such a king as will wipe the tears from every eye.)

In the days when men looked to the Bible for assurance on serious issues and found there all too many reasons for not being assured, for dread, in fact, and the near-certainty of damnation: in the days when men in trouble looked into the Bible for real consolation, they clung with all their hearts to the texts of good promise. One of them occurs in Isaiah 25:

> The LORDE God shal wipe awaye the teares
> from all faces

To judge by St John of the Apocalypse, this text meant much to the early Christians, for he twice refers to it, but the context More wishes to evoke is *Revelations*, ch. 21:

'And I sawe a newe heauen and a newe earth. For the fyrst heauen, and the fyrst earth were vaniszhed awaye, and there was nomore See. And I Ihon sawe that holy cite newe Ierusalem come down from God out of heauen, prepared as a bryde garniszhed for hyr huszband. And I herde a greate voyce from the seate, sayenge: beholde, the tabernacle of God is with men, and he wil dwell with them. And they shalbe his people, and God himselfe shalbe with them, and shalbe their God. And God shal wipe awaye all teares from their eyes. And there shalbe nomore deeth, nether sorowe, nether shal there be eny more payne, for the olde thinges are gone . . .'

& absterget Deus omnem lachrymam ab oculis eorum.

By its very exaggeration, however, the poem becomes a document of the greatest value—for More is here one with his age. There was an enormous surge of optimism in England when Henry came to the throne. People thought that a New Age had opened. The Humanists in particular thought that the New Jerusalem was really here on earth. We need not be too cynical. It is true that there was a great rush for jobs, and much joy among the successful and chagrin among those left out in the cold. But deeper than this was an almost religious feeling that now at last civilisation could begin. And it seemed a divine sign that the new king should be such a beautiful human specimen, a new Adam, or as More put it:

'The king who is as amiable as any creature in the realm of nature. Among a thousand noble companions he stands out taller than any. And he has strength worthy of his regal person. His hand, too, is as skilled as his heart is brave . . . There is fiery power in his eyes, beauty in his face, and such colour in his cheeks as is typical of roses. In fact, that face, admirable for its animated strength, could belong to either a young girl or a man. Thus Achilles looked when he pretended to be a maiden, thus he looked when he dragged Hector behind his Thessalian steeds.' [1]

The modern reader must rid his mind for the moment of the horrible, all-too-life-like portraits by Holbein of the ageing monarch, for Henry as a young man was in plain prose the beautiful human specimen of More's poem. There is a foreigner's report of the wonderful glow of his flesh as it shimmered through Henry's silk shirt when he began to sweat at tennis. For us, however, it is the Humanists' praise that we should listen to. Here, for example, is Mountjoy, Erasmus' English patron, reporting the news of Henry's accession:

'Oh, my Erasmus, if you could see how all the world here is rejoicing in the possession of so great a prince, how his life is all their desire, you could not contain your tears for joy. The heavens laugh, the earth exults, all things are full of milk, of honey, and of nectar . . . Our king does not desire gold or gems or precious metals, but virtue, glory, immortality. . . . The other day he wished he was more learned. I said, that is not what we expect of your Grace, but that you will foster and encourage learned men. Yea, surely, said he, for indeed without them we should scarcely exist at all.' [2]

I should like now to substantiate some of the remarks I have thrown out about More's epigrams by actual translations. Unfortunately, none is very distinguished, but at least they convey more than a bare prose crib. To support the argument that More's selection of poems from the Greek was made by a mediaeval taste, I have taken first an example on a well-known mediaeval topic, Fortune's wheel. And to hint at the relation between More's Latin and its context of English verse, I offer a stanza of More's own English poem on the topic. Here then is a version of his Latin epigram:

> Fortune observes no Method: for throughout
> Humane Affairs, her Wheel is turn'd about
> With great Inconstancy: Low things arise;
> High are confounded, by her quick surprize.
> Good Fortune, is transmuted into Ill;
> For to make Evill, Good; is at her will.
> Let not them grieve, who under hard Fates lie:
> Good Fortune's near at Hand: for shame don't die.[3]

---

[1] *Op. cit.*, pp. 139–140.
[2] Op. Ep., Tom. I, p. 450.
[3] Tho: Pecke, *Certain Select Epigrams, translated out of the Works of that upright Lord Chancellor, and facetious Poet, Sr Tho. More*, etc., 1659.

And here is More's own English:

> Alas, the folysh people can not cease,
> Ne voyd her trayne, tyll they the harme do fele.
> About her alway, besely they preace.
> But lord how he doth thynk hym self full wele
> That may set once his hande vppon her whele.
> He holdeth fast: but vpwarde as he flieth,
> She whippeth her whele about, and there he lyeth.

We are, I suppose, always in danger of preferring a slightly inferior English poem to a slightly superior Latin poem. Nevertheless I feel I should always prefer the vivid flick of

> She whippeth her whele about . . .

to

> sed rotat instabilem caeca subinde rotam.

What I have been doing in this single instance we should practise while reading the epigrams as a whole. We need, as it were, while holding the *Epigrammata* in our right hand, to have a mediaeval collection of verse in our left. I shall be doing something of the sort in a later chapter, but for the moment I should like to recommend the so-called *Bannatyne Manuscript* to give those unfamiliar with it an idea of what a late mediaeval *corpus* of poetry was like. This anthology begins with religious poems, passes to moral commonplace and ends with love poems. The love poems are divided into praise of women and mockery of women. This latter section has a heading:

Schort Epegrammis Aganis Women

Variants of the following poem were scattered over the English-speaking world and its author forgotten: the Bannatyne Manuscript ascribes it to Chaucer!

> Gif all the erth war perchmene scribable
> Maid to þe hand/ And all maner of wud
> Wer hewit/ and proportionat pennis able
> All watter ynk   In dame or in flude
> And euery man a perfyt scryb and guid
> The cursitness   And disset of wemen
> Cowld not be schawin be the mene of pen.[1]

Most of More's epigrams on women are in this mediaeval tradition. We can make ourselves more conscious of this if we read along with

---

[1] Page 572, fol. 258*b*.

them one of the mediaeval jest books. More is equally traditional on wives and marriage:

> A wife's a curse or worse;
> Still, good may come from ill,
> If she die soon—on her honeymoon—
> Remembering you . . . in her will.[1]

Or here:

> Thy wife is good when shee forsakes this light,
> and yealdes by force to natures destinie,
> she better is (thowe livinge) yf she die,
> but best when shee doth soonest take her flight,
> for soe to thee thine ease shee doth restore,
> which soonest hadd, doth comforte thee the more.[2]

These poems do *not* tell us anything of More's own feelings about marriage. Though he has left us some brutal jokes about his second wife, we must see here only a stock attitude. More is therefore not inconsistent in including among his epigrams a long poem about choosing a wife that is quite serious and not satirical.

By far the most popular stock joke throughout the Middle Ages was that turning on cuckoldry. Beatus Rhenanus was right to single the following epigram out for praise:

> *To Sabinus: whose wife conceiued in his absence*
> An helpe and comfort to thy life/ and to the age of thyne:
> A goodly childe is borne to thee/ haste hye thee home Sabine.
> Haste hye thee home to see thy wife/ the fruitful wife of thine:
> And eke thy blessed newe borne babe/ haste hye thee home Sabine.
> Haste hye thee home in poste poste haste/ thou nilt be there in tyme:
> Although thou hye thee nere so faste/ haste hye thee home Sabine.
> Thy wife doeth lye and long for thee/ thy brat doeth braule and whine:
> Both thinke thou tarriest ouer long/ haste hye thee home Sabine:
> Thou canst not be vnwelcome home/ when that a childe of thine
> Is borne, naie gotten to thy hands/ haste hie thee home Sabine.
> Haste haste I saie that yet at lest/ at sacred Fant deuine
> Thow maiest see dipt thy dillyng defte[3]/ haste hye thee home Sabine.[4]

More's epigrams on Astrologers really come under the head of cuckoldry, as we may see from the following example:

> *Of an Astrologer that was a Cuckold*
> To thee thou ayrie Prophet, all the starres them selues do show:
> And do declare what destinies al men shal haue belowe.

[1] Anon.

[2] Francis Thynne: *Emblemes and Epigrammes*, E.E.T.S., 1876 p. 59.

[3] A handsome last-born child.

[4] Timothe Kendall, *Flowers of epigrammes out of sundrie the moste singular authours*, 1577.

But no sterres (though they al things see) admonishe thee of this
That thy wife doth with euery man behaue her selfe amisse.[1]

More also gives us the stock joke on doctors in his epigram on
Nicolaus. The *Miles Gloriosus* is another perennial type; but the
following epigram is also a representative of another type of folk
jest, that in which the simple or countryman outwits the clever man
or the courtier:

A Iest of a Jackbragger

A Country clownish Coridon/ did vse abroad to rome:
And kept a bragging Thrasos wife/ while he was gonne from home.
When as the Souldier was returnd/ and heard this of the Clowne:
He stampt and stard and swore gogs nownes/ Jle beat the villen downe,
And went well weponed into feeld/ to seeke his fellow out:
At last by chaunce he did hym finde/ raingyng the feeld about.
Ho sirra, said the soldier, stay:/ you rascall villen vile
J must you bob: the clowne did stay,/ and tooke vp stones and tyle.
Shaking his sword the souldier sayd,/ you slaue you vsde my wife:
J did so said the clowne, what then?/ J loue her as my life.
O doe you then confesse, said he?/ (by all the gods J swere)
Jf thou hadst not confest the fact/ it should haue cost thee dere.[1]

Another mediaeval tradition is well represented in More's *Epigrammata*: satire on the clergy. Here again these epigrams do not tell
us anything of More's attitude to the clergy. We shall be seeing on
many a later page the difference between genuine indignation and
these stock jokes. But two other of More's satirical epigrams on the
clergy sound more like personal reflections: they both turn on the
illiteracy, the complacent illiteracy, of the clergy, and both turn on
the misuse of St Paul. In the Vulgate we find (in 2 Cor.)

> littera enim occidit, spiritus autem vivificat

and in Coverdale:

> For the letter kylleth, but the sprete geueth life.

Of an unlearned Bishop

The Letter killes, the Letter killes,
    thus alwaies dost thou crie:
And nothyng saue the letter killes
    thou hast in mouth, pardie.
But thou hast well prouided, that
    no Letter thee shall kill.
For thou dost know no Letter, thou
    in Letters hast no skill.[1]

[1] Timothe Kendall, *op. cit.*

54

In 1 Cor. we find

scientia inflat, charitas vero aedificat
(Knowledge puffeth a man vp, but loue edifyeth.)

The Portly Priest
Much knowledge puffeth up, thou say'st,
And what thou say'st is true,
But judging by thy breadth of waist,
Scant knowledge doth so too.[1]

Another popular type of verse, but one that also concerns More the man, is the attack on the foreigner. Here we touch on an extraordinary blemish in a many-sided character. But once again, I think, proper recognition of the blemish helps us to see More's self-conquest as the more heroic. This ugly trait comes out in the epigrams against the French (not German, as Peacham thought) Humanist, Germain de Brie. Apologists for More tend to gloss over the abuse he poured out in streams on this Frenchman who disparaged English martial and naval ability, and excuse More on the grounds that filthy abuse was a common Humanist failing. It is certainly true that great classical scholars have been noted for this failing—Bentley and Housman come to mind—but Erasmus was deeply shocked by More's lapse, and More himself eventually came to wish that he had not given way to his besetting vice. I call attention to it here since the scheme of this argument will not allow me to deal directly with More's religious controversial writings: for the same want of control and respect for his opponent are visible in them. Once More became blinded by passion, he lost all sense of proportion—he goes on and on and he hits lower and lower. The result is that many hundreds of pages written against what he thought heresy are virtually unreadable and constitute a large permanent blot on More's reputation as a Humanist, even if they contribute to his glory as a Catholic Saint.

The epigrams against Brixius, however, are not all dull, but an indirect attack, on the English affectation of French manners, is more telling:

A friend and chum I have, called Lalus, who
Was born in Britain and in Britain bred.
And though by seas, by manners, and by speech
We islanders are sever'd from the French,
Lalus holds British ways and fashions cheap,
Doting upon the French.
                    He struts about
In cloaks of fashion French. His girdle, purse,
And sword are French. His hat is French.

[1] *Philomorus*, 1878, p. 131 (adapted).

His nether limbs are cased in French costume.
His shoes are French. In short, from top to toe
He stands the Frenchman.
        Furthermore, he keeps
One only servant—This man, too, is French,
And could not, as I think, e'en by the French,
Be treated more in fashion of the French:
Lalus ne'er pays him wages,—that is French:
He clothes him meanly,—that again is French:
Stints him with meagre victuals,—that is French:
Works him to death,—and this again is French;
Belabours him full oft,—and that is French,
And in the street, the market, every place
Where men resort, delights in sorry French
To chide the knave, knowing as much of French
As parrots know of Latin. If he speak
Though but three little words in French, he swells
And plumes himself on his proficiency,
And, his French failing, then he utters words
Coin'd by himself, with widely-gaping mouth
And sound acute, thinking to make at least
The accent French . . .
With accent French he speaks the Latin tongue,
With accent French the tongue of Lombardy,
To Spanish words he gives an accent French,
German he speaks with the same accent French.
In truth, he seems to speak with accent French
All but the French itself. The French he speaks
With accent British. . . .
In short, of all the fopperies of France
He is an Ape, a very Ape.[1]

But though this is quite charming in a naive way, the Latin device gains by being transposed into English, as we can see from the following comparison:

He, like to a high stretcht lute string squeakt, O Sir,
'Tis sweet to talke of Kings. At Westminster,
Said I, The man that keepes the Abbey tombes,
And for his price doth with who ever comes,
Of all our Harries, and our Edwards talke,
From King to King and all their kin can walke:
Your eares shall heare nought, but Kings; your eyes meet
Kings only; The way to it, is Kingstreet.
He smack'd, and cry'd, He's base, Mechanique, coarse,
So are all your Englishmen in their discourse.
Are not your Frenchmen neate? Mine? as you see,

[1] *Philomorus*, 1878, p. 223.

I have but one Frenchman, looke, hee followes mee.
Certes they are neatly cloth'd . . .[1]

The other foreigner attacked by More is the Scot. Here we have an excellent opportunity to 'place' More, for Skelton wrote Latin and English poems at the same time and on the same occasion, the death of James IV at Flodden in 1513. They even use the same arguments. But while More writes better Latin than Skelton—he had, in a sense, made Latin a personal language, whereas Skelton seems to have had a merely external grip on the classical style—when we compare More's Latin with Skelton's English, we once again see how much More lost by writing his epigrams in Latin:

'While god-fearing Henry once again victorious in battle, subjects you, France, to your master, the Pope; non-god-fearing James, king of the Scots, invades England with a hostile army. He is not deterred by the treaties he so often swore to keep from making war on his wife's brother, or from allying himself with the Frenchman even though *he* is warring on the faith, or from desiring to sink Peter's little boat. 'Tis no wonder that now he is a man he should prove capable of such crimes, for while still a boy he dipped his tender hands in his father's blood. Consequently he perished by God's will amid great slaughter of his subjects. That is the end people who commit such crimes usually meet with.'

Contrast this with Skelton:

> Your lege ye layd and your aly
> Your frantick fable not worth a fly,
> Frenche kynge, or one or other:
> Regarded ye should your lord, your brother . . .
> Your souerayne lord most reuerent,
> Your lord, your brother, and your regent.
>   In him is fygured Melchisedec
> And ye were disloyall Amalec.[2]
> He is our noble Scipione,
> Annoynted kynge: and ye were none,
> Thoughe ye vntruly your father haue slayne . . .
> For your vntruth now are ye shent.
> Ye bare yourselfe somwhat to bold,
> Therfore ye lost your copyehold:
> Ye were bonde tenent to his estate:
> Lost is your game, ye are checkmate.[3]

---

[1] John Donne, *Satyre IIII*.
[2] For the point of this contrast, see *Epistle to the Hebrews*, ch. 7, and *Deuteronomy*, ch. 25.   [3] *Skelton Laureate against the Scottes*, lines 103–128.

Skelton is incoherent to a degree—he would have benefited by a Humanist training—but there is something fresh and forthright in his flashes of meaning, something that we miss in More's Latin.

The chief point that I hope has emerged from this rapid survey of More's Epigrams is that Latin is a drawback in a modern writer unless the writer is using it for purposes which his native language is unripe to fulfil. The utility of the survey will appear when we proceed to contrast this use of Latin with More's use of it for *advancing* thought. Advances in civilisation are always made in spurts, sudden local jumps: there is never a steady advancing line all along the front. I hope to have shown something of what it meant for a Humanist to be of the age. In the next stage of the argument I hope to show what it meant to make one of these spurts forward. We have seen sufficiently what passed for wit in More's day: my aim will now be to show More and Erasmus discovering a new kind of wit.

In leaving the Epigrams, I should like to qualify slightly the adverse judgement that we must pass on them when we are looking for the vital new thing in our period. They were not the kind of creative translation it is the business of this essay to bring forward and appreciate: they are not valuable pioneer work, but they had a deserved little success in their day and they gave pleasure for some hundred or so years later. More himself did not overrate their importance: he remarked to Erasmus on the publication of the 1520 edition (from which he excluded the poem on James IV):

'I have never been very fond of these Epigrams, as you very well know. If you and a few others had not found them more amusing than they have ever seemed to me, they would probably not be in print to-day.' [1]

[1] *Lucubrationes*, p. 481. *Op. Ep.*, Tom. IV, p. 254.

THE DISCOVERY OF WIT

The Identity of Spirit in More and Erasmus

The Praise of Folly *is the denunciation, on behalf of the humanists, of all the wickedness and folly of the age. Few read it nowadays. But it is a book which helped to make history. Yet, though the* Praise of Folly *was written in More's house, with More's encouragement, we must not make the mistake of identifying its spirit with the spirit of More.*

R. W. CHAMBERS

Aetas nostra sales, ac Mori *laudat acumen,*
Gratior haec eadem posteritasque canet

LELAND

I COME now to the contention that the More who counts as a literary force in England is virtually identical with *Erasmus*. And the point at which I should like to begin the enquiry is the moment when More and Erasmus began to translate *Lucian*. It is not clear whether we can speak of More as the initiator here or whether Erasmus had planned some translations before he met More. Erasmus, writing in 1506, says that the impulse came from More.[1] Both had been working hard to acquire a knowledge of Greek—a very difficult matter in those days, when helps were few—and both had overcome the beginner's pains and were beginning to enjoy their new mastery of this fascinating language. It is therefore of the highest importance to make out what

[1] Ep. 191: Quum annis iam aliquot totus Graecanicis in litteris fuerim, . . . nuper quo cum litteris Latinis redirem in gratiam, Latine declamare coepi, idque impulsore Toma Moro. . . .

59

these two gifted men were doing with an author that students are not nowadays encouraged to read either at school or at the university.

We may begin with the fact that even if More and Erasmus were pioneers in their cult of Lucian, they were in the first place leaders in what became a *European fashion*. It may surprise the reader who disparages Lucian to learn that, judging by the demand for editions, More's translations of Lucian were twice as popular as his *Utopia*; for during More's lifetime there were thirteen editions of his Lucian to five or six of *Utopia*. But this fact is not surprising when we consider the popularity of Lucian in Western Europe. There were 270 reprints of Lucian in Latin translation before 1550 and 60 editions of the Greek.[1] This is enormous, and makes it imperative to return to the topic of the essential triviality of the Humanists' interest in Greek, and their almost instinctive preference for the second-rate among the Classics.

This does not mean that we need make very heavy weather of the topic, as though it were a disgrace to be caught reading Lucian. He is quite entertaining in a light way, but his wit and irony are not Socratic, and his genius is at bottom parasitic on the glories of the past. No, it is the contrast between our modern verdict and the Humanists' that should arrest us. Why can such small fry as I so easily shrug off Lucian to-day, while such great men as More and Erasmus confounded him with the best authors of antiquity? I put the question in this way, because if we can approach an answer and say why the Humanists' approach to the Classics in general was trivial and could not help being trivial, then we have gone a long way towards understanding the Humanists themselves and the place they occupy in this enquiry into what matters in the literature of the early sixteenth century.

We can make a start, I believe, in the way I have suggested, by comparing our advantages in approaching the Classics with the position of the Humanists. If we ask ourselves about the extent to which the volumes of classical texts are now available to those who can read in the two languages, must we not say that they are accessible somewhat in the sense that Nature is present to us in a vaseful of cut flowers? (Though this analogy limps if we suppose that the surviving texts are a selection of the *best*, and that the action of Time has been to weed out the inferior flowers. In fact, the extant classical texts are largely a chance collection and contain along with the great masterpieces some rubbish and much inferior stuff.) But the obvious strength of the analogy lies in the fact that the collection

[1] Information taken from *The Translations of Lucian by Erasmus and St. Thomas More*, by C. R. Thompson, Ithaca, New York, 1940.

comes to us without any *roots*. The literary uses of the languages cannot be compared with their non-literary uses.

The misfortune of being cut off from the roots we share with the Humanists, and I shall be returning to underline what a misfortune it is. We have as one advantage over them a greater knowledge of the life of classical times derived from archaeology and other non-literary sources of evidence. But our greatest advantage is that of coming so many years after them—or rather so many generations after them. For generations of scholars have been able to sift and sort the body of extant texts and so gradually come to distinguish the value of the best from that of the second and third best. Our position is thus continuous with that of the Humanists rather than essentially different.

For it would be a wrong to these early Humanists to deny that they themselves were engaged in this task of sifting and sorting and distinguishing the first- from the second-rate. What it amounts to (very roughly) is this: the Humanists of the early sixteenth century were looking for principles of order, but lacking principles of their own, they turned to the Roman schoolmasters of the Empire, to men who had tried to do this very thing for Roman boys, who were not so very much more vitally linked to the past classics than the Humanists themselves. At first the Humanists are indistinguishable from their mediaeval contemporaries, except in the choice of books they read. For all men of the time supposed that if you wanted the Truth, it was to be found in Authorities, in the writings of people who lived many hundreds of years before they were born. At first the Humanists differed only in going to different Authorities: for instance, behind Scotus to Jerome. And I think we may resume the whole effort in this direction of the sixteenth, seventeenth and eighteenth centuries as an attempt to progress from unintelligent parroting of Quintilian to critical appreciation and possession of his judgements on classical literature and the relative worth of the famous names: from judgement resting on authority to judgement resting on Taste.

But the question here is: how in fact do we make the first step from the parrot stage? Merely knowing Quintilian—what Quintilian said—leaves us at that stage. What makes advance possible? A question easy to put, but hard to answer. At least we may say, to revert to my analogy, that we must supply the missing roots of the classical flowers from our own substance before the classical flowers will come alive. We must bring to the classics something corresponding to the spirit in which they were written before we can detect and enjoy that spirit in the classics. But, put in this general way, the problem seems insoluble: how can you become classical in spirit without the classics?

Here we can derive help from actual translations from the classics made at different times. If we take a passage that has been much translated we can see that success in translation is strictly determined by the state of civilisation (which includes the state of the language) in which the translation was made. It is a useful, though rough, way of grading the civilisations of different periods to compare what passed for a good translation in those periods. At least it forces us to see where the essence of the matter lies. All ages have access to the *words* of the classics. Why is the *spirit* invisible to some and visible to other ages? And why in particular do the classics sound trivial in early Tudor translations?

But before I proceed to give an instance, there is the prior question: are *we* in a position to judge? Do we know what the spirit of the classics was? Do we know better than Arnold, or Dryden or Ben Jonson? Here we had better be cautious and say with Mr Eliot that what we know are Jonson's, Dryden's and Arnold's attempts to render the spirit of the classics, and each successive effort sharpens our perception. I think we can go farther, but let me first give an example: the opening of the second book of Lucretius' *De Rerum Natura*. If we ask what we have got here, the answer I give myself is that we discover a set piece on a set theme, a conscious ornament: in other words, the rhetorical treatment of a commonplace. That, I admit, is a formal remark, and might cover a thousand treatments of this commonplace, all of which might be utterly without the power to move us. If this piece deserves a place in any short anthology of the great passages of Latin poetry, if it deserves translation as a separate piece and copying into our commonplace books, it is because the 'right' thing has been said as if it were the new thing, it is because Lucretius has supplied a feeling from his *unique* way of possessing a truth we all can share. Finally, it is because, in giving it his unique stamp, Lucretius has *simplified* the theme so that it is more adapted to universal significance than before he took it up. In other words, the rhetorical swell of the movement and the pathos of the simple language are not applied from outside to a neutral substance, but are themselves the substance, the life-matter, he has to express.

Let us therefore take two English versions in verse: the second is by Dryden and the first is from the only collection of verse I propose to examine closely in the first half of the sixteenth century, the collection usually called Tottel's Miscellany.

When dredful swelling seas, through boisterous windy blastes
So tosse the shippes, that al for nought, serues ancor sayle & mastes.

62

Who takes not pleasure then, safely on shore to rest,
And see with dreade & depe despayre, how shipmen are distrest.
Not that we pleasure take, when others felen smart,
Our gladnes groweth to see their harmes, & yet to fele no parte.
Not that we pleasure take, when others felen smart,
Delyght we take also, well ranged in aray,
When armies meete to see the fight, yet free be from the fray.
But yet among the rest, no ioy may match with this,
Taspayre vnto the temple hye, where wisdom troned is.
Defended with the saws of hory heades expert,
Which clere it kepe from errours myst, that myght the truth peruert.
From whence thou mayst loke down, and see as vnder foote,
Mans wandring wil & doutful life, from whence they take their roote.
How some by wit contend by prowes some to rise
Riches and rule to gaine and hold is all that men deuise.
O miserable mindes, O hertes in folly drent
Why se you not what blindnesse in thys wretched life is spent.
Body deuoyde of grefe mynde free from care and dreede
Is all and some that nature craues wherwith our life to feede.
So that for natures turne few thinges may well suffice
Dolour and grief clene to expell and some delight surprice:
Yea and it falleth oft that nature more contente
Is with the lesse, then when the more to cause delight is spent.[1]

And here is Dryden's version:

> 'Tis pleasant, safely to behold from shore
> The rowling Ship, and hear the Tempest roar:
> Not that anothers pain is our delight;
> But pains unfelt produce the pleasing sight.
> 'Tis pleasant also to behold from far
> The moving Legions mingled in the War:
> But much more sweet thy lab'ring steps to guide ⎫
> To Vertues heights, with wisdom well supply'd, ⎬
> And all the *Magazins* of Learning fortifi'd: ⎭
> From thence to look below on humane kind,
> Bewilder'd in the Maze of Life, and blind:
> To see vain fools ambitiously contend
> For Wit and Pow'r; their last endeavours bend
> T'outshine each other, waste their time and health
> In search of honour, and pursuit of wealth.
> O wretched man! in what a mist of Life,
> Inclos'd with dangers and with noisie strife,
> He spends his little Span; And overfeeds
> His cramm'd desires with more than nature needs!
> For Nature wisely stints our appetite,

[1] *Tottel's Miscellany*, edited by H. E. Rollins. Vol. I. pp. 152–153.

And craves no more than undisturb'd delight:
Which minds unmix'd with cares, and fears, obtain;
A Soul serene, a body void of pain.
So little this corporeal frame requires;
So bounded are our natural desires,
That wanting all, and setting pain aside,
With bare privation sence is satisfied.

Now though we do not know the name of the author of this first piece, it is just possible that he was as serious a man as Dryden and that in actual life he applied the doctrine he is putting into verse as constantly as Dryden may have done. Suppose it be so, why is the sixteenth-century author trivial, and Dryden comparatively serious? Surely we must agree that it is the jog-trot rhythm that prevents anything serious coming through, and that the author has not selected the necessary words? For instance:

Defended with the saws of hory heades expert . . .

This line alone suggests that for him Lucretius was writing prose. Yet he was nevertheless alive to the pathos: we can hear the authentic voice of the mediaeval lament here:

From whence thou mayst loke down, and see as vnder foote,
Mans wandring wil & doutful life, from whence they take their roote.
How some by wit contend by prowes some to rise
Riches and rule to gaine and hold is all that men deuise.

Compare that with this:

O Vanyte off vanytes & all is vanite!
Lo! how þis werld is turnyd vp [so] downe,
Now wele, now wo, & now tranquilyte,
Now werre, now pese, & now rebilyoun.
Iff þu wole daly labour fore renowne,
ffore profete, plesure, astate, ore grete degre,
The best þer-of schall ende in vanyte.[1]

We shall meet the same note of melancholy and resignation in Surrey:

Confesse vnder the sonne, that euery thing is vayne
The world is false, man he is frayle, and all his pleasures payne
Alas what stable frute, may Adams Children fynde
Jn that they seke by sweate of browes, and trauill of their mynde
We that lyve on the earthe, drawe toward our decaye . . .

Now if we glance back to Lucretius, we see that though he begins the phrase with the note of fragility, he ends with the note of power.

[1] MS. Ashmole, 61, f. 156v.

If he starts with a falling movement, he ends with a vigorous climb in which all our muscles are made to co-operate as when watching a tug-of-war:

> despicere unde queas alios, passimque uidere
> errare atque uiam palantis quaerere uitae,
> certare ingenio, contendere nobilitate,
> noctes atque dies niti praestante labore
> ad summas emergere opes rerumque potiri.

Dryden has the sweep, but not, to my mind, enough of the vigour:

> From thence to look below on Humane Kind
> Bewilder'd in the Maze of Life, and blind.
> To see vain fools ambitiously contend
> For Wit and Pow'r; their last endeavours bend
> T'outshine each other, waste their time and health
> In search of honour, and pursuit of wealth.

And if we make a corresponding enquiry of Dryden's version and ask what the voice of *his* age is contributing and dictating—both giving and at the same time limiting his power—then we can point at once to the all-too-neat arrangements of Nature for Man:

> For Nature wisely stints our appetite
> And craves no more than undisturb'd delight:
> Which minds unmix'd with cares, and fears, obtain:
> A Soul serene, a body void of pain.
> So little this corporeal frame requires;
> So bounded are our natural desires . . .

It reads like a 'fair copy' of Lucretius, after some schoolmaster has said: 'Take this muddled passage away and make it clear.'

One example cannot, of course, be conclusive. But if we took up these comparisons systematically, I think we could establish a law: we could go further than merely saying that one age allows one kind of translation, another another, and show that comparative success in translation depends on something in the life of the translator's times, and a capacity in the translator to isolate and refine out of that 'something' a sense of 'absolute' civilisation. But a translator's success is just as dependent on the contemporary poetry he can draw on. No translator can hope to rise very high—that is, to attempt a major classic with success—unless there is a contemporary literature which is nourished by and at the same time embodies the profoundest feelings underlying the way of life in the translator's day.

There, for the moment, I should like to leave the topic, with that bare formulation of a creed. For enough has been done to point to an answer to our starting question: why was the Humanists' approach to the Classics essentially trivial? We can see now that to grant that the approach was trivial, could not help being trivial, does not in the least imply that the Humanists were trivial-minded. But they were fatally without roots in the civilisation into which they were born. They did not know that the only sources of their strength were connected with the vernacular tongues so many of them despised. Or, to put it another way, they failed to analyse the civilisation they were born into, and they failed to see the true relations of literature and civilisation.

But the greatest weakness of the Humanists was their inability to conceive of a *worthy function for literature*. We can see this weakness in all their attempts at general literary theory. If we read through an impartial account such as that of the late Professor Atkins we can see at once what was wrong: they were trying to use a theory too advanced for them. Literary criticism cannot be carried on at a stage of refinement or sophistication in advance of the critic's capacity for appreciation. It was centuries before the Humanists came to understand this. They found Quintilian to hand, but though they could borrow the *words*, they could not discover his spirit.[1]

A further difficulty, with immense consequences for Europe, was that Roman critical theory is based on an understanding of *oratory*. The Romans, I take it, really understood oratory, it had taken a real hold on their imaginations, so much so that, long after the conditions for great oratory had disappeared, they continued to cultivate the ghost of their departed glory. The two consequences of this Roman bias are: a crudely utilitarian view of the function of literature, and a merely external account of Style. The Humanists had never known a world in which the command of speech could sway the fortunes of a powerful state. When they tried to wear the Roman clothes, they could only wear them with a mediaeval air. Consequently, their utilitarian view of literature, when it was not totally unreal, was far cruder than the Roman view.

Put shortly, roughly, and not allowing for brilliant exceptions, we may say that the Humanists' *impasse* was that they could find no justification for literature other than its moral instructiveness, that is, the only valuable thing they could find in literature was the boiled-down, abstracted statement, or moral of the poem, or the lifted statement taken from the poem, the wise saying or 'adage'. The first penalty, then, the Humanists paid for trying to use a too sophisticated critical vocabulary, was to have their literary vision narrowed to a crude view of Content, to the overstressing of what the poet put

[1] The partial exception of *Vives* is reserved for the epilogue.

into direct saying, and to a concentration on those sayings that bore directly on morals. Correspondingly, they were condemned to an equally abstract idea of Form. They became fascinated with mere forms, figures of speech, etc. And what was first an *impasse* for the writers of Latin became an *impasse* for all the early sixteenth-century writers in English.

My purpose in writing this excursion into generalities was not to rub in the obvious—that More and Erasmus were condemned to triviality in devoting their energies to making Latin translations of Lucian's Greek dialogues. On the contrary: having made the necessary point, I should like to add now that, in spite of all that has been said above, I think that More and Erasmus were guided by a right instinct in turning to Lucian. I think they appreciated Lucian for qualities they were the first Humanists to exploit. By turning to Lucian they overcame the difficulties outlined above. They were able to give a real meaning to critical terms they were unable to handle in their Latin contexts, whether in the work of Quintilian or of Horace. Through Lucian they advanced their critical insight by basing it on their own experience. This insight enabled them in their turn to produce a more complex type of wit than anything to be found in their epigrams.

In short, what I am arguing is that the start of a positive answer to the question: where does new literature *begin* in the sixteenth century? is not in the translations More and Erasmus made from Lucian, but in *the reasons they gave for making them*. Consequently, the prefaces More and Erasmus wrote for their translations of Lucian are primary documents in the history of *real thinking* about literature in this century. In keeping with the basic idea of economy in this study—that of working from as few texts as possible—I shall start from *Lucubrationes*, where More's preface and translations are re-printed, but I shall interject remarks from Erasmus's prefaces to show the *identity* of language they used to justify their joint work. Indeed, the letter More wrote to defend Lucian was long thought to have been written by Erasmus. In view of its cardinal importance, and for the benefit of the ordinary reader, I here offer a rough translation:[1]

'If any author can be said to have carried out Horace's recommendation to combine pleasure with instruction, I think the claim can be made for Lucian, for he avoids the two extremes of philosophy and poetry; on the one hand, a too severe and abstract treatment of

[1] For the original, see *Lucubrationes*, pp. 273–6.

morals, and, on the other, a too loose and light-hearted approach. Lucian is very witty, but always decent, and no human vice escapes his censure and rebuke. He aims his blows so skilfully and judiciously that, though no satirist strikes nearer home, his victim does not resist the stinging impact but cheerfully admits its force. . . . In selecting the dialogue on the Cynic, I rejoice to concur with the verdict of St John Chrysostom, a man of the keenest wit, the most Christian of the learned, and in my opinion the most learned of the Christians. He was so taken with this dialogue that he incorporated a great part of it into a homily he wrote on the Gospel according to St John. One can see why he did so, for what greater appeal to a serious-minded Christian could there be than this dialogue, which, while defending the life of the Cynics—so austere, so contented with the minimum of comfort—attacks the effeminate luxury of the pampered. Lucian is in effect here praising the Christian way of life, Christian simplicity, temperance and sobriety—"the strayte gate" and "narowe waye" "which leadeth vnto lyfe". . . .

'The *Philopseudes* is as pleasing as it is instructive. . . . We can derive clear profit from this dialogue, which puts us on our guard against the tricks of fake miracle-mongerers, which frees us from the superstitions which creep in under the name of religion, which helps us to lead our lives calmly, without falling a prey to those fears and terrors which are inspired by lying tales of supernatural horrors. . . . They think it piously done, I suppose, as though truth might be in danger of collapsing if a few lies were not present to prop it up. They have not been ashamed to adulterate with their lies the religion founded by Truth personified, which He wished to consist in naked, unadulterated truth, nor have they understood that, not only do these fictions do no good, they are more harmful than anything else. For, as St Augustine says, once we detect the admixture of falsehood, the authority of truth is undermined and ruined. This often makes me think that the greater part of these pious frauds were composed by the worst sort of crafty scoundrels and heretics with the design of making fun of the credulity of people too easily led astray, or, by thus dealing in false stories, of taking away our belief in the true stories of the Bible, for they often make up stories so close to those in the Bible that one can easily see that their object was to make religion a laughing-stock.'

The most surprising feature of this piece of literary criticism for the modern reader is the admixture of religious comment. This is a reminder to us that it is impossible to separate the man of religion from the Humanist in More. If in discussion we take up now one side and now the other, we must remember that it is the co-presence of both aspects that makes the interest of More's preoccupation with Lucian. I shall deal first with the religious aspect. It is not for nothing that both More and Erasmus recommend Lucian to bishops and men of religion. And it is interesting to see that at this date More's religion is like that of Erasmus, and that both attack the same vices in contemporary religious life.

The quickest way to describe this common religious attitude is to call it 'Puritan-evangelical', provided we import into the description no alien element from post-Lutheran times. By 'Puritan-evangelical' I mean no more and no less than is expressed in More's letter by his words, *Christianae uitae simplicitas, temperantia, frugalitas*. All these words are attacks on their opposites: More is against a religion of philosophical subtleties, against the pomp and luxury and indulgence in good living of prelates such as Wolsey. These are the two cardinal 'notes' of his religion: it is almost anti-intellectual and it is strongly in favour of plain living and even abstinence. But what are we to say of the vehemence of More's attacks on pious frauds, those little harmless fictions we find in devotional handbooks then as now? If we call this Puritan, we must also call Puritans all the purer spirits inside the Roman Church in all countries—even in the Vatican. For it is a fact that on all matters of integrity as distinct from dogma the distinctive virtues of the Puritan had their heroes in true children of the Catholic faith from the middle of the fifteenth century onwards. More, we see, is fiercely intolerant, but he cared for truth, since for him that was one of the names of God.

At the moment, however, the point we should attend to is not the measure of justice in More's violent attack on religious frauds, but the fact that in taking up with Lucian he was indirectly handling one of the things he cared most about, perhaps *the* thing he cared most about in life, and it is this which gives his literary arguments for Lucian all their force. It is my conviction that throughout his life More's passions were too strong for direct expression. Consequently, he was driven to exploit his great *forte* as a man, his gift of humour. He saw that the great interests of his life could be best advanced by appearing under a mask, that the profoundest truths could only be spoken by him if he assumed the clothes of the jester. More, as we shall see, was a master of foolery: his own 'fool' was an important person in his household, and occupies as much space in Holbein's sketch as More's only son.

The language of More and Erasmus is identical when recommending Lucian to clergymen, and I presume that this identity is the fruit of joint discussion. There is the same identity when we leave the religious for the literary grounds they give for taking Lucian seriously. The first and principal advantage the two friends derived from reading Lucian was that through Lucian they came to understand the basic principle of Roman literary theory: that literature is justified because it combines pleasure and instruction. The relation of these two aspects continued to bother Europe down to the time of Samuel Johnson: you can even find him oscillating between the alternatives, especially when he is not under the immediate impression of a poem, but is thinking of literary theory rather than practice.

Here, however, we must be careful not to exaggerate: More and Erasmus were not enabled by reading Lucian to enter into the *full* spirit of Roman literary criticism. They made one break-through, but, alas, only one. But in this one connection they grasped the real relation of these two functions, instruction and pleasure. Both stress this fact in their essays on Lucian. The language of Erasmus (Ep. 193) is almost identical with More's: *Omne tulit punctum (vt scripsit Flaccus) qui miscuit utile dulci. Quod quidem aut nemo, mea sententia, aut noster hic Lucianus est assecutus.*

The particular application of Horace's maxim they had learned to make was to the combination of levity with seriousness they found in Lucian. Now that Mr Eliot has made us all familiar with this combination in his attempts to define metaphysical wit, it begins to sound paradoxical to say that levity and seriousness do not *naturally* go together. We tend to forget that there is normally something shocking in treating serious things lightly: that it is the normal way of the flippant and the trivial-minded. More and Erasmus shocked as much as they delighted by advocating Lucian's mixture of levity and seriousness and his prevailing irony. We may see symbolic significance in the fact that Luther condemned Erasmus as the modern Lucian. It is also true that what More and Erasmus admired in Lucian's wit had always something equivocal about it. For there is in Lucian a fundamental uncertainty: he is sly with the reader and sly with himself. His sophistication is of the naive variety and pleases only the immature.

This makes it even harder to explain how they could see so much in Lucian. The answer, I think, is that what they found in Lucian they first found in each other. I should give this answer even if it had no other support than our two chief texts, *The Praise of Folly* and *Utopia*. The wit they admired was the wit they created between them. The sceptical reader may turn to the letters of Erasmus for the evidence he cannot derive from literature. One letter (Ep. 191) alone will settle the matter, for it is both contemporary with these translations and addressed to one who had seen More and Erasmus together—which removes any suspicion we might have that Erasmus was romancing. The telling phrase comes when he speaks of his competition with More in a literary wrestling match:

'cum amico omnium dulcissimo, quicum libenter soleo seria ludicraque miscere.'

If we look again at Erasmus on Lucian (Ep. 193), we find More described all over again in the description of Lucian:

'sic seria nugis, nugas seriis miscet: sic ridens vera dicit, vera dicendo ridet.'

Furthermore, in this letter to a common friend, Erasmus asks him whether he can find any difference in style between the rival efforts of two people he, the common friend, regularly considered as *born twins*:

'numquid in stilo sit discriminis inter hos quos tu ingenio, moribus, affectibus, studiis, vsque adeo similes esse dicere solebas, vt negares vllos gemellos magis inter se similes reperiri posse.'

We may note the comprehensiveness of the points of resemblance: *ingenium*—the inborn gift for literature, *mores*—the formed habits, *affectus*—common likings, *studia*, specific reading and literary tastes.

Erasmus contributes a point to the critical discussion when he singles out for admiration in Lucian his *dramatic* gift. Erasmus and More saw the superiority of enacting the moral over direct statement. They thus transcended the great literary blight of the age— the belief that by merely *saying* you are *doing* anything in literature. Now that Conrad and Henry James have demonstrated the necessity for dramatic presentation of a moral theme, we tend to forget how powerful is the pull the other way; to inject the moral from outside in the form of direct statement. It is still the French way of criticizing man and society. Nothing can be more deadly than the non-dramatic moral fable, nothing more powerful than such a fable when fully dramatic. We should therefore salute the triumph of definition when Erasmus says:

'sic hominum mores, affectus, studia (note the reapperance of these words), quasi penicillo depingit, neque legenda, sed plane spectanda

71

oculis exponit, vt nulla comoedia, nulla satyra cum huius dialogis conferri debeat.'

Finally, Erasmus and More make the identical claim that in this type of wit—this combination of levity with seriousness—they are being far more serious than the real triflers, the would-be solemn doctors of theology and the modern descendants of the warring schoolmen. Lucian's dialogue *Gallus*, says Erasmus, is conducted

'magis ridicule quam vllus possit γελωτοποιός, sed rursus sapientius quam theologorum ac philosophorum vulgus nonnunquam in scholis magno supercilio magnis de nugis disputat.'

Here we have the revolutionary claim to be redirecting men's minds from a false to a true notion of what really matters in life. But for the development of this theme, we must wait until we can discuss the two chief works of More and Erasmus. For it is, of course, only because of what they later wrote that I have been able to put my finger on these points in their prefaces to Lucian and say, here is the beginning of something new.

Before proceeding to these works, there are two darker notes to record. The reader may recall that in the discussion of More's epigrams I referred to a streak of coarseness in More's handling of the theme of love. I find a similar touch of coarseness in Erasmus' moral *taste*. For he praises (in Ep. 187) Lucian's dialogue on friendship, *Toxaris*, as though it could provide a model for the Christian's communion with Christ. Yet anyone who bothers to turn up the ten little stories illustrating perfect friendship which make up the substance of *Toxaris* will agree that they are drawn from unreal situations in light novels of a romantic kind. They represent extreme cases and their underlying morality is both vicious and crude.

The second darker note is that both More and Erasmus were also attracted to Lucian by their interest in declamation. The reader of R. W. Chambers' book on More will not find any mention of the fact that, not only did More translate Lucian's declamation, *Tyrannicida*, he challenged Erasmus to a competition in writing a counter-speech, and both published their efforts. Since this interest in declamation has an intimate bearing on the work of both Erasmus and More, we must look closely at what they were doing. Technically, they were practising a Greco-Roman form, a μελέτη or *declamatio*. Roman taste for oratory, we have seen, long survived the practice of oratory as a functional art. In fact we may say that mock-oratory took the leading place in the higher education of some young Romans, as it does for some English undergraduates to-day. Once oratory ceases to be functional it has no proper subject-matter, and attention has to be confined to manner, style and delivery. The Romans became connoisseurs of such things, and were as competent and keen to weigh the merits of a host of mock-orators as stage-struck people to-day are to compare and contrast the performances of modern Shakespearean actors or producers. The ancient and modern *fans*—or the better elements among them—had and have some interest in the great monuments of art, their Demosthenes and their Shakespeare, but not much. Once the shift in interest occurs from matter to manner, it becomes a virtue to select matter *for the sake of the manner.* The themes of these mock speeches were chosen for their *deliberate unreality.*

Thus we find More solemnly translating a speech by Lucian on the following set theme:

'A man went to the Acropolis to slay the tyrant. He did not find him, but slew his son and left his sword in the body. When the tyrant came and saw his son already dead, he slew himself with the same sword. The man who went up and slew the tyrant's son claims the reward for slaying the tyrant.'

Not only did More consider this speech as one of the best things in Lucian—the reader will recall how passionately More hated tyrants —he challenged Erasmus to compete with him in writing a counter-speech. The Humanists thought so highly of this speech of Erasmus' that it used to be printed in editions of Lucian.

I have dwelt at such length on this dubious development of a bad Roman habit, not so much to add one more to the list of charges that must be presented against the Humanists, but for a positive reason: since it is a further fact that out of this rivalry between More and Erasmus the first fruits were More's request that Erasmus would adapt this *declamatio* form to present what they had both discovered: a way of being serious while joking, a way of joking while being serious: out of this competition came *The Praise of Folly* and out of *The Praise of Folly* came More's *Utopia.*[1]

I hope, too, that the distinction I am trying to draw between translation and 'translation' is emerging. The translations More and Erasmus made from Lucian are dead: the 'translations' of Lucian— the two works mentioned above—are still alive.

R. W. Chambers wrote in his book on Thomas More :

'*The Praise of Folly* is the denunciation, on behalf of the humanists,

[1] Cf. Ep. 999 quin et mihi vt Morias Encomium scriberem . . . fuit auctor.

of all the wickedness and folly of the age. Few read it nowadays. But it is a book which helped to make history. Yet, though the *Praise of Folly* was written in More's house, with More's encouragement, we must not make the mistake of identifying its spirit with the spirit of More.'

Identity of spirit, strictly speaking, has, of course, never been recorded in human history. And if we survey the whole careers of More and Erasmus, the degree of identity and the amount of contact are slight. But if we confine our view to the *Praise of Folly* and *Utopia*, as works of a certain kind of *wit*, the close similarities are, I think, more striking than the divergencies.

The preface to *The Praise of Folly* may be divided into two parts: that which is addressed to More and that which is addressed to the public. On a first reading, one might think it a rather schoolboyish joke to link the title *Encomium Moriae* to More's own name. Yet this was a joke that More himself invited. At the very end of his life, he began his 'Second Booke of Comfort Against Tribulacion' with a confession of his predilection for treating serious things with levity:

'you maye see thys by our selfe, whyche comyng now together, to talke of as erneste sad matter as menne can deuyse, were fallen yet euen at the first into wanton idle tales: and of trouth cosin, as you know very well, my selfe am of nature euen halfe a gigglot[1] and more.'

But Erasmus saw More as one who could span the whole of society. This compliment permits Erasmus to open his manifesto declaring war on the enemies of Humanism with an appeal to the best title the Humanist has: 'homo sum: humani nihil a me alienum puto.' [2]

The part of the preface addressed to the public at least tells us what Erasmus thought were the popular prejudices he would have to overcome. In this part it is noteworthy that Erasmus does *not* say, as his modern interpreters do for him, 'I have merely joined the ranks of the so-called writers of "Fool Literature". You have read and enjoyed the *Ship of Fools* by Sebastian Brant, now read me. . . .' Instead he first appeals to classical precedent, and then turns to his serious arguments. One is the defence of literary fooling for its own sake. The Humanists devoted a great deal of time to the production of *Nugae*, trifling topics so handled as to display their command of elegant Latin. We can safely read between the lines of the following quotation that there was some prejudice against the apparent con-

---

[1] A gigglot is a woman no better than she should be—a female folly or Moria.
[2] Terence: *Heaut*, I, i, 23.

fusion of the lighter and the graver sides of life; that Erasmus expected to have readers who had lost the ability to appreciate the art of Chaucer:

'My critics can pretend, if they like, that I have been taking my mind off serious work by going in for small boys' or even nursery games. I don't see why intellectuals shouldn't indulge in some light relief, since every other class in society is allowed the privilege— especially if the fun and games lead on to something serious, and the clowning is so managed that a reader with the proper *flair* can derive more solid instruction from it than from some people's humourless display of logical analysis.'

The second half of this quotation gives us the main argument, that, in fact, the apparent fooling was more serious than . . . Erasmus does not make the odious comparison explicit, but, as we have seen from More's and his comments on Lucian, and as the book itself eventually makes clear, we know he meant 'more serious than the works of the professors of theology'.

If we say that the *Praise of Folly* is an attempt to laugh the Middle Ages off the stage of history, it is in the first place an attempt to laugh the doctors or schoolmen into oblivion: they are to be shown up as the true fools. The new world of Humanist values was not to triumph as a result of victorious *argument*, confuting the schoolmen on their own ground, but by jest and mockery, by the weapons of Lucian. The appeal was to the healthy instincts of the age to recognise the real and reject the sham in a grand burst of laughter. It is not for nothing that Rabelais acknowledged Erasmus as one of his masters.

The art of the preface, however, is to touch *lightly* on the painful sides of the book, while stressing the seriousness of the intention and the result. Yet the main claim is that the book is in the spirit of Lucian. In fact we might say that Erasmus in writing to Urswick in June 1506 was prophetically describing the *Praise of Folly*, as the reader can himself verify by turning back to the quotations I gave and comparing them with these from the preface and the following summary:

'Just as nothing can be more trivial than to turn serious topics into trivialities, so nothing can be wittier than to handle trifles in such a way that you seem to have been doing the reverse of trifling.'

We should in fact lose everything if for want of *flair* we missed this clue and instead thought the merit of the book derived exclusively from its classical side. The *Praise of Folly* would be tedious and unimportant if it were merely what Erasmus calls it, a *declamatiuncula*, a small-scale declamation on the Greco-Roman model. The only works of Erasmus that are worth reading are those in which the classical learning is wedded to observation of modern life. So here, if the speaker, Folly in person, were merely stringing together paradoxes in the manner of mock-oratory, we should have little reason to open the book save to admire the style and enjoy the allusions. It is because the speaker, besides commanding the greater part of 'bonae literae', is also the popular jester and the licensed fool that the book mattered in its day and matters now. It matters far less now than it did because it was so successful in showing later writers—for instance Shakespeare, Jonson and Molière—how to make a comprehensive criticism of society, how to vindicate essential human nature by blending the wisdom of classical comedy and satire with the common sense and the inherited sense of the spokesman of the people, the popular jester.

In taking this point, it should not be forgotten that Erasmus had a further reason for appearing before Europe as the Man in the Mask. The mask was necessary to make literature out of sermon material, but the livery of the licensed fool was also necessary to save Erasmus from the powerful enemies his satire created. It is no exaggeration to say that if Erasmus had cast his arguments into straightforward prose, he would have lost his life.

The *Praise of Folly* divides itself very conveniently for the expositor into two parts—though we shall have to ask whether the very ease with which we make the division does not point to a radical fault. The division has certainly led to a division among readers: some —particularly historians—have ignored the fooling and concentrated their attention on what they call the serious part, where Erasmus turns on the theologians and the abuses in the Church. Other readers have dismissed the second part as merely of historical interest and found the lasting value of the treatise in the first part, where they discover a Hymn to Nature, a vindication of spontaneous, instinctive life against the constricting powers of Reason.

The difficulty that faces us in attempting to decide between these views is the very mode in which the book is conceived; for the speaker in a *declamatio* is not on oath, it is part of his art to use startling paradox: there is no means of nailing him down. So we have no certain means of detecting from the speech of Folly what in fact Erasmus thought of the arguments he put into her mouth. We must suppose that some are meant to be preposterous, but how many?

Secondly, the wit has a wide range. Many of the jokes are such that the illiterate could share them: some would be confined to the learned. But *le fin mot de l'affaire*—which of Erasmus' readers would know how to take each stroke of wit? As we have seen, the preface itself hints that a special *flair* would be required—for that is the nearest equivalent to the word Erasmus borrows from that archidelicate nose-wrinkler, Horace. (And Holbein's portraits show us the tell-tale lines in Erasmus' own face.) The reader, then, who would profit from Erasmus' wit must be *non omnino naris obesae*. My comments were made before me by Lystrius in the preface to his commentary on the 1519 edition (based on notes supplied by Erasmus himself).

'There are very many things in the book which can only be understood by the classical scholar and those capable of close attention. For instance, there are the words and phrases in Greek, the numerous quotations from the classics, and the hidden allusions to famous classical passages. Then some of the jokes are so finely conceived as to be inapprehensible by all but those with the most delicate *flair* for wit—*qui naris sit emunctissimae . . .*'

Here again we have a phrase used by Horace to describe the wit of Lucilius. Caution is therefore necessary and extreme watchfulness or we may easily lose the scent. There is, however, no substitute for *flair*, since Erasmus' method is to embed his serious points in his ridiculous sallies in such a way that it is impossible to extricate one element, for each so colours the other that contamination is permanent. One example will show how great the difficulty is. There is no doubt, for instance, that Folly is loosely identified with Nature, and there are invitations to follow the identification as far as possible, even up to the sacred source of life. But consider in what context this phrase occurs; a phrase which some readers would have us take as solemnly as Mr Speirs, no doubt rightly, takes the cave in *Sir Gawain and the Green Knight*: 'Gawain is here at the hidden, secret source of life.' [1]

'To put the matter in a nut-shell, the philosopher will have to send for me if he thinks of becoming a father. And why shouldn't I use the franker language that goes with my office? I ask you, which part of the body is it that actually procreates gods or men? Not the head, the face, the breast, the hand, or the ear: none, in short, of the so-called noble parts, but, on the contrary, the

[1] *Medieval English Poetry*, 1957, p. 246.

propagator of mankind is a member so foolish, so laughable that you cannot even give it a serious name. This and no other is that sacred source from which all things derive life. . . .'

Here, in little, we see the difficulty of trying to press out of the mockery a firm conviction, a reverent attitude. I have written as though Erasmus were behind one Mask: the truth is, he uses so many that he can never be detected certainly behind any—at least in the first part of the *Praise of Folly*.

We meet with this ambiguity at the very outset in Folly's self-presentation. On the one hand, she likens her influence, which brings joy to gods as well as men, to the advent of spring which changes the face of the earth:

'. . . as when the sun shows his lovely, golden face to the earth or when after the bitter winter season the young spring comes breathing soft west winds, the whole world changes its appearance and colour, and, as it were, youth returns . . .'

which is in the spirit of our finest mediaeval poems:

> Lenten ys come wiþ loue to toune
> wiþ blosmen & wiþ briddes roune . . .

on the other hand, Folly asks her congregation to listen to her as they do, not to preachers, but to the entertainers of the market-place, clowns and jesters. But though these are the two elements in the self-presentation most easy for us to grasp, we must not overlook a third: Folly is also presented as an allegorical personage, presented as we should find her in a classical epic. There the rule was to group the associated qualities with the main quality of the allegory by supplying attendants to the main figure. So here, some of Folly's forms and attributes are brought on and exhibited as it were in the pulpit or on the bench as supporting figures: Self-Love, Flattery, Sloth, etc. We have lost this trick, even in sculpture, and, for an English parallel, must turn to the mock-epic, to Pope's *Rape of the Lock*, for example, where the Goddess Spleen

> sighs for ever on her pensive Bed,
> *Pain* at her Side, and *Megrim* at her Head.
> Two Handmaids wait the Throne . . .
> Here stood *Ill-nature* like an ancient Maid . . .
> There *Affectation*.

In fact, the wit of Erasmus is in large part mock-epic parody, deflating comedy. The claim of Folly to be the source of life, men-

78

tioned above, is put forward as a cheeky gloss on the wonderful hymn to the creative force which Lucretius put at the head of *De Rerum Natura*. But clearly Moria's pleading stands merely in a sly relation to Lucretius' powerful affirmations. She 'nothing affirms', but herely hints.

Where we might see a deep affirmation is in the flow of varied images on the theme of youth. Here, perhaps, Erasmus was allowing himself to indulge his own feelings of regret for the loss of youth. Not that even here he did not contemplate his regrets with irony. In the copy of the book illustrated by Holbein, there is a drawing of Erasmus working at his *Adagia* and looking a good deal younger than 48. When he saw this drawing, Erasmus is said to have exclaimed: 'Ohe! ohe! si Erasmus adhuc talis esset, duceret profecto uxorem.' As we note a certain exuberance in the references to the desirability of youth, we do not, however, focus our attention on the age of the author. In so far as we can focus on anything, I think it is on the dream of perpetual youth enshrined in the legends of the 'fountains of youth'. The spirit of Erasmus' satire seems to me very like that I have seen in contemporary paintings. The belief in these fountains has never been English, so far as I am aware. But in France and Germany one finds frequent reference to them as *Jungbrunnen* or *Fontaines de Jouvence*.

'Let the foolish world then be packing and seek out Medeas, Circes, Venuses, Auroras, and I know not what other Fountains of restoring Youth. I am sure I am the onely person that both can, and have made it good. 'Tis I alone that have that wonderful Juice with which Memmon's daughter prolong'd the youth of her Grandfather Tithon. I am that Venus by whose favour Phaon became so young again that Sappho fell in love with him. Mine are those Herbs, if yet there be any such, mine those Charms, and mine that Fountain, that not onely restores departed Youth but, which is more desirable, preserves it perpetual.' [1]

When we read these lines and enjoy the humour of hearing Folly denouncing the folly of all the legends of restoring youth, we do not altogether exclude the idea that she is speaking on behalf of a great and beneficent natural power. We never forget that this is one more sophistical argument, but because of this, we can safely entertain the imagination of a bliss we know to be impossible.

[1] This and all subsequent quotations, unless otherwise stated, are from the translation of the *Praise of Folly* by John Wilson, edited by Mrs. P. S. Allen. Oxford, 1913.

Whereas here Folly seems to be appealing behind and over the head of common sense, when she comes to the claim that she is the cement of society, the whole argument rests on solid sense. We all know that illusion is necessary if we are to carry on like so-called reasonable beings. It was a fine stroke to make Folly the advocate of reasonable good sense against a narrow and theoretical Reason. In this part of the argument Erasmus joins the More we shall meet in *Utopia* in regarding and enjoying Nature as a kindly figure.

These passages are more interesting than the commonplaces of wisdom in which the only wit consists in placing them in the mouth of Folly. Here is a comparison dear to the Elizabethans:

'And what is all this Life but a kind of Comedy, wherein men walk up and down in one another's Disguises, and Act their respective Parts, till the property-man bring 'em back to the Tyring House. And yet he often orders a different Dress, and makes him that came but just now off in the Robes of a King, put on the Raggs of a Begger.'

Thus Erasmus canalised the aphorisms of the Greek and Roman moralists for the benefit of Elizabethan essayists and playwrights:

'All the world's a stage
And all the men and women merely players;
They have their exits and their entrances,
And one man in his time plays many parts . . .

Yet Erasmus' drift is not toward the copy-book maxim of his beloved *Adagia*, but towards a definition of the truly human, the human condition. He begins by contrasting true humanity with the unnatural behaviour of the Stoic philosopher, who, in seeking to make everything subordinate to Reason, loses the human touch:

'A man dead to all sense of Nature and common affections, and no more mov'd with Love or Pity than if he were a Flint or a Rock . . .'

To this monster Folly opposes the Fool, who is the true Humanist:

'one that thinks nothing of Humanity should be a stranger to him'.

Similarly, against the Absolutist, *l'homme absurde*, as M. Camus called him, who is ever complaining of the deficiencies of *la condition humaine*, Erasmus sets the man who knows how to put up with the inevitable limitations of Man:

'But methinks I hear the Philosophers opposing it, and saying 'tis a miserable thing for a man to be foolish, to erre, to mistake, and know nothing truly. Nay rather, this is to be a man. And why should they call it miserable, I see no reason; forasmuch as we are so born, so bred, so instructed, nay, such is the common condition of us all.'

We have a similar progression from commonplace to insight when Erasmus opposes Nature to Art, the life of instinct to the life of civilisation:

'So are they most happy of all others that have least commerce with Sciences, and follow the guidance of Nature, who is in no wise imperfect, unless perhaps we endeavour to leap over those bounds she has appointed to us. Nature hates all false-colouring, and is ever best where she is least adulterated with Art.'

Yet Erasmus presses the point further: he makes Folly equate nature and human nature with the life of bees and beasts, and so praises the Fool because he is nearer them than us:

'They . . . seem as little miserable as possible, who come nearest to Beasts and never attempt any thing beyond Man.'

This brings Erasmus to the most daring of his paradoxes: that to be truly human is to be mad. But at this point—just where we expect something deeper than the jokes Erasmus offers, he branches off into ordinary sensible satire of men's occupations, and only when he has exhausted what we might call his serious satire, his *direct* attack on the abuses of the day, does he return to the topic that opens the possibility of profundity. But by then the spirit of the book has changed and the suggestive approach has been lost.

Before I pass to the end of the book to note this contrast, I should like to resume the impressions made by the first part. There is, it now appears, something that needs qualification in the remark I threw off about the classical and popular elements *blending*. Certainly, the piquancy of some of the classical borrowings matches the tone of some of the more unexpected claims of Folly, yet the brilliance of the book as a piece of Latin is something separate from the intrinsic interest which I have been trying to make out. The Latin has what the French would later call a 'solid brilliance'. The *Praise of Folly* was almost immediately used as a text-book in schools—no doubt in the higher forms—and it could still be used to-day if our main interest in the Classics were to extract from them proverbs, pithy sayings and mythology. The book is so packed with references to passages in classical authors that I cannot believe that it was composed without the help of a library or a copious book of extracts. I could say more about the work as a Latin composition, but at the end of it there would always remain the question: what would Horace have made of it? Since this question is unanswerable, we might try another: does it not resemble the other productions in Latin by European scholars, in that it would have been better in one of the vernaculars, if the vernaculars could have been made to embody it? This again is hard to answer. The *Encomium Moriae* is far better than any of the English translations I have read: it has a genuine raciness and a variety of tone that have not been reproduced by the translators. Yet, if we compare it with Rabelais, who never, to my mind, exhibits the *finesse* of Erasmus, we can see that it would make a greater impact to-day if written in Rabelais' old French, than it does in any English translation. The reason, I think, is that the element of 'translation' in it, the assimilation of classical modes, would be more effective if digested into a vernacular. For, after all, we do not want a second-hand guide to Classical proverbs, pithy sayings and mythology. Once we leave the lower forms of school, we go to the classical originals. What we want is to see the wisdom in the classics applied to modern material. I think it is a fair criticism that in this book we find the classical spirit only on the surface: much of the book is merely parasitic on the classics.

In fact it is surprising to find Erasmus so little dependent on the Classics for what he really has to say. If I have made out the kernel of his message, although he invokes Nature in language taken from the Classics, the simplicity and exuberance he seems to value in nature do not seem to be qualities derived from classical reading. The feelings he evokes seem to me to come from genuine participation in the life of the times and in the living tradition. Yet when we probe these feelings, we find they are painfully insubstantial. It is hard to be certain that we have in fact got to the bottom of the matter. The manner in which the various hints are thrown out does not invite us to go much further with them. After all, Erasmus did not go on to write the works of Rabelais. The *Praise of Folly* is a kind of farewell to youthful fantasy: no other work by Erasmus attempts to see the whole of life and society from this point of view.

There is in fact a fatal want of responsibility towards his own insights: by adopting the sly, shifty, dodging mode of Lucian, Erasmus confines himself to the limited kind of success obtained by Lucian. 'Yet,' Erasmus might here interrupt, 'you are speaking only of my preface. I did not write the first half for its own sake. I was not concerned to give the public my whole view of Nature's simplicity and exuberance, but to prepare my contemporaries for a knock-out blow against certain abuses. I did in fact deliver that blow and strike home in my second part.' The facts speak for Erasmus—but at the cost of his literary reputation. As we shall see, when he deals with society, the whole elaborate play of Folly in her multiple rôles drops away, and we hear one voice only, that of Erasmus himself. Of course, we may treat the first half of the book as mere protective camouflage. We may say that Erasmus filled it with manifest absurdities in order to be able to reply to those who were hurt by the second part, 'Can't you see that the whole thing is a joke?' But if we see in this first part the establishing of a point of view, we must admit that it is at the same time too radical and too fanciful to support a straight attack on specific actual abuses. For the idea of Folly as Nature makes all activity foolish: it does not matter whether the theologians continue in the mediaeval way or give place to classical scholars of the new school, for they would be equally vulnerable from Folly's angle of shot. The comic spirit generated in the first part of the book could only expand in further exaggerations. Consequently something peters out when we come to Erasmus' actual survey of society.

For this reason the close of the book is disturbing. We have been for so long in the presence of a clear, convincing point of view, of a man conducting responsible satire, making true distinctions and conveying strong, genuine feelings—Erasmus' attacks on his enemies resemble those of Pascal on the Jesuits: they are unfair, but telling, and justified by the rightness of the animus—that we note with dismay that when he has finished his survey he drops back into one of Folly's inferior rôles and offers us a parody of a learned text-book and lets Folly pretend to establish her position by quoting authorities. This might have been very amusing if Folly had continued to be the mouth-piece of wisdom. But we soon make out that Erasmus has reduced her to the rôle of strict Folly: she may say wise things but she thinks them foolish.

The creation of this new rôle might have been amusing to an audience familiar with the fault satirised, of establishing nonsense by a nonsensical use of Authorities—we shall see in a moment More making clever use of this mode of attack. But when Folly seeks to justify herself on Scriptural grounds, we become uneasy. What gave

83

and gives particular offence was the claim that Christ himself was the chief of fools:

'. . . christ him selfe mindynge the relefe and redempcion of mankyndes folie, although he was the ineffable wisedome of the father, became yet a maner foole. Euen as Paule saieth, he was made sinne also, to cure and heale the sinnes of the world, to which sinnes yet it pleased hym to ministre none other medecines than the Folie of the crosse . . .' [1]

What makes this frigid is that Folly does not identify herself with this supreme folly but treats it from a point of view at bottom hostile. For the wisdom of Folly throughout is *human* wisdom. Folly represents good sense, a right attitude to life. But it is one which recognises the harmony of Man and Nature, Body and Soul. Consequently, when she comes to speak of the religious, she treats them as she did the studious, all those in fact who violate the harmony of man's nature, or prefer illusions to reality.

When I have commented on the second part of the *Praise of Folly*, I shall deal with the defence of the book made both by More and Erasmus. Here I should like to anticipate that part of the defence which refers to this passage. There Erasmus admits that the language he used does not suit the speaker. This line of defence is damaging to the claims of artistic unity that are made for the book:

'I was so afraid lest I should offend and come short of the dignity of the theme and the demands of piety, that I preferred to break the rules of art and injure the dramatic credibility of the book.' [2]

I take this as a hint that we are on the wrong track in seeking to make the book *primarily* an affirmation of the spontaneous, instinctive and anti-intellectual element in life. Certainly, as we shall see in *Utopia*, these two men had intuitions that transcend their times. In their play they throw out notions that have since fructified. But these fruitful seeds do not come from their integrated selves. For them the struggle against false religion was the serious matter. So here: the first part of the *Praise of Folly* is like the witty conversation that we can imagine was often the prelude to their serious discussions. At bottom neither More nor Erasmus knew what to do with the overflowing of their wit, or rather they were content to let it remain in the world of *play*.

I come now to the part of the book that hurt, and was meant to

[1] Chaloner.   [2] *Op. Ep.*, Tom. II, p. 105.

hurt: the attack on the theologians and their claims to be the leading faculty in the world of learning. Here Erasmus does not hurt by saying the very worst things that were open to him to say: he does not rail or curse, but presents his charges in such a way as to make the theologians *ridiculous*. His art is therefore that of the satirist, and his aim is consequently to make the Humanist point of view appear the central, the truly human point of view. Moderation is therefore one of his chief weapons; another is to appear to have no personal animus. It is for this reason that he places himself among the fools: he is in fact the only fool to be named in the book.

One of his chief means of giving point to his satire was to provide a sense of proportion by placing the theologians in their social setting. Erasmus therefore offers us a satire of the whole of society from the Humanist point of view—at least, that is the pretention. In fact, he concentrates on a few of the topics dearest to the hearts of the Humanists. It is clear that he is more interested in bringing the Humanist standards to bear on the religious life of the times than on any other aspect of society. Yet, by dwelling for a moment on these lesser topics, we can obtain a summary view of the Humanist battle front.

A topic common to all Humanists was their attack on the feudal aristocracy. Speaking broadly, we may say that their aim was to make the lord into a gentleman. If we could travel backwards in time and find ourselves in the company of English lords at the court of Henry VIII, we should no doubt sympathise with the Humanists and long as they did for an aristocracy embodying the ideals of Plutarch or Cicero. Yet, with the whole course of subsequent history before us down to the present when the peculiar virtues of a landed aristocracy have almost vanished, we cannot help noticing how blind the Humanists were to the good inherent in the old feudal traditions. When Erasmus accompanied his noble English patrons to the hunt, he could only scoff, and he introduced into his picture of Folly the elaborate ceremonial at the kill, which is so vividly presented in *Sir Gawain*, lines 1325 ff. There, of course, the ceremony is treated with respect:

> Gedered þe grattest of gres þat þer were
> & didden hem derely vndo as þe dede askeȝ:

The poet describes the cutting up of the animal in great detail and the proper distribution of the parts to each according to his rank:

> Vche freke for his fee as falleȝ forto haue.

85

Erasmus viewed all this with scorn:

'And to this Classis do they appertain that sleight everything in comparison of hunting, and protest they take an unimaginable pleasure to hear the yell of the Horns and the yelps of the Hounds, and I believe could pick somewhat extraordinary out of their very excrement. And then what pleasure they take to see a Buck or the like unlac'd? Let ordinary fellows cut up an Ox or a Weather, 'twere a crime to have *this* done by any thing less than a Gentleman! who with his Hat off, on his bare knees, and a Cuttoe for that purpose (for every Sword or Knife is not allowable), with a curious superstition and certain postures, layes open the several parts in their respective order; while they that hemm him in admire it with silence, as some new religious Ceremony, though perhaps they have seen it an hundred times before. And if any of 'em chance to get the least piece of 't, he presently thinks himself no small Gentleman. In all which they drive at nothing more than to become Beasts themselves, while yet they imagin they live the life of Princes.'

Erasmus was not tilting here at the occasional 'backwoodsman' among the courtiers, but at the very cream of English nobility and at the king himself. (How often ambassadors reported that important business was delayed because the king was out hunting!) Even a refined courtier put hunting before reading. We have the testimony of Sir Thomas Wyatt, who, when describing the delights of country life, speaks of leaping hedge and ditch after the hounds and stalking with his bow, and hawking, as his main pleasures. Reading was reserved for the days when the weather made hunting impossible:

> This maketh me at home to hounte and hawke
> And in fowle weder at my booke to sitt
> In frost and snowe then with my bow to stawke.

The Humanist, in fact, found the Court setting him the most serious of his life-problems. We might call it the chief problem of the century for all concerned to 'make it new'. For it was clear that if civilisation were to return to Europe, it could only spread by taking root in the centres of each society. In semi-feudal countries, such as England, it was the court or nothing. When the Humanists came to court, as come they must, if they wanted responsible posts, they contrived a sort of civilised community among themselves, but they did not set the tone at court. It is remarkable to find how More and Erasmus, men fond of company, hated the life of the court and avoided it as much as possible. It did not provide them with a fit setting for their social lives, for it offended their practical morality at every step. This problem, of course, was never solved: there is little difference in Erasmus' picture of the court and that we find in Donne's Satires: 'I do hate/Perfectly all this towne . . .'

We must, however, look to More's *Utopia* for the serious treatment of the relation of the Humanist to practical life. In the *Praise of Folly* Erasmus directs his attention principally to religion. We can draw a fairly accurate picture of the Humanist outlook here from observation of his selected topics and the manner in which he treats them. What is most striking at a first reading is the apparent similarity between this outlook and that of the leading Protestants. Indeed, the Protestants later argued from this book that Erasmus had shown he belonged to them, and they could not understand how Erasmus could hesitate to join them. Yet they were mistaken. It is more significant to stress the identity of outlook between Erasmus and More. If we can rightly apply the word 'evangelical' to Erasmus' outlook, we should all the more emphasise the fact that in attacking these religious abuses Erasmus had the sympathy of all men of good will and good sense in his day.

Erasmus spoke for the protestant conscience of good Catholics, and on many of the pages of his book his laughter was painful to share. Too much of what he said was *vero verius*, as the commentators wrote in the margins of the *Praise of Folly*.

This wide survey of religious life in the *Praise of Folly* is the true setting for the peculiar Humanist battle, the central issue in the transvaluation of values that is still being fought out at this moment. Because everyone of good will in Erasmus' day agreed with him in his general satire, it was hard for the opponents of the Humanists to resist the particular attack Erasmus made in the name of Humanism on contemporary theologians. For it would not be so obvious to all contemporaries that the theologians needed to be supplanted from the position of authority they had so long enjoyed. This was a necessity apparent only to their rivals. For the sake of accuracy, it would be as well here to cease simplifying all the Humanists into one, and ask instead: in the name of what were More and Erasmus attacking the authority of the theologians in the world of learning? If we do this, we see at once that Erasmus was not calling on *all* Theology to cease: he is careful to state that his enemies are certain theologians. More, we shall see, wanted the whole of scholastic theology to close down. Both wished theologians to return to the early fathers, in particular Augustine and Jerome. They wanted the theologians to become more like themselves. In later life Erasmus summed up his aims as follows:

'My whole purpose in life has always been twofold: to stimulate others to cultivate *bonae literae* and to bring the study of *bonae literae* into harmony with theology. My reason for seeking this harmony has been, first, thereby to initiate a process which would impart to *bonae literae* a truly Christian note. (You are well aware that in Italy the characteristic note of Humanism has been hitherto notoriously pagan.) Secondly, that the study of theology on its present conventional lines might itself be improved and enlightened by theologians acquiring a better knowledge of Classical Latin and Greek and an improved critical taste in literature as a whole.' [1]

Put like this, the purpose sounds very moderate and conciliatory. In fact, however, it would have involved a total revolution in the presuppositions of worth entertained by the last scholastics. And though Erasmus safeguarded himself in words, and managed to live on good terms with some theologians of the old school, he had in fact declared war, and his enemies, as we shall see, knew it at once. If they were slow to grasp the full implications—for the notes on the New Testament had not yet appeared—they saw at once that Erasmus had made them ridiculous, and ridiculous because of the truth of his caricature. We have the evidence of Colet that Erasmus had truthfully portrayed his enemies, for in a letter to Erasmus of 1516 he speaks of some English theologians as 'theologi illi quos tu in Moria tua et aliis locis non minus vere quam facete describis'. [2]

In his sketch of the state of religion in his day Erasmus reserves his hardest blows for his main target, the theologians: here the charges in order are, a fondness for smelling out heresy in those who oppose them, a dexterity in evading awkward conclusions in argument, claims to knowledge of fantastic and abstruse matters, impious suppositions and paradoxes. Here again Erasmus works by contrast:

'Paul knew what Faith was, and yet when he saith, "Faith is the Substance of things hop'd for, and the Evidence of things not seen", he did not define it Doctor-like. . . . [The Apostles] knew the Mother of Jesus; but which of them has so Philosophically demonstrated how she was preserv'd from Original sin, as have done our Divines . . .

---

[1] Ep. 1581.   [2] *Op. Ep.*, Tom. II, p. 257.

They Baptized far and near, and yet taught no where what was the Formal, Material, Efficient, and final cause of Baptisme. . . .'

He further accuses them of not knowing the Gospel or St Pauls' Epistles, of claiming that the Church Universal rests on their foundations and not on those of the Bible. Coming nearing home, he charges them with contempt for good writing. And chief of all:

'Lastly, they look upon themselves as somewhat more than Men, as often as they are devoutly saluted by the name of 'Our Masters', in which they fancy there lyes as much as in the Jews Jehovah and therefore they reckon it a crime if Magister Noster be written other than in Capital Letters . . .'

or, as he puts it when he returns to the charge:

'Here they erect their Theological Crests, and beat into the people's ears those Magnifical Titles of Illustrious Doctors, Subtle Doctors, most Subtle Doctors, Seraphick Doctors, Cherubin-Doctors, Holy Doctors, Unquestionable Doctors . . .'

That precisely this was the main point of the book can be demonstrated very neatly from contemporary evidence. For when the *Praise of Folly* reached the theologians of Louvain, they put up one of their number, a certain *Martin Dorp*, to answer Erasmus. Erasmus took the opportunity to make a classic reply. Not only this: when More read the exchange of pamphlets, he was provoked to join in the controversy and thus provide us with further evidence that he was heart and soul with Erasmus, and, indeed, went much further than Erasmus in denouncing both the abuses of religion and the false claims to authority of contemporary theologians.

Dorp reported[1] that the theologians were up in arms against the *Praise of Folly*, saying, 'Why attack *us*, have we ever provoked *you*?' One tell-tale phrase is worth retaining:

'Some of the accusations may be true, but think of the scandal if they were known to the common people! Where would our authority be then?'

And, true to type, Dorp darkly threatens accusations of heresy. Secondly, Dorp objects to the satire as such. Thirdly, Dorp and his friends rightly saw as the main point of the *Praise of Folly* the

[1] *Op. Ep.*, Tom II, p. 12.

Humanist's claim to raise the study of *bonae literae* above their own. He invited Erasmus to put things right by a palinode, a *Praise of Wisdom*. It further appears from this letter that what was really worrying the theologians was that Erasmus was following up his satire on them with a piece of real undermining of their authority: his practical work of restoring the sense of the New Testament by going back to the Greek. The theologians were afraid that once the authority of the Vulgate were questioned, there would be no end to the process of doubting.

All this provided Erasmus with an occasion to write a defence of the *Praise of Folly*, which used to be printed with all the editions of that work. It is indeed a classic defence, and, as the persevering reader will learn, was one of the texts of the Humanists Ben Jonson knew by heart.

I call this defence a classic because it is an attempt to go back to first principles, to re-found the right to moral satire in the conditions of a Christian world, to distinguish between satire and libel, between the gratification of personal grievances and the duty to public morals. But, as with More, it is impossible to separate the Christian from the literary critic. Erasmus claimed that in the *Praise of Folly* he was merely doing in the form of satire what he had been doing in his devotional treatises. His purpose, he asserts, had been moral— to do good to his contemporaries. He claims that *euangelica veritas* is conveyed more effectively in the form of satire than by straightforward preaching. Consequently, if we call the *Praise of Folly* a monument of true Humanism, we must add, of *Christian* Humanism.

As this is the second piece of real thinking about literature in the century, I make no apology for an extensive quotation. I have in fact put together the passages that commended themselves to Ben Jonson before me:[1]

'What is wrong with their eyes, I ask you, what is the matter with the ears or taste of these people you mention as being offended by what they call the biting wit of my little book? In the first place, what right have they to call my wit biting, when the only person attacked by name in the whole book is . . . myself? Have they forgotten, I wonder, one of Jerome's favourite maxims: that there can be no question of harming the reputation of any individual in a general arraignment of vices? If anyone *does* feel himself under attack, that gives him no grounds for complaining of the satirist who sticks to generalities. If he *must* quarrel, it will have to be with himself, for giving himself away by discovering a particular reference to his own

[1] For the original, see *Op. Ep.*, Tom. II, pp. 90–114.

behaviour in what is written with such generality that the reference could only be made by one voluntarily applying the remarks to himself.

'Perhaps you will quote Persius against me:

> Your Satyrs, let me tell you, are too fierce:
> The Great will never bear so blunt a Verse.

If you think that there is no way of speaking out freely that can be justified, and that the truth should never be brought into the light of day if there is the slightest danger of giving offence by it, why do doctors use bitter medicines to effect their cures, and count bitter antidotes among their sovereign remedies? If they use these methods to cure the ills of the body, haven't we a much greater right to use similar methods in healing the diseases of the mind? I grant you that as there are some events which are too horrible to be shown on the stage and are therefore merely narrated in tragedies rather than acted before our eyes, so some vices of human beings are too loathsome to be mentioned if decency is to be preserved.

'People who take offence, though no names are mentioned, strike me as being all-too-feminine in temperament. For whenever women hear anything said to the detriment of their sex, they take the insult as a personal offence, but if they hear any praise of the few virtuous women in the world, they suppose it applies to the whole of womankind. If (in a satire) a fault is touched on from which I myself am free, I am not offended by the mention of it. On the contrary, I congratulate myself on being an exception to a charge I see so many people are open to. If the fault touched on is one of my secret vices, and, by complaining, I reveal its presence in myself, I still have no right to blame the author. If I am wise, I shall not let anyone see that I wince, I shall not give myself away. If I have a conscience, I shall take warning in good time, and so prevent myself being exposed to public scorn for the vice which is now being singled out for general censure.

'I fail to see why I should not be allowed in the *Praise of Folly* to take the same liberties as are thought legitimate in the theatre. Consider what comedians are permitted to say without blame when they attack kings, bishops, monks, wives and husbands, and all ranks of society. Because they eschew personalities, the audience laughs at them and the spectators either cry *touché* if they are honest with themselves, or else pretend that their withers are unwrung.'

No doubt we should wish to add and qualify nowadays if we had to re-state the justification of the moral satirist. We should, in particular, wish to introduce into the defence more of the ways poetry affects us as distinct from prose. But this defence was found adequate down at least to the time of Pope. For it was a genuine translation of a classic position—of Horace, for example—adapted to the needs of modern writers. The letter to Dorp ought to figure in any anthology illustrating the development of literary criticism.

But to return to Erasmus' attack on the theologians. He adopts in this letter the same tactic as in the book: he excepts all good theologians and is only concerned with the few bad ones—those who complain of their treatment in the *Praise of Folly*! These, he asserts, are practically illiterate and draw their knowledge from secondary sources. Yet they claim to be treated with the utmost respect. In particular he accuses them of hating *bonae literae*:

'Hii magno studio conspirant in bonas literas. Ambiunt in senatu theologorum aliquid esse, et verentur ne, si renascantur bonae litterae, et si resipiscat mundus, videantur nihil scisse, qui antehac vulgo nihil nescire videbantur.'

Here the cat is out of the bag: *bonas litteras metuunt et suae timent tyrannidi*. But Erasmus twists the knife in the wound. He reminds Dorp that in the *Praise of Folly* he had not said all that could be said against the theologians: there was, for instance, the topic of their morals. But he presses further in claiming that what he did say was only a shadow of what good theologians say about their weaker colleagues. Here again Erasmus comes close to what Luther and others would soon be saying: that the theologians preferred their own notions to those to be found in the sources of theology, the Bible and the early Fathers. But here again, as the next pages will show, Erasmus is only saying mildly what More wrote with passion. Finally, Erasmus raises the war-cry of the new age: *quid commercii Christo et Aristoteli?* What has scholasticism to do with Christianity?

The most interesting point in Dorp's reply to this is his readiness to join with Erasmus in attacking the bishops. He speaks of the *mira paucitas* of bishops who live up to the standard set by St Paul:

'But a Biszhoppe must be blamelesse, the huszbande of one wife, sober, discrete, manerly, harberous, apte to teach: Not geuen to moch wyne, no fighter, not geuen to filthy lucre: but gentle, abhorrynge stryfe, abhorrynge coueteousness. . . .'

Dorp's second point is one that can still be made against anyone who thinks that 'poetry can save us'. Where do you draw the line? Is *all* poetry to be included? This had even more point against Erasmus since he himself did not know how to justify many of the authors he read and recommended. How can fiction and poetry be made to advance the cause of Christ? Or rather, how can they be defended from the charge of either distracting or corrupting Christians? Dorp's arguments were later much used by Puritans and are still to be met with to-day. Finally, he returns to the central issue: which of the two has the responsibility for Christ's flock, the theologian or the poet—or your new Greek scholar?

Dorp actually goes on to press home the theologians' side of the battle, but I shall not give his further arguments here, because at this point More steps in. When he read these three letters he was so indignant that he at once wrote off a long letter attacking Dorp and all theologians. Not only that, when in 1520 a monk attacked Erasmus, More wrote the most outspoken of his attacks against the people Erasmus had merely made fun of in the *Praise of Folly*.

The next stage in this argument will be that the *Praise of Folly* and *Utopia* have their origin in a strikingly similar conception both of the way serious topics should be handled in literature and of the values which it mattered to assert in the face of a hostile world. It is therefore an essential preliminary to a discussion of the *wit* in *Utopia* to present the evidence which proves that More shared Erasmus' point of view on the matters of fact underlying both parts of *The Praise of Folly*.

When Erasmus received this last letter from Dorp, he wrote a long and bitter reply, which he afterwards suppressed. This has now disappeared. At the same time, and independently, More wrote a letter to Dorp of some 1,600 lines, which he in turn suppressed, but which was not lost. It became an item in the 'protestant' version of More's works, where it appears under the title:

APOLOGIA PRO MORIA ERAS =
mi, qua etiam docetur quam neces =
saria sit linguae Graecae co =
gnitio.

What is extraordinary about this Humanist manifesto is the heat and confusion. More pours out his indignation and mixes together arguments of all kinds. This makes for difficult reading. Fortunately, for our purposes it is enough to note this fact, that More is thoroughly aroused both by the attack on Erasmus, and, what is even more important for this argument, by his hatred of current theologians.

In spite of the title given to the letter in *Lucubrationes*, it is not a defence of the *Praise of Folly*, for More considered that Erasmus had said before him all that was necessary. It is rather a supporting attack on the pretensions of theologians, and, in particular, on their underlying philosophy and logic. More's case is that the spirit in which contemporary theologians treated divine matters was both trifling and impious: they were fools and dangerous fools. What was more, they were ignorant of the true sources of theology, the Bible and the Early Fathers. Since the letter is so badly constructed I cannot summarise the argument. Fortunately, More had a gift which redeems even the dullest parts of his controversial treatises: the gift of summarising his case in an unforgettable anecdote. As he himself wrote, 'from this one story you can judge what all the theologians I am attacking are like:

'Some time back I was having dinner at the home of a very rich Italian merchant, who was as learned as he was rich. At this party there was a certain theologian, a monk famous for his powers of disputation, who had come to England from the Continent to give this country a taste of his ability in religious argument.[1] And if I had time, I would give you an account of the propositions he defended here: they would make you laugh. But at this dinner the theologian showed his skill by extempore refutation of everything advanced in the company or by immediate support of everything denied—and this on topics having nothing to do with Theology or Philosophy or any of the things he was supposed to be an authority on. And when the host brought the discussion round to theological topics, the theologian proved to be equally efficient there. The merchant then proposed as a joke a very topical question: that it was better to keep one concubine in your house than to run after many whores in the town. The theologian embraced this proposition eagerly and began to prove the contrary from one of his *limpidissimi Doctores*, who had written a treatise on the subject which had just been printed at Paris. There was a long wrangle, but in the course of it the merchant noticed that the theologian, who could quote so well from his fellow-theologians, did not seem to be so familiar with the Bible. So he began to support his side of the argument by quotations, which, he said, came from the New Testament—and he gave chapter and verse. But, supposing the epistle he named as his authority had sixteen chapters, he would quote from chapter twenty, and so on. The theologian, who had no idea he was having his leg pulled, either defied the authority of the Bible or found some clever way of making the plain

[1] 'In the masterly handling of *quaestiones*', for which see p. 95 below.

sense of the quotation mean the very opposite. And if he was hard pressed, he would even claim that though he knew the merchant's verse, it was given a different interpretation by one of the famous commentators on the Bible, Nicholas de Lyra.'

More was right: although the story may not have been so neat in fact, and gains by More's way of telling it, it was *ben trovato* in that it makes the point of the *Praise of Folly* in an even sharper form. More adopts the same tactic to make the allied point, that the modern schoolman missed the truth by trusting to secondary compilations and neglecting the sources, or rather the contexts from which the schoolmen's quotations had been torn:

'I met an old man once in a bookshop, who, as the saying goes, had one foot in the grave, and would soon have both. He was a Doctor of Theology of more than thirty years' standing. When I chanced to remark in his hearing that St Augustine held that the devils all had substantial bodies, the theologian scowled and tried to browbeat me for advancing so daring a heresy. "I don't hold the view myself, Father," I said, "nor do I blame Augustine for holding it. To err is human. I believe most of what he writes, but I don't believe every word either in his books or in anyone else's." The man was already in a rage because I had dared to insult one of the Church Fathers. "Do you think I haven't read my Augustine?" he said, "I finished him before you were born." And he would have floored me and finished *me* off if a convenient means of settling the question had not presented itself. There was a copy of Augustine's book on devils in the shop. I opened it, found the passage, and showed it to the theologian. He read it once, he read it twice, and when, with my assistance, he managed to make out the sense at a third attempt, he said, "I can't understand what Augustine is driving at in this book of yours. He didn't say *that* in the *Magister Sententiarum*, which is a book of far greater authority than yours.'

Here again More fixes and sums up in an anecdote the following information, which I have copied from a modern scholar:

'Peter Abelard was as radical an innovator in the twelfth century as Erasmus was in the sixteenth. Abelard turned Scholastic philosophy into a literature of questions by collecting some 1,800 texts from the early Church Fathers and sorting them out under 158 controversial "quaestiones" or seeming contradictions in the *Sic et Non* ... The followers of Abelard continued the development with the integration of Biblical statements into a systematic whole. Rarely, if ever, did they feel the need of examining original texts in an attempt to resolve contradictions by a closer study of the sources. They were satisfied with the second-hand knowledge of the Bible and the Fathers garnered in little snippets from the *Glossa Ordinaria* of Walafrid Strabo or the *Decretals* of Gratian.

'Erasmus, on the other hand, devoted his life to the re-editing of original sources . . . Thus he reoriented the study of theology to a careful study and grammatical explication of the original texts. Erasmus was forever insisting upon a return to the sources—"ad fontes"—because an examination of the correct text frequently resolved the "quaestiunculae" of the Schools, and a close attention to the historical context removed further difficulties.' [1]

What the modern scholar sets out coolly as dead history, More resumes with all the heat of battle about him:

'To sum up: I do not attack all theologians, nor condemn all the "questions" of the neo-scholastics. But I think we should not only condemn but abhor all those pointless questions which contribute nothing to learning but much to impiety. And as for those which are serious in their treatment of Man and reverent towards God, provided they are kept in their place, I grant they are good for sharpening the wits. But I utterly deny that the salvation of the Church Universal depends on them. I approve the cultivation of these questions as an addition to the learning of a man who has first gone to the sources, but I do *not* approve the life-long study of them and only of them to the neglect of the Classics and the very Gospel itself.'

The tone of this letter is sharp, but never offensive: More writes as to one capable of appreciating his arguments and taking his points. (It is interesting to learn that Dorp eventually recanted and that he, More and Erasmus became friends and remained friends until the untimely death of the theologian.)

I shall pass over the other controversies in which More continued to support Erasmus—particularly over the translation and editing of the New Testament—and turn to the so-called 'Letter to a Monk', for here we see More at his most passionate. (It is dismissed in three lines in Chamber's book on More!) It appears from this letter (of 1,555 lines) that the monk was a man of some standing whom More had known for many years, since he refers to the days before the

[1] Taken from P. Albert Duhamel in *Studies in Philology*, vol. LII, April 1955, Number 2, pp. 101–2.

monk retired to contemplation in his monastery. This monk had written to warn More of the dangers of consorting with such a near-heretic as Erasmus. For this impudent attack on the faith and morals of Erasmus, More gives the Contemplative such a magisterial dressing-down that the letter was included with others by More in a collection printed at Basle in 1520, designed to show the solidarity of the Humanists with Erasmus on the question of the right to go to the original Greek for the true meaning of the New Testament. It would be convenient to have the whole of this letter in English, for although much of it deals too closely with the monk and affairs of the time to interest us, it would be desirable to see two things *in their context*: More's praise of Erasmus and his attack on the monkish orders as a whole.

More's praise of Erasmus is as high and as comprehensive as we could wish. Against the charge of near-heresy, he asserts:

'There can be no question of the quality of Erasmus' faith: his so long studies, so many late nights, so many dangers undergone, such vicissitudes in fortune and health, all for the sake of the Scriptures, are themselves a very store-house or source of faith.'

Against the charge of bad style, More ridicules the monk and declares that no-one who ever wrote Latin had an easier style or was more careful in the choice of words. The monk had also attacked the *Praise of Folly*, but once again More considered that Erasmus had settled this question in his Letters to Dorp. More does, however, break out once to say that 'there is less folly and more piety in that book than in most of your . . .' but the aposeiopesis cuts off what might have been an indiscreet tirade.

Towards the end of the letter, More gathers together all the points he has been making:

'I am not going to write a formal eulogy of Erasmus: I doubt whether my powers would be equal to it. And in any case his reputation with all the good and learned is secure. His own works speak for him, and when the present attacks die down Erasmus will be famous.'

We may compare this with a sentence from a contemporary letter to Edward Lee (February 29, 1520), who had attacked Erasmus' edition of the New Testament:

'Quum augurer atque praesagiam, aut euictis hostibus aut desistentibus, Erasmi labores aeternum esse victuros.'

To conclude: for More, Erasmus was the great model of the Christian Humanist—a term to be defined in the following pages. He was eminent because his classical studies increased the possibility of a genuine religious life. This letter is all the more precious because in later years More was bound to feel disappointed that this eminent Christian Humanist did not regard the struggle between the Pope and Luther as truly central.

But the letter is equally precious for showing that, though More was to become almost the official spokesman of a persecuting orthodoxy, he was not blind to the abuses, the crimes indeed, of the clergy. It is, then, in the course of giving the monk a lesson in spiritual manners that More incidentally illustrates the similarity of views between himself and Erasmus. Here is an instance. In the *Praise of Folly* Erasmus wrote, while giving an account of the typical mediaeval sermon:

'Lastly, such is their whole action that a man would swear they had learnt it from our common Tumblers, though yet they come short of 'em in every respect. However, they are both so like, that no man will dispute but that either these learnt their Rhetorick from them, or they theirs from these.'

When we read this, we might pardonably suppose Folly was indulging in one more extravagance. Yet here we have More attacking the monk for using quotations from the Scriptures *mal à propos* in order to ridicule Erasmus: 'you play the fool,' he says, 'with the Bible as the jester does in comedies; a trick both shocking and cheap:

'A rascal of a minstrel recently mimicked the manner, voice, appearance and gesture of a preaching friar, and put into his 'sermon', which was entirely made up of a string of Biblical quotations, an obscene and ridiculous story of the habits of certain friars. It was a shameless account of a friar wooing and seducing a poor woman. The rogue made up the whole filthy story in all its unsavoury episodes out of quotations from the Bible, never once using a word or phrase not to be found in the Scriptures, and applied them so cleverly to such disparate matter that the most serious person there could not help smiling, nor could the most wanton-minded spectator fail to be revolted by this disgusting treatment of the Scriptures. Some of the spectators thought the whole thing providential: for, since most friars habitually adulterate the Word of God, it was right that there should be people to mimic the friars and employ their own methods against them, so cutting their throats with their own sword.

'If it is impious, as it surely is, to abuse the Scriptures for the sake of raising a dirty laugh, how much more impious is it to do what you

are doing: misusing the words of the Bible to take away the reputation of Erasmus.'

If we came upon this anecdote by itself without More's comment,
should we not say it was from an unexpurgated edition of the *Praise
of Folly*? Is not this what Erasmus would have written if he had in
fact been speaking in his own person and not under the Mask of
Folly?

More, however, was not primarily concerned to make the monks
ridiculous: he was in too serious a mood for that. He was concerned
to strike a central, knock-out blow. The gravamen of his charge is
that the monks cared more for their special position in society than
for the Christian religion: they stood in fact for a rival or substitute
religion hostile to Christianity. They attacked Erasmus, not because
he was a danger to Christianity, but because he was a danger to the
monks' *prestige*. The bitterness of More's attack was due in part to
personal feelings:

'There cannot be a good man in this world to whom all the religious orders are not especially dear. My feelings towards them have
been more than love: I have always felt for them a religious veneration . . .'

The contrast between the ideal and the actual was hard for More to
bear. First, there was the war between the rival orders, a war of petty
details, such as the colour of the monks' dress. Worse was the
monks' pride: not only, he says, did they treat the common people
like dirt, but all the clergy not subject to their rule. Their true religion, he says, was adoration of that which separates them from the
Christian community. And this religion consisted in swallowing the
camel while straining at the gnat—or as More puts it, of swallowing
an elephant whole. (The claim, for instance, that it was a *mortal* sin
to omit one verse in a prayer.)

More, however, goes further and reports a story—unfortunately
shrouded to prevent identification of the criminals—of a group of
monks who were eventually caught committing the worst crime More
could imagine. Before proceeding to their crime these monks used to
go into the Lady chapel and ask for the blessing of the Blessed
Virgin. 'That,' says More, 'was a shocking exception. Let me quote
you an example of the normal thing:

'There was at Coventry a friar of the unreformed Franciscan
branch who used to go round the town, the suburbs, and villages

around Coventry, preaching that whoever read over the Hours of the
Blessed Virgin once a day could never be damned. The people were,
of course, only too ready to believe that there was such a sure and
easy road to Heaven. The local priest, a decent and learned man,
because he thought this nonsense, at first, did not speak his mind:
but when he saw that his congregation were being seriously infected
by the disease, and that it was the worst element who became regular
readers of the Hours, and regarded their reading as giving them complete protection for all their sins—a licence, in fact, to be wicked for
the rest of the day—then he began to warn his flock that even if they
said the prayers over *ten* times a day they would not on that account
alone be nearer salvation. Better, he said, to drop the prayers
altogether if they dropped at the same time the sins they committed
because they thought the prayers made them safe. The audience
were wild; hissed and stamped. The next day the friar went into
the pulpit and invoked the aid of Mary against her enemies. He
soon converted the people to the belief that their parson was a
heretic.

'Now, while this scandal was at its height I paid a visit to Coventry
to see my sister in a nearby convent. I had just had time to get off my
horse when the question was served up to me: could a man be damned
who once a day recited the Psalter of the Virgin? "What a foolish
question!" I said, and laughed the matter off. I was warned on the
spot that I had given the sort of answer that might endanger my life
and my soul, for a Holy and Learned Father had somewhere pronounced the contrary opinion. That made no impression on me and
I thought no more about it. I was then invited to a dinner party.
When I arrived, this friar came in: an old man, a gloomy deathshead
in fact, followed by a boy carrying his books. I grasped the situation
in a flash: the stage was being set for a battle. As soon as we sat
down to eat, my host repeated the question and the friar gave the
substance of his sermon. I kept my mouth shut: I don't like taking
part in such hateful and time-wasting discussions. But the time came
when I saw I should have to say something, so I gave my opinion
briefly and carelessly. Then the friar brought out his prepared speech,
longer than two sermons. His case turned and rested on certain
miracles many of which he cited from a *Mariale*, and others from
foolish collections of tales which devotees of the cult of the Virgin
treat as gospels. He had some of these laid out on the table as his
authorities. Well, at length he finished his long speech and I replied
in a quiet voice that what he had said had no force of persuasion on
anyone who rejected his miracles—and it was not a matter of faith
to believe them. And even if you did believe them, they would not

prove his case. For instance, it is quite possible to suppose that a prince might occasionally pardon one of his subjects—or even a conquered enemy—at the instances of his mother, but no prince would be such a fool as to give it out as a law that you could commit any crime or treason provided you first applied in a set form to his mother for pardon. There was a long squabble, but the effect of my speech and the subsequent argument was that the friar was praised to the skies and I was laughed at as a fool. In fact matters finally got to such a point in Coventry that the Bishop himself had to bring his whole weight to bear to suppress this friar and his cult . . .

'This is the sort of thing that Erasmus was attacking in his *Praise of Folly*.' [1]

I hope that I have now made my point: that More and Erasmus speak as one voice on the issues at stake in the *Praise of Folly*. I now wish to proceed to show the close connection between the *Praise of Folly* and *Utopia*. Before doing this, however, I should like to comment on the significance of this coincidence of views for the whole spiritual history of these times. For we have now come to one of the great dramatic moments in history: a moment that recurs again and again in various forms, a moment, therefore, which is highly instructive for us to-day. Put broadly, the problem is the relation of men of ideas to the forces of society. More and Erasmus in their attitude to religion were the spokesmen of the best element in society. We can in fact speak of a Catholic Reform movement. This movement is in danger of being forgotten: the Protestants regarded it as a timid precursor of their own movement, and Catholics have not until recently cared to know just how radical the attitude of good Catholics was at the moment when Luther appeared on the scene.

For it is Luther who personifies the force that makes this moment in history so dramatic: he raises the usual farce of human affairs almost to the heights of tragedy. We shall miss the true significance of the writings of More and Erasmus in our literary tradition if we do not see their bearing on the whole life of the sixteenth century and on our own.

We must, we cannot help testing the values of Christian Humanism by what its professors did when challenged by Luther. For it was Luther who put Christian Humanism to the vital test. Before Luther came, More and Erasmus were unaware of a split in their *Weltanschauung*. They had seen such a split occur in Italy. There, some of

[1] For the original, see *Epistolae Aliquot Eruditorum* (1520).

the Humanists had in fact ceased to be Christians—a few openly, the majority secretly. Perhaps this shows that they were truer humanists than those who read the Greek and Roman classics north of the Alps. For we now know that to absorb the classics passively must involve absorbing a philosophy which is humanist in a pagan sense. The values of the Greco-Roman world are largely the values of that world only—a world in which this life on earth counts for more than any life to come.

Neither More nor Erasmus embraced the classics in this thoroughly passive way. And we may argue that their appreciation of the classics was less inward because they took from the classics only what suited them as Christians. Actually, their relation to the classics was less simple than *that*, but in practice they were able to cover the inner contradictions of their relation. In practice they were Christians first and classics second. Luther forced them to decide in what sense they were Christians.

We therefore cannot avoid the question: did More and Erasmus commit *la trahison des clercs*? Did they come to deny the positions they held in the *Praise of Folly* and *Utopia*? We have seen that it is no easy matter to say what positions Erasmus held, and we shall soon see that it is equally difficult to say what positions More held in his *Utopia*. But we know how they answered when Luther put them the question: for me or against? We cannot study More or Erasmus without forming an opinion of their answers. We know that More answered clearly to Luther: against you: and that when he came to the further test put to him by his king, he said: for God and the Pope, against you, my master. And we know that Erasmus said to Pope, Emperor and Luther: neither with you nor against you: and that, though eventually forced to write against Luther, if Luther regarded him as an enemy, the Pope and probably More himself did not consider that Erasmus had done what they wanted.

I shall not pursue the careers of More and Erasmus any further, but I could wish that the reader who follows out More's steps to his voluntary martyrdom would also consider the painful dilemma of Erasmus in *his* last years and perhaps bear in mind these words of Donne:

> Oh, to some
> Not to be Martyrs, is a martyrdome.

One task, however, cannot be avoided: to define what More and Erasmus stood for in the years before these terrible questions were put to them. This is a topic that is usually avoided and, it is true, we need to walk delicately and allow for all that we do not know. What

I wish to insist on is the fact (with all its consequences) that they were
civilised Christians. There is no difficulty in accepting the *adjective*
for Erasmus: to appreciate the noun, we need to soak ourselves in
the *Enchiridion* and in the preface he wrote for it when it was repub-
lished in 1518. But for some Christians and some civilised persons,
the whole phrase may seem a contradiction in terms: a Christian,
they say, cannot be civilised: and these Christians reply, a civilised
person cannot be a Christian, if we use both terms in a strict sense
and as implying high values. It is true that if we look in history for
eminent Christians who have been eminently civilised, we do not at
once find names. All would agree that to combine these two qualities
unusual mental powers are needed: it requires *great play, great
flexibility of mind.*

This is the quality I discover in Thomas More. I think he was
virtually, what Erasmus was actually, an escaped monk turned man
of the world. Both were men who 'knew how to undervalue the world
with good breeding' – though their refinement was not that of the
eighteenth century, nor had they its coarseness. As for More's
Christianity, I do not think it is an exaggeration to say that if More
had died of the plague in 1517, his works would sooner or later have
been put on the Catholic index a'ong with those of Erasmus. The
reader will recall the significant difference between the two collected
editions of More's work which appeared after his death. Some of his
works are virtually on the index to-day.[1] No reader of Chambers'
book on More would guess that More put his heart into the letter to
the monk. Not that anything More wrote smells of heresy: but it
exhibits far greater freedom and play of mind than his biographers
seem able to allow him.

I have hinted that this may mean that More was fundamentally
inconsistent. Neither More nor Erasmus shines as a philosopher.
They did not grapple with the great philosophical achievements of
the mediaeval schoolmen. As I have written above, they did not
argue them off the stage of history, they laughed them into limbo.
No, the strength of these two Christian Humanists lies in their poise
of mind. More, in particular, strikes me as being admirably balanced
—but not in the least static. I see in him two violent pulls: More was
drawn powerfully to enjoyment of life: he was drawn even more
powerfully to reject that enjoyment. His wit, as I see it, was genera*ed
from the violence of this conflict, from his ability to see life from
opposing points of view. That, at least, is the hypothesis I shall put
to the test in commenting on his *Utopia.*

[1] Or were until recently: see page 124.

103

MORE'S 'UTOPIA'
The Vindication of
Christian Humanism

Mᴏʀᴇ's *Utopia* presents us at once with the greatest challenge to and the finest vindication of the point of view I have been endeavouring to put forward in this essay. For this book is admittedly the most important document of Christian Humanism that we possess. It is so important that whatever judgement we form of its merits will have a bearing on the greatest issues in life—what finally matters for people capable of choosing their modes of life. This very importance has made it impossible to read More's book without somewhere or other falsifying the evidence. Such a judgement may sound arrogant: taken by itself, it may suggest that, whereas all previous commentators have had to wander blindly in a twilight of mingled reason and superstition, I alone have been granted a clear, unerring light, which enables me to bring centuries of tentative discussion to a final, triumphant close. Needless to say, I do not stand in this relation to my predecessors. On the contrary, I owe almost all my understanding of the book to them, and in particular, to two recent commentaries: Chambers' account in his book on More and H. W. Donner's admirable *Introduction*. What strikes me as right about *Utopia* will be found in their pages. Where I differ from them is in arguing that the book demands to be read in a different spirit from theirs, and that we must regard it primarily and all the time as *literature*.

Utopia has in a sense proved too exciting to be treated as literature. It is not, for instance, as literature that it is recommended reading in the Soviet Union. Nor is it as literature that it is praised by the ultra-reactionaries who see More as the rigidly orthodox champion of a mediaeval point of view. What these two opposed views have in common is a disregard for the book as it stands and a passionate regard for what More himself in his private capacity really thought about the great issues of life. For both views presuppose a simple relation between the man and the book: they suppose that it matters whether the More who died a martyr did or did not hold the views put into the mouth of one or other of the speakers in *Utopia*.

To claim that the way out from this *impasse* is to return to literary criticism is not to express indifference to the 'ideas' that can be extracted from *Utopia*. But it does imply hostility to the way in which the 'ideas' are treated in Moscow and Rome. To take the Moscow view first, it is true that many of the features of Utopia have either been realised since or are within reaching distance, in the sense that a political party could seriously include them in a programme. This is a remarkable fact, and it is undoubtedly a credit to the Humanist More that it should be so. Yet this does not make *Utopia* a book like Huxley's *Brave New World*. In Huxley's book, if I am correctly informed, what is predicted is something that the author had every right to suppose was within the possibilities of science and technology at the time he was writing. Huxley's science was the science of the day. And when—if it happens—the world is run on the lines predicted by Huxley, nobody will call Huxley a prophet. We have no evidence to support the view that More conceived of his ideas as referring to things already started or that he looked forward to their inevitable triumph in the future. He certainly puts forward the case for a kind of communism through his characters, but, judging by the book, and that is what we must do, we cannot say that More is in any obvious sense historically linked to those who also advocated communism, but as a programme of action for the nineteenth century. What we have to discover is the meaning of communism as put forward in *Utopia*. We might also go on to enquire into the meaning of communism in More's own life: yet this will have nothing to do with *Utopia*.

For this reason those who are shocked by the idea that a canonised saint should have written so strongly in favour of communism in his book do not interpret *Utopia* by producing statements from More's later writings in which he repudiates the doctrine. But where they are on stronger ground is in appealing to general probability, and, in particular, to the impossibility of men of one century anticipating the point of view of later centuries. We may note in passing that the arguments used by Christians—who rightly insist that More's pronouncements must be treated as pronouncements within the limitations of his century—can also be turned against the use of the

Scriptures when applied to the social conditions of our day. These, however, are difficult problems and I am not competent to argue them. But it does seem sensible to me, when trying to discover the meaning of *Utopia*, to consider the times in which it was written.

Here, however, we must be careful not to decide *a priori* what were the limits of thought in More's day. What Christians and especially Catholics must guard against is another form of anachronism: that of reading into the past the self-conscious orthodoxy of Catholics *after* the emergence of Luther. Here again I am not competent to say very much. But I would ask those of my readers whose chief interest is in the martyr and saint, the man who died for loyalty to the Pope and the Church of Rome, to allow that More's relation to his religion suffered a subtle change when Luther's challenge and Henry's challenge forced him to become self-conscious about his allegiance. For my purposes I do not need to define closely what the change was. All I ask for is permission to suppose that More's mind could enjoy greater play in the years in which he was closely associated with Erasmus than in the years in which he was combating Tyndale or his King.

As the reader will have discovered, the point of view I advocate is that we should look on *Utopia* as a piece of *wit*, and that if we keep tight hold of this fact we shall not find ourselves willing to discuss the book on the lines favoured either by Moscow or by Rome. After the discussion of the *Praise of Folly*, I shall not need to distinguish this point of view from that of those who take wit to mean pure fooling. For some commentators, who also reject Moscow and Rome, do so in order to claim that *Utopia* belongs to light literature: they call it a work of pure entertainment. As we shall see, it *is* a work of entertainment, and it is important to grasp that its greatness cannot be separated from the element of entertainment. And here I differ from those who regard the book as foolery *alternating with* seriousness. The whole difficulty for the reader is that More does not mark the passages 'to be regarded as a joke' from those to be taken as deadly earnest. He is nowhere present in his work as a commentator on the drama. The form of his humour is to leave everything to the reader. As with the *Praise of Folly*, the serious and the trifling are inextricable, and each reinforces the other.

In the effort to make this point of view triumph and replace that of Chambers and Donner, I think it is worth while to glance at the way the book was presented to the public. This does not *prove* anything: it is still open to us to argue that the book was totally misunderstood until the nineteenth or the twentieth century. Yet I should think it a point of some interest for our general enquiry into the significance of Humanism in the early sixteenth century to make out how Humanists of this period took the book when it appeared. Perhaps I can make my point first in a trivial way by saying that I wish we could divert our attention from what leads us to call the book *Utopia* to the conception of the book as it was first presented in the Louvain edition of 1516. At least we could then say that it is a book with the same title as the *Praise of Folly*! For the 1519 edition of the *Praise of Folly* is entitled: 'libellus uere aureus, nec mi/nus eruditus, & salutaris, quam festiuus', and if we could look at the first edition of *Utopia* (1516), before we came to the word 'Utopia' we should find:

LIBELLUS VERE AUREUS NEC
MINUS SALUTARIS QUAM FESTI=

uus

The book, then, is presented as a work of wit serving serious purposes. And if we read on to find out what this work is witty about, we discover 'de optimo reip. statu', that is, on the best form of ordering society.

This in itself tells us very little for we cannot be sure that More had a hand in the printer's title. But, as we shall see, there is every reason to suppose that Erasmus was present while More was writing his book, and this is in fact how Erasmus introduced the book to the wittiest Humanist in Paris, a man for whom he had the greatest respect, William Cop:

'If you haven't read More's *Utopia* yet, do send for it, if you want to have a good laugh, or rather, if you want to see the very sources from which practically all the ills of society rise.' [1]

Here again we must not press a single sentence too far. But I hope to make it plain that this sentence shows how the book ought to be read. Positively, it argues that we should take the whole thing as a game, yet, in doing so, we should be inspecting, not the details of a system, but the fundamental causes of social evils: that is, we should look at the details of *Utopia* separately, not as elements in a possible state, but as embodying points of view which might enable us to see what is wrong with our own society.

I wish Erasmus had himself enlarged on this in a preface, for if Erasmus did not understand *Utopia*, I should like to know who did. But as he was anxious that the book should not appear to be recommended merely as the work of a friend to whom he was known to

[1] Ep. 537, 24 Feb. 1516–17.

be partial, he encouraged others to supply the readers with hints
how to take the book. We may therefore begin with the verses of
Cornelius Grapheus:

> Vis qui uirtutum fontes? uis unde malorum
>   Principia? & quantum in rebus inane latet?
> Haec lege . . .

given the task of picking out the heart of the matter in a few lines, it
is interesting to see that he stresses as the fundamental character of
the book the sources of good and evil, the vanity of life. *Gerardus
Noviomagus* had the same thought:

> Hic fontes aperit, recti prauique . . .
> The hid welles and fountaines both of vice and virtue
> Thou hast them here subiect vnto thine eye . . .

Busleiden stresses the model of a commonwealth and claims that
More has shown how to prevent modern states from following the
unhappy fate of Sparta, Athens and Rome. He takes More's solution to the problem of greed, intrigue, luxury, envy and wrong, which
are promoted by the possession of private property—the causes of
ruin to all other states—to be the institution of communism. *Guil-
laume Budé*, too, sees as the great contemporary evil, rivalry over
private property. To this he opposes the Christian ideal:

'But the founder and regulator of all property, Jesus Christ, left
among His followers a Pythagorean communion and love; and
ratified it by a plain example, when Ananias was condemned to
death for breaking this law of communion.'

He therefore praises the Utopians for holding to three Christian
principles: equality of property, love of peace, contempt for gold:

'Three things these, which overturn, one may say, all fraud, all
imposture, cheating, roguery, and unprincipled deception.'

By the observation of these three rules in Europe

'We should soon see pride, covetousness, insane competition, and
almost all other deadly weapons of our adversary the Devil, fall
powerless:'

Peter Gilles uses words very similar to those of Erasmus in summing
up his praise of the book:

'his singular prudence, who so well and wittyly marked and bare away al the originall causes and fountaynes (to the vulgare people commenly most vnknowen) whereof both yssueth and springeth the mortall confusion and vtter decaye of a commen wealth . . .'

In the light of all this we cannot doubt that More's fellow-Humanists took the references to communism seriously and used them to stress the contrast with the prevailing evils of the day, pride, avarice and greed.

If the first demand on the literary student is to read *Utopia* as a work of wit, the second is to read it as a piece of Latin. It is to the lasting disgrace of English scholars that they have allowed their readers to suppose, as it were, that this classic of Humanism was not written by More but by Ralph Robinson. His translation has merits; it may even be urged that it is not unlike what More would have written had he himself translated his Latin, but the point is, not merely that he did not do so, but that More's personality in Latin is not identical with his personality in writing English. We must therefore not neglect the obvious fact that, like the *Praise of Folly*, More's *Utopia* is a piece of show Latin. More has an original style, a personal style, full of faults if you like, but of deliberate faults. It is also full of rare words to 'show his reading', as we may learn from the authority on this subject:

'C'est dans le choix des mots que sa coquetterie d'humaniste se donne carrière. Il va chercher chez Plaute ou chez Ennius une expression archaïque, chez Pline un terme technique, dans la langue chrétienne une façon de dire détournée de son sens ancien. Le mot le plus rare est toujours celui qu'il préfère.' [1]

We should therefore do two things: in the interests of accuracy, we should go to More's text whenever we wish to make an important factual reference to the content, and we should go to the Latin when we wish to gauge whether More is 'behind' any particular passage: for it is only by listening to the Latin that we can detect whether any part is written with unusual warmth.

The third demand on the literary reader is to consider the relation of the two parts of the book. Here we have an excellent guide in an essay by J. H. Hexter: *More's Utopia: The Biography of an Idea.* In the famous biographical sketch of More which Erasmus wrote on July 23rd, 1519, we find, 'He wrote Book II at leisure and composed Book I hastily soon after under the pressure of events . . .' Professor Hexter tries to show that it is most unlikely that the whole of our

[1] *Thomas More: L'Utopie*, ed. Marie Delcourt, 1936, p. 29.

Book II could have been written before any of our Book I was composed: the narrator, for instance, must have been in More's mind from the beginning. The details, however, of his attempted reconstruction do not matter here: what does matter is to discover the *point* of adding a Book I to an almost complete Book II.

Here I am delighted to be able to report that such an able investigator as Professor Hexter, writing from a different point of view, stresses the community of outlook between More and Erasmus. I shall therefore suppress for a few pages my own account, composed before Professor Hexter's book appeared, in order to give the reader a taste of the superior version, which, however, should be read in its proper context, where many valuable thoughts lying outside the scope of my argument may be gleaned. Here, then, is an independent argument which wonderfully reinforces the point of my essay. Professor Hexter starts from a word used by More when sending the completed text to Erasmus:

'Nusquamam nostram, nusquam bene scriptam ad te mitto.' [1]

Why does he say 'ours'? Professor Hexter's answer is that More was referring to the Dialogue in Book I. Certainly Erasmus did come to London and stayed with More. Here Professor Hexter writes:

'We may be sure that while he lived with the Mores Erasmus read, pondered, and discussed with its author the lively book Giles had told him about. We may be sure, too, that during the midsummer evenings the two old cronies, irrepressible lovers of good conversation, talked of many other things. . . . Less than three weeks after Erasmus left More's house his friend sent him *Utopia* with the Dialogue added. . . .' [2]

This was the reason why Erasmus was able to be so precise about the composition of Book I. Professor Hexter conjectures that the Dialogue reproduces the substance of an actual discussion.

He points out that circumstances had made the problem discussed in Book I of *Utopia* a personal problem for each. It is true that it was a less pressing problem for Erasmus: for though he had been made a councillor to Charles V, and was urged to attend court, he did not find his sovereign difficult when he politely declined. He made his contribution, he paid for his sinecure, by writing a treatise on the model Prince, a work, as we shall see, very unlike that on which Machiavelli was engaged. For More, however, matters were more

---

[1] Ep. 461, September 3rd, 1516. [2] *Op. cit.*, pp. 101–2.

serious: he had made a good living by his law practice and his municipal business, but he found the need to provide for a growing family of girls—for in those days a dowry was a *sine qua non* if they were to marry—a hateful business. He was an unwilling though very able lawyer. The temptation to accept the pressing invitation of Wolsey was therefore great: it was also dangerous to decline a favour conferred by the new Cardinal. It was out of a discussion of these affairs, Professor Hexter concludes, that the idea of writing Book I arose.

Whether this is true history or not does not affect the point that the *function* as distinct from the *origin* of Book I is to serve as a guide to the reader how to take Book II. This view is admirably stated by Donner, but this time I shall take the liberty of choosing my own way of formulating the argument. Book I, to my mind, does two things: it attempts to explore the duty of the Christian Humanist to society, and it attempts to overcome the besetting sin of the Humanists, which may be expressed crudely as an inability to think or to talk to the point. If we open the treatise Erasmus wrote for Charles on the way a Christian prince should govern, we could see from this work alone what this besetting vice was like. Faced with the duty and opportunity to give advice to his sovereign, Erasmus offered him an ideal picture of the good prince and the good councillor. At hardly any point does Erasmus take into account the actual conditions in which Charles had to govern or his ministers advise. The book has therefore no practical value. It is a beautifully writt..n summary of the wise things sa:d by the Greeks and Romans and by the authors of the Gospels. Yet apart from the style and the choice of authorities it is a thoroughly mediaeval work. If the reader consults the admirable *History of Political Thought in the Sixteenth Century* by J. W. Allen, he can confirm the verdict that, save for Machiavelli —and even Machiavelli shares in the prevailing fault—there is not much that can be called *real thinking* in the political writing of the early years of the sixteenth century. For real thinking implies a close relation between the general truth and the particular political fact.

This weakness lies at the heart of Humanism. At best the scholars did little but possess the wisdom of the past as we might possess a set of copy-book maxims. The maxims certainly make us aware of a difference between the actual and the ideal, but they do not of themselves enable us to penetrate the actual; still less do they show us how to bring the actual nearer to the ideal. It is pathetic to see the Humanists in all walks of life supposing that the mere writing up on the wall of a wise saying will make a difference to those who read the writing on the wall. Yet these very Humanists were now taking a prominent part in government: they were being called in to advise their king, along with the huntsman, the lawyer and the cleric—three rôles often filled by one and the same actor. This fact made the discussion of the duty of the Humanist extremely actual.

Let us therefore survey the elements of the Humanists' problem. We may allow, for the time being, the claim that the Humanists did in fact know, as one of them put it, *quam sit humaniter vivendum*; for it is still true that civilisation is in part the maintenance in an active state of certain ideas or ideals. Few people are really alive in the present, while most of us are about twenty-five to fifty years behind our present, living off the insights of the civilised minority who were present and alive in the years 1918–25. We may also allow that it is the duty of the civilised minority to spread their ideas or ideals and as far as possible see to it that they prevail over the ideas of fifty years ago. The question is: have they a special duty to seek to gain control of power? Or should they be content to be politically insignificant during their lifetimes with the reward of being obeyed fifty years after they are dead? A poor reward, usually, since the actual form in which a man's ideas are realised fifty years after he is dead is most often a travesty of the ideas he expressed when alive. In our society the intellectual in the strict sense of the word is a revolutionary, and he is permitted the luxury of professing to subvert the foundations of our settled ways. In More's day there was no such safe position for an intellectual in politics. For him the problem was narrower: he had to ask himself: is it my duty to share in the active government of the day, to sit in council with the huntsman, the lawyer and the cleric? This meant in practice to devise means to compass ends the scholar would never himself propose, and most often ends at variance with his whole set of beliefs. To this the modern intellectual may reply: 'More's problem is ours: if we enter politics, even revolutionary politics, we cannot hope to dictate policy, though we may hope to modify it.'

More put this case admirably in Book I and makes it unnecessary for me to continue with crude restatement. The question is: what light does this debate on the duty of the Humanist throw on the Utopia of Book II? My answer is, that by contrasting what he has to say in Book I about the real England of the early sixteenth century with what he says in Book II about an imaginary England (though, of course, More is not strict in making every detail of his Utopia apply to our island), he reminds us that his treatment belongs to another order of thought than the practical. The key sentence here is:

'This philosophical way of speculation is very pleasant among good friends, in a free conversation: but there is no room for it in the council chambers of princes, where decisions on matters of importance have important results throughout the kingdom.'

I shall postpone the discussion of the significance of the phrase 'free conversation', for I wish to consider first More's remarks on the state of England in Book I. Here I would argue that they do not show More as more enlightened than some very indifferent contemporaries, and he is in some ways inferior to them. To substantiate this remark, I could point to the dialogue written on the same topic by Starkey;[1] but more interesting than that piece of ineffectual Humanism masking mediaeval commonplace is a piece of actual thinking by an unknown author: *A Discourse of the Common Weal of this Realm of England*. Instead of these, however, I should like to take a parallel of a different kind, in order to support previous casual references to More as a *puritan*.

The reason why a dual purpose can be served by a single reference to a full-blown Protestant is that both he and More were traditional, that is, mediaeval in their attitudes towards society. The chosen Puritan, *Henry Brinklow*, was in real life in the position discussed in Book I of *Utopia*, that is, he was offering in the form of sermons practical advice to Parliament on the conduct of the main business of the day. Brinklow also shows that More's prudent and despondent account of the limited amount of liberty allowed to the advisor of Princes was well-grounded, for Brinklow was not permitted to preach his sermons: they were written in exile and smuggled into England.

As a sample of topical interest to the reader, let me outline one or two points from the sermon Brinklow wrote on the consequences of current high prices and extortionate rents. Here it is interesting to note that one of the causes of trouble and want, in his eyes, was a result of the sale of monastery lands. Coming from a Protestant to whom the original owners were 'impys of Antichrist' it is valuable to have the admission:

'it had bene more profytable . . . for the comon welth, that thei had remayned styll in their handys. . . .'[2]

It is characteristic of the common, traditional attitude that Brinklow

[1] Conveniently edited by K. M. Burton.
[2] *Complaynt of Roderyck Mors*, ed. J. M. Cowper, p. 9.

regards the raising of rents and eviction of poor tenants as an offence against religion:

'if another rich couetos carl, which hath to moch already, will gyue anything more than he that dwellyth vpon it, owt he must, be he neuer so poore; though he shuld become a begger, and after a thefe, and so at length be hanged, by his owtgoing: so lytle is the lawe of loue regarded, oh cruel tyrannys! Yea, it is now a comon vse of the landlordys, for euery tryfyll, euyn for his fryndys plesure, in case his tenant haue not a lease, he shal put hym owt of his ferme; which thing is both agaynst the law of nature and of charyte also, he being an honest man, payng his rent, and other dutys well and honestly. I think there be no such wicked lawes nor customys in the vnyuersal world agayne. What a shame is this to the whole realme, that we say we haue receyued the Gospel of Christ, and yet is it worse now in this matter than it was ouer fyfty or .iij. score yearys, whan we had but the Popys law, as wicked as it was, for than leassys were not known.[1]

Nothing, however, can better illustrate the common note than the outcry against enclosures. (The economists are puzzled to reconcile the spate of tracts, verses and books attacking this practice with the small amount of enclosure recorded and the correspondingly small degree of hardship inflicted — to say nothing of the 'material benefits' it brought in its train.) Here it will be sufficient to place two passages alongside. The first is from Book I of *Utopia*:

'. . . your shepe, that were wont to be so myke and tame, and so smal eaters, now, as I heare saie, be become so great deuowerers, and so wylde, that they eate vp and swallow down the very men them selfes. They consume, destroy, and deuoure hole fieldes, howses, and cities. For looke in what partes of the realme doth growe the fynyst, and therfore dearist woll, there noble men and gentlemen, yea, and certeyn Abbottes, holy men god wote, not contenting them selfes with the yearely reuennues and profyttes that were wont to grow to theyr forefathers and predecessours of their landes, nor beynge content that they liue in rest and pleasure, nothyng profytyng, ye, muche noyinge the weale publique, leaue no grounde for tyllage: they enclose all in pastures: they throw downe houses: they plucke downe townes: and leaue nothing stondynge but only the churche, to make of it a shepehowse. And, as thoughe yow loste no small quantity of grounde by forestes, chases, laundes, and parkes; those good holy

---

[1] *Op. cit.*, pp. 9–10.

men turne all dwellinge places and all glebe lande into desolation and wildernes.

'Therfore, that one couetous and vnsatiable cormaraunte and verye plage of his natyue contrey may compasse abowte and inclose many thousand acres of grounde to gether within one pale or hedge, the husbandmen be thrust owte of their owne: orels other by coueyne or fraude, or by vyolent oppression, they be put besydes it, or by wronges and iniuries they be so weried that they be compelled to sell all.'

And here is a true companion-piece from Brinklow, written some thirty years later:

'Oh Lord God, that it wold please the to open the earys of the kyng, lordys, and burgessys of the Parlament, that thei may heare the cryeng of the peple, that is made thorow the reame, for the inclosing of parkys, forestys, and chasys, which is no small burden to the comons. How the corne and grasse is destroyed by the dere many tymys, it is to pytyful to heare! It is often sene, that men, ioynyng to the forestys and chasys, haue not repyd half that thei haue sowne, and yet sometyme altogether is destroyed. And what land is your parkys? Be not the most part of them the most batel and fruteful grownd in Ingland? And now it is come to passe by wicked lawys, that if a man kyll one of those beastis which beare the mark of no one pryuate person, but be indifferent for all men, commyng vpon his own ground, deuouryng his corne or grasse, which is his lyffelod; and yet if he kyl them vpon his oune ground, being chase or forest, it is felony, and he shal be hanged for it! But what sayth the prophete to the makers of this wicked act, and such other lyke? "Woo be vnto you which make wicked lawys," &cete. To wryte of what vnreasonable length and breddyth thei be is superfluos: the thyng is to many-fest. God grant the king grace, to pull vp a great part of his oune parkys, and to compel his lordes, knyghtys, and gentylmen to pull vp all theirs by the rootys, and to late out the ground to the peple at such a resonable pryce as thei may lyue at their handes. And if thei wil nedys haue some dere for their vayne pleasure, than let them take such heathy, woddy, and moory ground, as is vnfruteful for corne or pasture, so that the common welth be not robbed; and let them make good defence, that their poore neyhbors, ioynyng vnto them, be not deuouryd of their corne and grasse. Thus shuld ye do, for the erth is the poor mannys as wel as the rych. And ye lordys, se that ye abuse not the blessing of the ryches and pour which God hath lent you, and remember, that the erth is the Lordys, and not

115

yours. For ye be but stewardys, and be ye sure that ye shal gyue account vnto the Lord for the bestowyng of your ryches. And to you burgessys, seing such thynges wyl not be reformed, but only by your pour and auctoryte, I say to you, . . . Consyder whereunto ye be called and for what purpose; not for your oune particular and pryuate welth, nor yet for the kynges, in any thing preiudycyal to the comon welth.' [1]

After these necessary preliminaries, I must now try to sketch the significance of *Utopia* for this enquiry and indicate in what its importance lies. In a general way, it ranks high as one of the finest expressions of that for which the Humanists deserve to be remembered; their aspiration towards a better way of life, towards civilisation; their power to conceive ideals that might be operative at least in conduct. Here is where we should lay the emphasis: not on the actual things they yearned for or dreamed of, but on the spirit in which they conceived their ideals. Therefore, for us, the greatness of *Utopia* is hinted at in the wood-cut made by Ambrosius Holbein for the 1518 edition (Basle). There we see the artist attempting to reproduce the setting in which the whole discourse and dialogue took place, as given in the words:

'and there in my gardeyne, vpon a benche coueryd wyth grene torues, we satte downe talking togethers'.

The artist there depicts the ideal situation: the point where the world of the sixteenth century came into closest contact with the ancient classical world. Holbein has stylised or even idealised this ideal picture; the scholar, Clement, becomes a real *puer* acting as a servant, presumably bringing refreshments to the three discoursing figures seated in an arbour—a significant compound of nature and art—on the confines of town and country. The house suggests opulence and civilisation, but it looks out on hills and fields.

That the claim to have found the 'objective correlative' of the Humanist dream in this situation is not a whimsy or a personal 'construct' to bolster up my argument, may be seen by a reference to Huizinga's book on Erasmus:

'In order to understand Erasmus's mind and the charm which it had for his contemporaries, one must begin with the ideal of life

---

[1] *Op. cit.*, pp. 16–17.

that was present before his inward eye as a splendid dream. It is not his own in particular. The whole Renaissance cherished that wish of reposeful, blithe, and yet serious intercourse of good and wise friends in the cool shade of a house under trees, where serenity and harmony would dwell. The age yearned for the realization of simplicity, sincerity, truth and nature. Their imagination was always steeped in the essence of Antiquity, though, at heart, it is more nearly connected with medieval ideals than they themselves were aware. In the circle of the Medici it is the idyll of Careggi, in Rabelais it embodies itself in the fancy of the abbey of Thélème; it finds voice in More's *Utopia* and in the work of Montaigne.[1]

The link with antiquity is not directly with Plato, but with Horace, as we may clearly see if we look at the *Convivium Religiosum* of Erasmus. Here we have perfect continuity from Horace through Erasmus and More to Ben Jonson, for the ideal setting of this supreme value—good conversation on things that matter—is the surrounding of simple but cultivated manners exhibited when the civilised man invited his friends to a meal in his country house. Horace in the archetypal poem, the sixth 'sermo' of his second book, unwillingly detained on business in the big city, meditates somewhat as follows:

'As the long day wastes on, I feel depressed and yearn for home— my little bit of land with a garden and running stream and a few trees—and wonder how long I must wait before I can get back to my old books, to doze and do nothing and forget the worries of town life. And eat my home-grown food, dining like a prince in front of my own hearth, with my cheeky, home-grown, too familiar, servants around me. Or inviting friends of an evening with no damned etiquette to govern our drinking: the one who likes his whisky neat next to the other chap who sips his sherry and mellows at his own speed. And the talk that comes of it! We don't discuss our richer neighbours or their smart modern residences, nor what is going on at the Old Vic. We talk about what really concerns us, things it is bad not to make up your mind about: what makes people happy? money, or their own inner worth? what holds friends together? the advantages each gets from having the other, or an impersonal bond, an ideal? We exchange views about what 'good' really means and what is the supreme aim in life—and we don't mind driving home our philosophical points by repeating old wives' tales or nursery rhymes. . . .'

There is real continuity, but not, of course, identity, when the

[1] *Erasmus of Rotterdam*, by J. Huizinga, Phaidon Press, 1952, p. 104.

conversation is Christian and takes place north of the Alps. 'I wonder how anybody can endure to live in a smoaky Town,' says the first speaker in Erasmus' dialogue, 'when everything's so fresh and pleasant in the Country.' [1] But the Humanists were not what we might call 'nature-lovers':

'In the *Country*, 'tis true, ye have Woods, Gardens, Springs and Brooks, that may entertain the Eye; but these are all mute; and there's no Edification without Discourse.'

The Humanist ideal is to be in the country in the company of the philosophers:
'A *Country Life*, I must confess, in such Company, were a Paradise.'

This exchange introduces the invitation to the classical meal: the material simplicity to mirror the spiritual:

'If you have a mind to make Trial of it, take a Dinner with me to morrow, a step here out o' the Town: I have a plain little House there, but I'le promise you a cleanly and a hearty Welcome.'

Here Erasmus makes one of the speakers refer to the description of the Happy Life in the Country, presented by Horace with exquisite irony in Epode II, for his notion of the ideal meal:

'And if on top of all this the man has a self-respecting woman for a wife, one who does her share in the running of the farm and in creating a happy family—a woman of the old school or the coarse red-faced type you see bustling round farm houses in Southern Italy —who keeps a good fire blazing with seasoned logs and has everything ready by the time her husband comes in tired from his work, and before his coming has penned the goats and relieved their tight-swollen udders of the last drops of their milk, and drawn a jug of this year's wine from the cask and laid on the table a meal no money can buy. . . .'

'In one word,' says Erasmus, 'you are to expect only a *Garden Treat*.'
There is ample evidence that this ideal mode was not hopelessly out of touch with actual conduct. More and Erasmus often enough

[1] All the quotations from the *Convivium Religiosum* are taken from the translation by Roger L'Estrange: 'Twenty Two Select Colloquies out of Erasmus Roterodamus—The Third Impression. Corrected and Amended', 1699.

refer to real conversations in which the pleasure lay as much in the wit as in the serious discussions. Very often a conversation in these informal circumstances did give rise to written works in which the pros and cons of a topic so discussed were elaborated at leisure and after further reflection. But what it is crucial for my argument to claim is that in the conversations between More and Erasmus there was *greater play of mind* than many commentators are willing to concede. I assume that More enjoyed trying out paradoxes without being committed to them in practice or to all of their consequences.

This at least provides us with an experimental approach to a judgement on the place and value of the discussion of communism in *Utopia*. We should at least approach the question with open minds. We have no right *a priori* to say that More could not have found serious support for communist views in his own thoughts or in those of his contemporaries. On the contrary, I should like to try out as an initial hypothesis the view that the relation of the free ideas thrown out in *Utopia* to fully-embodied life-convictions was something like that holding between the ideas of a young man of twenty-five and those of the same man at fifty. We must, of course, be extremely wary in using such an analogy, but surely, we mean something like this when we speak of a civilisation as 'maturing', surely, we must make some such judgement when we compare More's *Utopia* with Shakespeare's *The Tempest?* I think, too, we can acquire a hint of the distinction we require in a classic formulation by W. B. Yeats:

'I am persuaded that our intellects at twenty contain all the truths we shall ever find, but as yet we do not know truths that belong to us from opinions caught up in casual irritation or momentary fantasy. As life goes on we discover that certain thoughts sustain us in defeat, or give us victory, whether over ourselves or others, and it is these thoughts, tested by passion, that we call convictions. . . . We begin to live when we have conceived life as tragedy.' [1]

Since this hypothesis—that the discussion of communism in *Utopia* was both the *result* of thought and was meant to *provoke* thought, though by 'thought' I mean something analogous to the thoughts of a poet in his twenties—runs counter to views I respect, notably those of Donner, it becomes a duty to state explicitly where and how I diverge. In all disputes of this sort, the best method is first to review the facts. In looking for what *Utopia* was meant to be, it is natural to turn to the close. There we find the speaker using his completed

[1] *Autobiographies* (1926), p. 234.

119

sketch of Utopia to make a criticism of contemporary society as the speaker and his audience knew it. This shows that the interest of the fiction for More lay in its bearing on contemporary fact.

Hythloday begins by saying that in no society known to him or his hearers can justice and equity be found. The reason he gives reads very like that put forward by communists, namely, that there can be no justice or equity as long as the rewards of labour and capital are so different as they are in contemporary society. These modern terms 'capital' and 'labour' are hardly an anachronism, for under what I have called 'capital' Hythloday groups the landed aristocrat, the banker and the money-lender, and under 'labour', the hired man, the carter, the blacksmith and the farmer. The speaker regards the capitalists as drones, useless members of the community, who, if they are not utterly idle, perform no *necessary* function, whereas without 'labour' there would be no *respublica* at all. He contrasts the life of splendid ease of these drones with the miserable struggle of 'labour' to keep alive, a struggle that makes all provision for old age impossible and existence itself a doubtful blessing.

But to complete the parallel with modern communist propaganda, he adds: not only are the drones ungrateful, they pervert the laws in order to defraud 'labour', and call the result justice. This sounds remarkably like what would be known in the nineteenth century as 'class justice'. Hythloday sums up his arraignment of contemporary society in memorable words:

'When I look closely at and consider all the commonwealths that flourish anywhere in the world to-day, God help me if I can find them anything but a conspiracy of the rich handling things for their private advantage and calling *that* a true common weal.'

For Hythloday, money and the longing to acquire wealth are the curses of society: they give rise to all the crimes and they rob men of their peace of mind. But Hythloday does not give the last word to the economic motive; he says that Christ himself would easily have brought all societies to live under communism as the Utopians do, were it not for ineradicable human *pride*: 'omnium princeps parensque pestium' (the contriver and parent of all the evils of society). We must not therefore accuse Hythloday of a one-sided preoccupation with economics. In trying to decide whether More is 'behind' any of Hythloday's arguments, we should not forget that he sees pride rather than greed as the chief obstacle to a durable form of society.

I take it then that this closing speech by Hythloday was meant to concentrate attention on the main point of the book, as we saw that

More's contemporaries understood it. There remain the very last words of *Utopia*, More's dramatic comment when Hythloday's discourse came to an end:

'When Raphael had completed his account, a great many objections occurred to me, since many of the features of Utopia struck me as utterly absurd; their manner of making war, their religious observances and their religion itself. But what I chiefly objected to was the chief and most fundamental feature of their way of life: their abolition of private property and of money and their institution of communism; for this effects a radical and utter overthrow of all aristocracy, all show of magnificence, and all that is popularly understood to give a commonwealth real style and dignity.'

We must certainly weigh these words, though we must take them with the final summing-up:

'I readily admit that there are very many features of Utopia which I should like to see realised in our society, though I have not much hope of seeing their realisation.'

Whether or not this conclusion was written before More thought of adding Book I, it is clear that as the work now stands we are meant to take the conclusion of Book II with that of Book I, for in fact *for the reader* Book II here merely amplifies what Hythloday said in Book I:

'Wherever there is private property and money is made the measure of all things, it is hardly possible that the commonwealth should be governed justly or be prosperous. . . .'

As long as there is private property there will be two nations, a few rich and many poor. To this in the dialogue the objection is made that in a communist state there will be no incentive to work and no respect for the magistrates: two objections which are shown in Book II not to hold for the people of Utopia.

How are we to take all this? If we turn to Donner, we find there is nothing in it to cause disturbance. But Donner, to my mind, assumes what he ought to prove. His assumption is 'that unique consistency which marks More's life and writings': but this is a mere counter-assertion against those who, like Tyndale in More's lifetime, and socialist commentators in our day, have asserted that More's practice in his last years was a betrayal of his principles in *Utopia*.

Nobody doubts that at the end of his life—that is, before it was cut short by judicial murder— More, faced with the practical communism of the wilder Anabaptists and the encroachments of Protestants of different colours, made various statements repudiating any possible identity of his views with those of political or religious extremists. But to suggest that these later statements are the true context in which we should read *Utopia* is to be guilty of anachronism: More wrote his book in something like intellectual freedom and before Luther appeared.

In fact, much of what Donner adduces reads to me more like an attempt to explain away than to explain. For the question remains: why did More put these arguments into *Utopia* at all? Why do they figure so largely if they were not meant to make the reader think? Donner supposes that More could have demolished Raphael's claim, but, if he had done so, he would have destroyed his own book. This is to say that *Utopia* is a very fragile creation if it could not stand up to criticism, and criticism, I suppose, that any other reader could bring. Now, since Donner admires *Utopia*, we must ask what it is that he admires. It is, apparently, a clever trick. After quoting the final remarks at the end of Book II, Donner writes:

'It must be admitted, I think, that More could not have argued more strongly against communism without destroying his own fiction. We accept it as a potential reality because More tricks us to accept it.[1] Evincing a consummate skill in the manipulation of the dialogue he makes us first accept reason, and not human ability, as the standard by which to judge whether something may be realised or no. Secondly, he deliberately deceives us into blaming institutions, instead of human nature, as the cause of abuses and injustice. In this way he persuades us that society can be cured of all the evils besetting it, if only the institutions were reasonable. Raphael Hythloday's argument in favour of "cure" is allowed to get the better of More's own, which is that we should so contrive that "what you cannot turn to good, so to order it that it be not very bad", and which is dismissed by Raphael as effecting at the best no more than a "mitigation" of evil. This is the manner in which More brings about his brilliant *jeu d'esprit*. Without this deception there would have been no Utopia, or if there had, it must have been taken to be More's own ideal.' [2]

This seems to me totally at variance with the spirit of the book

[1] Sc. 'into accepting it'.
[2] *Introduction to Utopia*, by H. W. Donner, Uppsala, 1945, pp. 70–1.

as a whole, which I take to be that in which a radical criticism of society as More knew it is mounted in such a way that the reader's mind is led by a hundred different channels to the essential point. More is not so much *for* communism as *against* the evils of society which he thought sprang from the evil passions which the evil institutions of the day fostered. Professor Hexter seems to me to come nearer the truth when he writes:

'More simply did not believe that all the evil men do can be ascribed to the economic arrangements of society, and that those evils and the very potentiality for evil will vanish when the economic arrangements are rectified and set on a proper footing. More believed no such thing because in his view of men and their affairs there was a strong and ineradicable streak of pessimism. More's pessimism was ineradicable because it was part and parcel of his Christian faith. He knew surely, as a profoundly Christian man he had to know, that the roots of evil run far too deep in men to be destroyed by a mere rearrangement of the economic organization of society.' [1]

Professor Hexter therefore argues, as I have tried to do, that we must adopt a view neither of the Left nor of the Right. For him, as for me:

'the Utopian Discourse is the production of a Christian humanist uniquely endowed with a statesman's eye and mind, a broad worldly experience, and a conscience of unusual sensitivity, who saw sin and especially the sin of pride as the cancer of the commonwealth'.[2]

Recent Catholic scholarship, however, is free from the faults of Chambers and Donner, who are, to my mind hysterically over-eager to load the scales in favour of a reactionary More, and in so doing do harm to their cause. The question under discussion here—how to take the communism in *Utopia*—has been notably advanced if not permanently settled by a Jesuit Father, *E. L. Surtz*,[3] from whom I trust we shall shortly have a definitive volume on More.[4] He has raised all the questions under discussion so far and has tried to answer them by considering what the Church tradition on communism and private property was before More discussed them. According to him, there were two rival views: one, that Christ enjoined communism on the whole of society, but that, owing to man's weakness, the institution of private property was founded, not on natural law, nor on divine positive law, but on human positive

[1] *Op. cit.*, pp. 71–2. [2] *Ibid.*, p. 78.
[3] In PMLA, vol. LXIV, 1949, pp. 549–64.
[4] A hope partially realised in *The Praise of Pleasure* (1957).

law, and this view he attributes to Duns Scotus. Aquinas, however, held that private property was an addition made to the natural law by human reason.

After repeating the portion of Hythloday's last discourse, in which Christ is said to have been trying to bring the world to the Utopian standard, but was defeated by human pride, the Jesuit Father does a remarkable thing: he quotes from the letter to a monk about which Chambers was so reticent. He thus shews that More expresses the same view as Hythloday only three or four years after he wrote *Utopia*. The passage is worth noting:

'God shewed great foresight when he made all things common: so did Christ when he tried to bring men back from what was private to what was common. For he surely felt that our corrupt nature does not so love what is private without what is common suffering loss or harm: all experience verifies that this is so.'

The Jesuit Father, however, goes further and sees that Hythloday is the mouthpiece of the Christian Humanists:

'One cannot escape the conviction that there is an underlying consistency in the attitude toward Christian communism in Hythloday's views as propounded in *Utopia*, in More's mind as revealed in his letter to a monk, and in the writings of such humanists as Budé, Lister, and Erasmus. In its most simple terms, this common attitude may be expressed as follows: God originally intended communism to be the social system best suited for human beings. Fallen man, however . . . introduced the right of private property . . . Christ tried to recall . . . his followers to the original arrangement made by God, Christians were aided in this thwarting of Christ's wise provision by the authority of Aristotle and the ingenuity of clever preachers who trimmed Christ's doctrine to suit the evil times.'

The Humanists realised that communism would only work where men were good, but they wished men to acquire the spirit of the early church in Jerusalem, where, they thought, communism was actually practised.

The Jesuit Father then turns to the question: where do we find More in the *Utopia*, in Hythloday or in the objections? and he answers, as we might expect: in both. More favours communism as the ideal, but he sees objections to applying it to society as it is. This view is supported by the arguments in Book I. There, the reader will recall, when Hythloday enunciates the ideal, More objects on practical grounds. Hythloday does not reply because the practical grounds do not exist in Utopia: there men are *not* idle and the magistrates are held in respect. But, after we have heard the account of Utopia, More's objection at the close of Book II is no objection at all. It is a stroke of subtle irony:

'For the whole purpose of Utopia has been to prove that (nobility, magnificence, splendour and majesty) are *not* the qualities which should distinguish a commonwealth.'

More's view is that

'it is the mad striving for nobility and majesty, magnificence and splendor, which is bringing Christian princes and peoples to their downfall and which is causing the poor and needy to suffer unutterable hardships'.

This strikes me, as it struck Professor Hexter, as unanswerable. It enables us to see the interest and value of the discussion of communism in *Utopia*. It is clear that what makes the discussion worth having is the *tension* it creates. If it were *obvious* either that communism or private property were right in all cases and under all conditions it would not be worth raising the matter, but once we see that the rival claims are an example *typifying the nature of real life*, then *Utopia* can be seen to have serious point. For real life presents a clash between what reason demands to be done and nature permits to be done. By showing sensitive appreciation of this issue More overcomes the besetting weakness of the Humanists. More was able to do justice to the complexity of the issue because he was himself complex, because in him you cannot separate the Christian from the Humanist, nor the man of the world from the man of the spirit. The discussion of communism admirably exemplifies the poise, balance, and good sense of More, and his powers of dramatising one of the real tensions felt by the finer spirits of his day.

So far I have considered *Utopia* as if it were designed to make one single point, namely that the radical ill of society, the sickness at the root, was the love of money fostered by ineradicable pride. I have no doubt that this *is* the main point, and that More's contemporary commentators were taking the author's meaning in stressing greed, avarice and pride as the sources of all social evil. Yet the book contains more than this one lesson, and it is not great because ot this lesson. For the lesson itself is as old as humanity, and as More expresses it, as old as Christianity. Indeed, the reader may complain that in exploring my theme—what it meant to be a Christian Humanist—by concentrating on the discussion of communism I had found the Christian but had lost sight of the Humanist in More.

Yet this would not be the whole truth: for the course of the discussion showed that More's point was *not* to say with dramatic force only what all Christians were saying, but to examine the bearings of the truth on life as it had to be lived. The value of More's book, it appeared, lay in the contrast and opposition of the possible, the ideal and the actual. The book, on this view, has power only in so far as it brings together and forces to inter-act, views which More's contemporaries were content to keep separate. This is the function and definition of More's wit.

This very conclusion, however, must lead us to say that although the discussion of communism enabled More to make the sharpest possible judgement of the society of his day and to set out the difficulties in the Christian Humanist's descent into the political arena—in short, though the topic is handled with vigour and point, it does not really constitute a profound, new reintegration of man's nature. More, that is to say, is not really deeply involved in this theme. It would have been a different matter if he had seen practical possibilities opening before him, if he had chosen to work against the official policy of his day. More, I think it is clear, did not see any such possibility: it did not seem to be his duty to found a communist party or even a party in opposition to the main official line. His duty was rather a negative one: not to pretend that the present arrangements of society were satisfactory or could be tolerated as Christian arrangements. The tendency of his argument in *Utopia* had been against entering politics, which could only mean the king's service. The Humanist's duty was rather to remind people like himself of what the demands of faith and reason were: namely, to condemn if not to remedy the social abuses of Christianity in Christendom: to promote a longing for a better order: to prevent oblivion of the standards: to keep open continuity with the primitive teaching of the early Church.

Where then in *Utopia* is More deeply involved? Where does he explore and exploit the conflicts in his own nature? If we follow Chambers and Donner, names which, as always, I choose as the most respectworthy, we must answer: nowhere. For they are convinced that for More *Utopia* allowed only a limited part of his nature expression: the narrow area of experience that can be attained by the use of reason. Here is a sample from Chambers of what Donner calls the Roman Catholic version of *Utopia's* significance:

'We must never forget that More's education fell not in the Nineteenth but in the Fifteenth Century. To a man educated in that century, the distinction was obvious between the virtues which might be taught by human reason alone, and the further virtues taught by Catholic orthodoxy. It was part of the medieval system to divide the virtues into the Four Cardinal Virtues (to which the heathen might attain) and the Three Christian Virtues. The Four Cardinal Virtues—Wisdom, Fortitude, Temperance, and Justice—are the foundation of Plato's commonwealths. . . . These virtues were taken into the medieval system—part of the immense debt it owes to Greek philosophy. The Three Christian Virtues—Faith, Hope, and Charity—come of course from St. Paul's *First Epistle to the Corinthians*. Four and Three make Seven—the Perfect Number, which was extremely comforting. The perfect Christian character must comprise all seven. But the four heathen virtues were sufficient to ensure that a man or a State might be a model of conduct in secular matters. . . .

'In basing his *Utopia* upon these four heathen virtues, More is following medieval tradition; further, he is following his great examples, Plato's *Republic* and *Laws*; but, above all, he makes his satire upon contemporary European abuses more pointed. The virtues of Heathen Utopia show up by contrast the vices of Christian Europe. But the Four Cardinal Virtues are subsidiary to, not a substitute for, the Christian Virtues. More has done his best to make this clear. It is not his fault if he has been misunderstood. . . .' [1]

Although Chambers sounds so confident and has everything so pat, my trouble is that on re-reading More's *Utopia* in the light of these words, I cannot see that More was trying to make this point at all. And if he had been, I cannot see that he was doing his best. There were many little hints More might have given which would have made the Chambers' line plausible: for instance, he might have let Raphael say that those of the Utopians who embraced Christianity came to see that the ideal republic fell seriously short of the 'orthodox' Catholic ideal. But it is not very satisfactory to leave the matter with a simple disclaimer of *non possumus*. Can it be that the opposition More intended is not between a heathen Utopia and a Christian Europe, but an opposition within Christianity itself?

[1] *Op. cit.*, from the section entitled 'The Meaning of *Utopia*'.

The ultimate answer lies, as does my objection to Chambers' at bottom anachronistic dogma, in the impression the book makes as a whole. But we may derive a hint as to the nature of this opposition from an important letter (Ep. 1039) Erasmus wrote to a Bohemian who had appealed for help in creating unity in his country, so dreadfully torn by religious dissensions. That this letter was no casual throw-off we may see from Allen's note:

'This letter is important, as indicating in detail Erasmus' views of moderate reform in the Church; just at the time when it was becoming plain that Luther's call for reform could not be stifled. Erasmus made no secret of what he had written, but published it in his next volume of *Epistolae*. . . . Some years later it was translated into German and printed . . . the title showing that it was regarded as exhibiting 'die eynigen waren Mittel . . . durch welche gegenwertige Zweyung in vnserm heyligen Glauben möchten fruchtbarlich hingelegt werden'.'

Here Erasmus makes a distinction between what he calls articles of faith and 'those from which Evangelical piety flows as from a spring—contempt for money, honours, control of the passions, anger, hatred and envy. What advantage is it to profess the Articles if we are a slave to these passions? If avarice, ambition, lust, hatred, envy, detraction, are held in greater honour among us and weigh more with us, what is the point of professing to believe in Christ, who was made man to call us away from these very things? If I give offence to anyone by saying this, let him quarrel with the Apostle James who said:

'Goo to nowe ye riche men. Wepe, and howle on youre wretchednes that shal come vpon you. Youre riches is corrupte, youre garmentes are motheaten. Youre golde & youre siluer are cancred, & the rust of them shalbe a witnes vnto you, & shal eate youre fleszhe, as it were fyre. Ye haue heaped treasure togedder in youre last dayes: Beholde, the hyre of the labourers which haue reped downe youre feldes (which hyer is of you kept backe by fraude) cryeth: and the cryes of them which haue reped, are entred in to the eares of the LORDE Sabaoth. Ye haue liued in pleasure on the earth and in wantannes. Ye haue noryszhed youre hertes, as in a daye of slaughter. . . .'

This, it seems to me, is the challenge Utopia makes to the Christian: the Utopians perform what Christ came to teach: and I think it is in this spirit that we should read what Raphael says about the society of his day and of the society of Utopia.

In searching for the real wit and the real 'engagement' of More in *Utopia*, we must distinguish between topics which More regarded as open to debate and those which represent views that he does not offer for discussion. For instance, everybody notices that the people of Utopia do not tolerate the view that man's soul is not immortal. Yet this view was seriously held in More's day, but More regarded it as not worth discussing. Nor did Erasmus, as we may see from the letter mentioned above:

'It is incredible that people should still be found to profess the folly of Epicurus and deny that our souls survive death. Yet many people can be found even here who live as though they did not believe that anything at all survived death. But nobody is so crazy as to be either the leader or fellow-traveller in promulgating this belief as an -ism.'

Similarly we must pass over many witty strokes in *Utopia* as merely representing favourite ideas of More, but not matters for internal debate, such as the advocacy of Greek, the attacks on Swiss mercenaries, and many more.

Where then do we find a serious conflict in More's own mind, something to which it was not easy for him to find an answer? I think we find it when More tries to resolve what I have described as the opposite pulls in him exerted by his love of pleasure and his love of an ascetic life. In *Utopia* one of the most striking features of a society in many ways repellent to us by its drabness and harsh discipline is the surprising fact that these intellectual robots were Epicureans in their philosophy, though they rejected the Epicurean view of man's end. Here, I think, More is dramatising his own conflict. In Utopia we find that the normal view was that God is to be worshipped in Nature, but a considerable minority, in the name of their religion, did not engage in the intellectual pursuits which the rest of the community followed in their leisure, but sacrificed their leisure to the service of the community, and hoped thereby to earn everlasting felicity after death. These men did not boast of their superiority to what we may call the Humanists in Utopia, and the Humanists honoured them for doing the dirty work of the world. Secondly, these people held divergent views about pleasure. Some were out-and-out ascetics and regarded the pleasures of this life as harmful; others thought that they owed it to Nature to marry and have children. They accepted all pleasures that did not hinder them in their work. Now the Humanists of Utopia thought the latter were *prudentiores* but the former were *sanctiores*, that is, in so far as they were guided by reason, they thought that pleasures were to be accepted, and that it was ridiculous to refuse Nature's gift. But they respected the claims of the ascetics' religion.

Yet if we turn back to More's discussion of pleasure in Utopia, we do not find such a clear-cut distinction. Here, then, if I am right, we find a genuine debate in More's mind arising from the two contrary impulses in More's nature: a debate that could not be resolved by the victory of one or the other side. Whether or not it is the heart of the book, the discussion of pleasure is certainly the part in which More comes nearest to possessing and recreating the spirit of Horace. Here he is translating and here he makes his most valuable contribution towards founding a truly civilised attitude.

The opening words of the section on pleasure read very like the words of Horace, paraphrased above on p. 117.

'In that part of philosophy which has to do with morals, they discuss the same topics as we do: they inquire about the meaning of "good" for mind and body and whether the word can be applied to anything outside the mind. They argue, too, about the meaning of virtue and pleasure, but their principal interest is in the question: what constitutes human happiness—one thing or many?'

And here we come to a remarkable point:

'On this question of man's happiness they have a strong leaning to the side of pleasure as constituting if not the whole, at least the greater part of that happiness. And what is more remarkable, they go to religion—in itself a matter grave, strict, even gloomy and severe in principles—for support of a doctrine in favour of the reverse of these qualities. And this on the general principle that in discussing happiness the fundamental arguments must be taken both from philosophy based solely on reason and from religion—for without religion they think reason alone a weak and defective guide in the search for true happiness.'

This alone would demolish the view that the Utopians are mere rationalists, and it suggests that those who favour pleasure are not mere heathen Epicureans, since Utopian religion is a different matter from the Greek or Roman. The whole point lies, I think, in this contrast between the bright and the gloomy, the bright being based on the gloomy. Their god and their religion, however, are benevolent. Their doctrine rests on the belief that the soul was made by god to be happy, but that its final state of happiness will depend on a judgement after death. The pleasure they seek must at least be consistent with virtue in this life. On rational grounds they argue that if there were no after-life, it would be foolish to suffer for virtue's sake and the pursuit of pleasure would not have to reckon with the claims of virtue. The wise man would choose the greatest available pleasure in this life with the minimum of pain.

As it is, they differ from their Stoic opponents who think virtue itself to be happiness. The Utopian view is that virtue draws our nature to good pleasures—for they define virtue as living in accordance with Nature. They think we were made by god for that end. But once again religion and reason chime, for, says More, we are following Nature's way when we listen to reason in choosing or rejecting things. Reason, too, first fills us with love and reverence for god's majesty. Thirdly, it is reason that both warns and stimulates us to lead our lives with the minimum of worry and the maximum of joy, and to assist our fellow-men with whom we share the bond of nature to enjoy the same happiness. The same Nature which tells you to procure pleasures for others, lays down as a rule that you yourself should pursue a life of pleasure as the end of all your actions. Yet you cannot pursue pleasure at other people's expense. On the contrary, there is more pleasure to be got by diminishing your own immediate pleasure for the sake of increasing another's— especially as god will reward such self-sacrifice with everlasting joy. So much for the reasons for placing pleasure as the ultimate goal.

Now as to the definition of pleasure: true pleasure must be distinguished from false. True pleasure is that in which we delight when Nature is our guide: it is that to which both instinct and true reason lead us. False pleasures are unnatural, but we are often deluded into thinking them true, and we come to prefer the false to the genuine. An instance of false pleasure is the love of fine clothes and the belief that you are a better man for being better dressed.

And here we plunge into the topics of the *Praise of Folly*, for the value we put on fine clothes and the claim to be respected for wearing them are only instances of a general folly: that of putting value on outward honorific signs. 'What is nobility,' says Raphael, 'but being descended from wealthy landowners, and what is left of nobility when the lands are gone?' It is still in the vein of the *Praise of Folly* that More groups under false pleasures both hunting and gambling.

Now though the Utopians prefer the pleasures of the mind to those of the body, it is remarkable how much space (and how much extension!) More gives to the latter. For instance, when he is listing the sensual pleasures, he includes that of voiding excrement and of scratching where it itches. First of the pure pleasures is that of music: by a secret unseen virtue it affects the senses, raises the passions and strikes the mind with generous impressions. Second, comes the pleasure of being perfectly healthy, which the Utopians regard as the foundation of all the other joys of life:

'If it is said that health can not be felt, they absolutely deny it, for what man is in health that does not perceive it when he is awake? Is there any man so dull and stupid as not to acknowledge that he feels a delight in health?'

Indeed though these are called the inferior pleasures, More rises to a pitch of eloquence in speaking about them that allows us to call this section of the book a hymn to Nature:

'They think, therefore, none of those pleasures are to be valued any further than as they are necessary, yet they rejoice in them, and with due gratitude acknowledge the tenderness of their Mother Nature, who has with the sweetest blandishments enticed her children to do those things which are necessary for their preservation. How miserable a thing would life be if those daily diseases of hunger and thirst were to be carried off by such bitter drugs as we must use for those diseases that return seldomer upon us!

'They therefore gladly cherish as the peculiar and pleasant gifts of Nature, physical beauty, strength, and nimbleness of body. More than that, they entertain themselves with the other delights let in their eyes, their ears, and their nostrils, as being Nature's special gifts to man, since no other living creatures consider the beauties of the world or are delighted with smells save for distinguishing food, nor do they apprehend the concords or discords of sounds. These are what men regard as the peculiar relishes of life. But in all this they take care that a lesser joy does not hinder a greater and that pleasure may never breed pain, which they think always follows wrongful pleasures.

'But they think it the extreme of folly, and a sign of a mind cruel to itself and ungrateful to Nature, to give up all Nature's benefits, because we disdain to be beholden to her: to despise physical beauty, to wear out our strength, to turn nimbleness to torpor, to waste the body by fasting, to injure our health, and to reject the other kind gifts of Nature—unless a man were to neglect these things for some public service or service to others for which he expects a greater

132

recompense from God. But most ridiculous they think it is to afflict oneself for the empty shadow of virtue for no better end than to render oneself capable of bearing misfortunes that may never happen.'[1]

Raphael does not defend these notions, he merely reports the opinion of the Utopians that this is the best and truest view man's reason can attain unless holier views are sent to man by inspiration from heaven—though what this can mean, seeing that their views were already based on religion, I cannot guess. Raphael is content to say that, whether true or not, these views work in practice: there is no happier state in the world.

When we seek to value this moment in our civilisation, it is natural, coming from *Lear* at the one end or from Cicero at the other, to find very little 'done' and much borrowed. Yet by a comparison nearer in time—in fact by a comparison with one who had studied *Utopia*—we can, I think, see this passage in its true dimensions; for *Rabelais* handled this same topic. He, too, comes under the formula 'escaped monk turned man of the world' which I thought fitted the authors of the *Praise of Folly* and *Utopia*. It will be helpful, therefore, to show an important difference between our two creators of the Northern Renaissance and Rabelais. Both parties are drawing on the same set of doctrines. Life in accordance with Nature, was a Stoic view, which our Humanists absorbed through Cicero, and to some extent through Seneca. In discussing More and Rabelais, however, we should keep in mind a further source of interest in this doctrine coming from the discoveries in the New World of Amerigo di Vespucci, who said that the natives 'live according to nature and may be called Epicureans rather than Stoics'. And at the same time we should keep in mind those portions of the *Praise of Folly* in which Folly is equated with Nature and Pleasure. Finally, though we do not here need the details, we have to remember that Rabelais borrows directly from More and Erasmus.

The portion of Rabelais which challenges comparison is the description of the Abbey of Thelema in *Gargantua*, written before the end of 1533. I shall for the moment pass over the physical details of this abbey to end all abbeys and quote the 'manner of living of the Thelemites':

'All their Life was laid out, not by Laws, Statutes, or Rules, but according to their Will and free Pleasure. They rose from their Bed

---

[1] Adapted from Gilbert Burnet's translation.

when it seemed good to them, they drank, ate, worked, slept, when the Desire came upon them. None did awake them, none did constrain them either to drink or to eat, or to do anything else whatsoever; for so had Gargantua established it. In their Rule there was but this Clause:

DO WHAT THOU WILT.

because that Men who are free, well-born, well-bred, conversant in honest Company, have by nature, an Instinct and Spur, which always prompteth them to virtuous Actions and withdraweth them from Vice; and this they style Honour. These same Men, when by vile Subjection and Constraint they are brought down and enslaved, do turn aside the noble Affection by which they are freely inclined unto Virtue, in order to lay aside and shake off this Yoke of Slavery. . . .' [1]

In making this comparison I have been drawing on an essay by Arthur Tilley, from which I should now like to quote directly.

'The whole point of Rabelais's abbey is that it is the complete antithesis of the monastic system. In it there was to be no constraint, no regulations, no fixed hours, not even a clock. *Fay ce que vouldras* was its only rule, but in practice this led neither to an exaggerated individualism nor to an undue licence. For in the first place the knights and ladies are in such perfect harmony with one another that the wish of one is the wish of all; and secondly they "have by nature an instinct and spur which always prompteth them to virtuous actions, and withdraweth them from vice; and this they style honour". But they are so prompted because they are *free, well-born, well-educated, conversant in honest company*. These are essential conditions: you must be well-born, that is to say, have inherited virtuous propensities: well-educated, that is to say, have been trained to virtuous endeavour; conversant in honest company, that is to say, live in a virtuous environment. Nothing is said about the grace of God; we have only the natural man—selected and cultivated, it is true, but still the natural man.' [2]

Before going into details, I should like to resume my sense of the resemblance and difference. The resemblance lies in the conception of Nature as a benevolent power: the difference lies in the conception of human nature. What a Frenchman, Brunetière, said of Rabelais and what Shakespeare was to call Great Creating Nature in the

[1] *Rabelais,* tr. W. F. Smith, 1893, vol. I, p. 190.
[2] *Studies in the French Renaissance*, 1922, p. 241.

Winter's Tale hold with very little modification for Erasmus and More:

'Pour Rabelais, la croyance à la bonté de la nature était en quelque sorte le résultat d'une intuition et plus même d'une intuition, d'une révélation véritable. Il l'a en effet célébrée en poète ou en philosophe métaphysicien, comme s'il était enivré par elle; il la vénère et la chante; il chante la diversité de ses manifestations, la puissance et la fécondité de ses créations, la bienveillance quasi maternelle qu'elle montre envers ses créatures.' [1]

Yes, in all that makes our three Humanists supreme jokers, we can trace the filiation back to an optimistic view of Nature and God as fundamentally on the side of happiness. Yet, if we return to the Abbey of Thelema after reading *Utopia*, the difference is striking; for if the Abbey is the antithesis of the monastery, Utopia might be called its apotheosis. More has taken all that was best in the monastic life and shown how discipline is required to regulate the good life. This difference is as profound as any could be. It explains why More's ideal had no future, whereas Rabelais's was to, as the French say, *faire fortune*. For More was condemning the very heart of his civilisation, while Rabelais was releasing some of its tendencies.

The heart of civilisation as it was to be found at the courts of Western Europe was a rotten core: outward ceremony, idleness: pomp without function. No doubt More was indulging in his own personal dislike of show in making Utopia so drab, and indulging in his own love of intellectual activity in making Utopia so industrious. Yet in insisting on these two points he was making the most telling criticism of his age. What gives harmony and depth to his vision is that More's social and religious views go hand in hand: for the age needed evangelical simplicity as much as it needed classical simplicity of manners. When More and Erasmus spoke of returning *ad fontes*, they were at bottom asking for two things: the New Testament *and* the wisdom of Horace.

To see that this is so we have only to return to the *Convivium Religiosum*, Horace's simple meal where the talk is purely Christian. Let us take it up at the point where Erasmus introduces the topic expressed by Rabelais in his motto: Do What You Will. One of the diners takes out St. Paul's Epistles and reads from the sixth chapter of the first epistle to the Corinthians: 'All things are Lawful unto me, but all things are not Expedient,' which he interprets: 'The Liberty

[1] *Ibid.*, p. 243.

135

of the Gospel makes all things Lawful.' [1] After a theological speaker
interprets this text in the light of its context and the commentaries
of the Fathers, another begins to discuss the question by reference
to the Classics:

'The first place must be granted to the Authority of the Holy
Scriptures; and yet, after That, I find among the Ancients, nay the
Ethniques, and, which is yet more, among the Poets, certain Precepts,
and Sentences, so clean, so sincere, so divine, that I cannot perswade
my self but they wrote them by Holy Inspiration. And perhaps the
Spirit of Christ diffuses it self further then we imagine. There are
more Saints then we find in our Catalogue. To confess my self now
among my Friends, I cannot read *Tully, Of old Age, of Friendship*;
his Offices; or his *Tusculane Questions*; without kissing the Book;
without a Veneration for the Soul of that *Divine Heathen. . . .*'

And after quoting some words Cicero put into the mouth of Cato
in *De Senectute*, Erasmus goes on:

'What could a Christian have said more? The Dialogue of this
Aged Pagan, with the *Youth* of his times, will rise up in Judgment
against many *our Monks*, with their *Holy Virgins. . . .*'

Parallels are then found in the epistles of the New Testament:

'Now who can hear these words of Cato, *Oh that glorious Day!*
without thinking of St. *Paul's, I desire to be dissolved, and to be with
Christ*?—How happy are they that wait for Death in such a state
of Mind? But yet in *Cato's* speech, tho' it be great, there is more
boldness, and Arrogance in it methinks, then would become a
Christian. No, certainly, never any *Ethnique* came nearer up to us,
then *Socrates* to *Crito*, before he took his Poyson. *Whether I shall be
approved, or not, in the sight of God, I cannot tell, but this I am certain
of, that I have most affectionately endeavour'd to please him. And I
am in good hope that he will accept the Will for the Deed.* This great
Mans Diffidence in himself, was yet so comforted by the Conscience
of Pious Inclinations, and an absolute Resignation of himself to the
Divine Will, that he deliver'd up himself, in a dependence upon Gods
Mercy and Goodness, even for the Honesty of his Intentions.—
What a wonderful Elevation of Mind was this in a Man that only
Acted by the light of Nature! I can hardly read the Story of this
Worthy without a *Sancte Socrates Ora pro Nobis*. Saint Socrates

[1] *Op. cit.*, pp. 84 ff.

pray for us, and I have as much ado sometime, to keep my self from wishing well to the Souls of *Virgil* and *Horace*.'

The speaker then contrasts the behaviour of many Christians when about to die:

'— And 'tis no wonder to find those disorder'd at their Deaths, who have spent their whole Lives in the Formality of Philosophizing about Ceremonies.

'— What do you mean by *Ceremonies*?

'— I'll tell ye; but with this Protestation over and over, before hand; that I am so far from Condemning the Sacraments, and Rites of the Church, that I have them in high Veneration. But there are a wicked, and superstitious sort of People, (or, in good Manners, I shall call them only Simple, and unlearned Men) that cry up these things as if they were Foundations of our Faith, and the only Duties that make us truly Christians. These, I must Confess, I cannot but infinitely blame.

'— All this is not yet enough to make me understand what it is you would be at.

'— I'll be plainer then. If ye look into the ordinary sort of Christians, you will find they live as if the whole Sum of Religion rested in *Ceremonies*. With how much Pomp are the Antient Rites of the Church set forth in *Baptism*? The Infant waits without the Church door; the *Exorcism*, the *Catechism*, is dispatch'd; the *Vow* is past; the *Devil* with all his Pomps and Pleasures is *abjur'd*, and then the Child is *Anointed, Signed,* Season'd with *Salt, Dipt*, a Charge given to his *Sureties* to see him well brought up, and then follows their *Oblation*; and by this time the Child passes for a Christian, as in some sense it is. After this, it comes to be Anointed again; and, in time, learns to *Confess*, take the *Eucharist*, Rest on *Holy-Days*, to observe *Fasts*, and *Publick Prayers*, and to abstain from *Flesh*, and observing all these things, it goes for an absolute *Christian*. The Boy grows up then, and Marries, which draws on *another Sacrament*; he enters into *Holy Orders*, is *Anointed again*, and *Consecrated*, his *habit chang'd* and so to *Prayers*. Now, the doing of all this, I like well enough; but the doing of it more out of *Custom* than *Conscience*, I do not like; as if this were all that is needful to the making up of a *Christian*. There are but too many in the World, that so long as they acquit themselves in these outward Forms, think 'tis no matter what they do else: but Rob, Pillage, Cheat, Quarrel, Whore, Slander, Oppress, and Usurp upon their neighbours without Controll. And when they are brought through this Course of Life, to their last Prayers, then there follow *more Ceremonies*; *Confession* upon *Confession*, more *Unction* Still, the *Eucharist, Tapers*, the *Cross, Holy Water, Indulgences*, and *Pardons*; if they be to be had for Love or Money: Order is then given for a *Magnificent Funeral*, and then comes *another Solemn Contract . . .*'

I have quoted so much in order to be able to say: transpose all this passage on religious ceremonies to the secular sphere and you have the picture of society More is attacking in *Utopia*. This unhealthy effloresence of ceremony had its parallel in the flamboyant outward display that accompanied it. 'Burgundo-French culture of the expiring Middle Ages tends to oust beauty by magnificence . . . the border-line between pomp and beauty is being obliterated. Decoration and ornament no longer serve to heighten the natural beauty of a thing; they are over-growing it and threaten to stifle it. . . . In the art of costume, the essential qualities of pure art, that is to say, measure and harmony, vanish altogether, because splendour and adornment are the sole objects aimed at. Pride and vanity introduce a sensual element incompatible with pure art. No epoch ever witnessed such extravagance of fashion as that extending from 1350 to 1480 . . . All the forms and dimensions of dress are ridiculously exaggerated . . . A state costume was ornamented by hundreds of precious stones. The taste for unbridled luxury culminated in the court fêtes.' [1] The extreme point of decadence in outward display was well past when More as a young man first watched the entry of the Queen in 1501:

'On November 12th, the most illustrious daughter of the Spanish King, wife of our most glorious Prince, made her royal *entrée* into the City and was received with greater pomp and circumstance than was ever accorded to any personage within living memory. So magnificent was the show of our knights and nobles that it could easily have amazed you. But, heavens, if you had seen the proud Spanish train, you might have ruptured yourself with laughing at their ridiculous appearance.'

With this we may contrast Halle's naïve approval of the same spectacle:

'the ryche apparell of the pryncesse, the straunge fashion of the

[1] *The Waning of the Middle Ages*, by J. Huizinga, from chapter XIX, 'Art and Life'.

Spanyshe nacion, the beautie of the Englishe ladyes, the goodly demenoure of the young damoselles. . . .'

and his account of the coronation banquet of 1509:

'The kynges estate on the right hand, and the Quenes on the left hand, the cobard of ix. stages, their noble personages beyng set: first, at the bryngyng of the first course, the trumpettes blew vp. And in came the Duke of Buckyngham, mounted vpon a greate courser, richely trapped, and enbroudered, and the lorde Stewarde, in likewise on an horse, trapped in clothe of Golde, ridyng before the service, whiche was sumpteous, with many subtleties, straunge devyses, with severall poses, and many deintie dishes. At the kynges fete, under the table, wer certain gentelmen. And in likewise with the quene, who there continued, during that long and royal feast. What should I speake or write, of the sumpteous fine, and delicate meates, prepared for this high and honorable coronacion, provided for as wel in the parties beyond the sea, as in many and sundery places, within this realme, where God so abundantly hath sent suche plentie and foyson? Or of the honorable ordre of the services, the cleane handelyng and breaking of meates, the ordryng of the dishes, with the plentifull abundaunce.'

In fact Halle's account of 'the triumphant reigne' of Henry VIII is the perfect foil to More's *Utopia*.

It was in this world that the instinct for health drew More in two directions: he tried to break away from the unhealthy traditions of the Middle Ages in two ways: by asserting against the underlying pessimism he had inherited an optimism and confidence in the goodness of the universe and its creator; by asserting in the face of this empty pomp and magnificence the virtues of simplicity and inwardness. The result is a precarious balance, not a neat system. The contradictions in More are not pressed home to what might be thought their logical conclusions: More does not reject the extreme ascetic ideal, nor does he subordinate to it the cult of sensual pleasure. They are held together without resolution. Similarly in the world of religious ideas, the heathen and Christian elements are not opposed, as Chambers would have it, but held together.

Christian Humanism based on such a precarious poise could not hope to last. Sooner or later damaging choices would have to be made. Neither Luther nor the Pope could tolerate the evangelical piety of Erasmus. More himself was forced out of it by the needs of his polemic with Tyndale and others. And in the secular sphere, all

the restraining forces More invokes would have to give way before
the powerful impulses to extravagance and splendour could exhaust
themselves. The finery and magnificence of the Abbey of Thelema
represent the dream of the greater part of the sixteenth century:

'The Men were apparelled after their Fashion . . . Their Gowns,
as costly as those of the Ladies. Their Girdles, of Silk, of the Colours
of the Doublet. Each one had a gallant Sword by his side with the
Handle gilt, the Scabbard of Velvet of the Colour of his Hose, the
Tip of Gold and Goldsmith's Work; the Dagger was of the same.
Their Cap was of black Velvet, adorned with many Jewels and
Buttons of Gold; the white Plume above it was daintily parted by
Rows of gold Spangles, at the End of which hung in Sparkles fair
Rubies, Emeralds, etc.' [1]

But if Christian Humanism was fragile, it does not mean that it
was less valuable than what took its place. For me, at least, the plain
façades of the streets of Utopia with the gardens behind form a more
sustaining image than the splendid rooms and courtyards of the
Abbey of Thelema:

'A long row of by no means inelegant buildings can be seen forming a façade on both sides of the street. Behind the houses run a series
of large gardens in which the streets are embowered . . . They think
highly of their gardens, and have brought the cultivation of vines,
fruit trees, vegetables and flowers to a pitch both of fertility and
elegant arrangement that I have never seen equalled in Europe.
The care they give to these gardens is in part due to the pleasure
of the cultivation itself, but their ardour is stimulated by a kind of
inter-street competition for the best kept display of garden produce.
Nothing in the whole city can compare with these gardens for the
combination of pleasure and profit, and the founder of the city seems
to have given more attention to the institution of these gardens than
to any other feature of Utopia.'

[1] For the whole passage see *op. cit.*, pp. 179–189.

PART TWO

Poetry in the Early Tudor Period

THE PEOPLE AND THE COURT

The Relation of Wyatt's 'Devonshire' Poems to the 'Popular' and 'Courtly' Traditions

Wyatt's reputation rests, or should rest, on his lyrics or ballets.

Wyatt doubtless overvalued his translations because they were more difficult achievements than the songs which came to him as naturally as the leaves to a tree.

PROFESSOR KENNETH MUIR,
in his introduction to the
Collected Poems of Sir Thomas Wyatt.

I⊤ is an unfortunate, but inevitable, feature of this argument that in pressing towards what is uniquely valuable in Erasmus and More it left behind what is typical or characteristic of the Humanists as a body. It is certain that we cannot generalise about Humanism from the best parts of *The Praise of Folly* and *Utopia*. It is doubtful whether more than a handful of their contemporaries appreciated the peculiar combination of levity and seriousness in these works of Erasmus and More. The common temper of mind among Northern Humanists is a lesser thing than the spirit I have tried to discern and define in these two minor masterpieces. And what I did circumscribe does not amount to a clearly-thought-out and co-ordinated view of life.

The grasping of a fugitive moment does not take us very far in the search for the true literary history of the early sixteenth century. But if we turn our attention to the surrounding *ambiance* from which More and Erasmus were unconsciously drawing sustenance, the task of definition grows much harder. We must in fact give up the hope of precision for the simple reason that most of our material has disappeared. We can be fairly sure that if we wished we could survey all that the Humanists had to offer. They were usually anxious to get into print, and, though some of their works remained in manuscript and some have been lost, we may say that the bulk of their work is in print in the great libraries of Europe and America. This very fact makes the More-Erasmus 'moment' look so small. For although I have not sifted a thousandth part of these printed books, those who have turned it all over have not brought forward a single work to rival *The Praise of Folly* and *Utopia*. Now the whole production of the Humanists is similarly dwarfed in comparison with the total imaginative use of words (legends, stories, songs, etc.) in the various European vernaculars. But hardly any record has survived of this vast literary production, whether committed to writing or depending on oral transmission.

For reasons to be developed in the next chapter, the poems of *Thomas Wyatt* mark the second significant 'moment' for our study. We cannot place them in their context and contrast their unique virtues with the common qualities of contemporary verse with the same precision with which we could estimate the comparative worth of the best parts of the printed work of More and Erasmus. The loss is great among Wyatt's contemporaries and immediate predecessors at court. But for a few accidents we should not even have any poems of Wyatt to study. Even if the court poet writing in the vernacular were not averse to printing his works, the poems were not thought of as destined for a 'public'. For what public could there be outside the court? The poems were private papers allowed a limited and confidential circulation. The printer of Tottel's Miscellany (addressing the reader) describes his collection of the poems of Wyatt, Surrey and other courtiers as 'those workes which the vngentle horders vp of such treasure haue heretofore enuied thee'.[1]

But great as is the loss of courtly writing, it is as nothing compared

[1] He may, however, be thinking rather of *owners* of manuscripts than of poets. Compare 'Wyllyam Awen' in his prefatory letter to the translation of *Aeneid IV* by Surrey: '. . . my desyre was greate, at one time or other, yf by a meanes conuenient I might, to publyshe the same: and that the rather because I coulde vnderstand of no man that had a copye thereof, but he was more wyllyng the same should be kept as a private treasure in the handes of a fewe, then publyshed to the common profyt and delectacion of many.'

with the loss of the verse that is commonly styled 'popular'. The bulk of Wyatt's verse presupposes an immense tradition: Wyatt inherited a mass of metrical forms and poetical attitudes. In a general way we can be sure that this verse is the result of a blend of the 'popular' and the 'courtly', and that our task should therefore be to define these two elements. But only a fragment of the necessary 'popular' context has come down to us. This fragment, by its chance survival, bears not the slightest guarantee of being representative. Unfortunately, slight as are the remains, they are enough to assure us that we have lost in the unwritten and the written 'popular' poetry the voice of a civilisation we have hardly any other means of reconstructing for our appreciation. One thing, however, is certain. This 'popular' literary tradition on which Wyatt drew did not long survive his death. 'Popular' poetry changes in character and pursues a different course after about 1550. Wyatt, in this respect, belongs to an epoch that comes to an end with Tottel's Miscellany.

We already have had a hint of what to expect when we move out of the world of Humanist Latin: the reader will recall that the epigrams of More suggested that More as a poet is a much more mediaeval figure than the author of *Utopia*. Let us therefore take the road suggested by the epigrams and seek to define the context of English verse in which More's poetry was conceived. Accident provides us with a convenient approach. If More's English Works had not been collected by his friends and relations, we might never have known that he wrote English poems. Thanks to an accident we know that these poems had currency outside the family circle, that at least one London contemporary thought two of them worth copying out. One was the poem on Fortune of which I quoted a stanza in a previous chapter:

Alas! þe folyshe people can not cease . . .

the other was a funeral elegy on Henry VIII's mother, who died in 1503. It is a purely mediaeval poem untouched by Christian Humanism.

This accident is one of a kind: we owe the preservation of these poems to a habit which persisted down to the nineteenth century, that of writing into a single book all the memoranda required by a practical man. We should know very much less about 'popular' poetry and its place in the life of its audience if all the commonplace books written from the fourteenth century onwards had disappeared. Unfortunately few such commonplace books have survived. They were usually lost or destroyed when the composer died. The book which contains More's poems survived only because it somehow found its way into a college library, where it was fortunately forgotten.[1] The composer, one Richard Hill, is otherwise known as a London merchant. His commonplace book will at least give us an imaginative starting point. We shall never *know* very much about the kind and quality of poetry reading and writing in the early years of the century. But we may with guarded licence make certain suppositions by turning over the pages.

Merely to list the table of contents tells us something, for we can thus sample the other needs which accompanied that for poetry and song. Here are random extracts:

Item 1: The cheff placis wher faires be kept in Ynglond
    2: The grace þat shuld be said affore mete & after mete/ all the tymes in the yere
  3-4: Two English versions of tales from the *Gesta Romanorum*
    5: The crafte to brewe bere, etc.
       The maner to make ynke
    8: The birth of children of me Richard Hill . . .
10-20: A selection of stories from Gower's *Confessio Amantis*, including
       The tale of Pyramus & Thesbee which slew them self vpon on swerd
  22: Rules for purchasing land
  23: A treatise of wyne
  30: An oyle for harnes
  33: To clarifie the stomacke (receipt, 7 lines)
  43: For anybody þat is takyn in þe on side all lame & sumwhat swart & thowgh he haue yelow pympilles
  46: The boke of curtasie (in English verse with French interlinear translation)
       Formula of a business letter in English and French
49-64: Religious and moral poems

Item 65 is worth quoting entire:

> Lully, lulley, lully, lulley!
> þe fawcon hath born my mak away.
> He bare hym vp, he bare hym down,
> He bare hym in to an orchard brown.
> Lully, etc.
> In þat orchard þer was an hall,
> þat was hangid with purpill & pall:
> Lully, etc.

[1] It is now MS. 354 in the Library of Balliol College, Oxford.

And in þat hall þer was a bede,
Hit was hangid with gold so rede:
      Lully, etc.
And yn þat bed þer lythe a knyght,
His wowndis bledyng day & nyght:
      Lully, etc.
By þat bedis side þer kneleth a may,
& she wepeth both nyght & day:
      Lully, etc.
& by þat beddis side þer stondith a ston,
Corpus Christi wretyn þer on.
      Lully, etc.
      Explicit.

Where, we may ask, did Richard Hill get this, and why did he want it? More than three centuries later, in 1862, some one was still reciting it in a slightly different form in North Staffordshire. Later in the century, Vaughan Williams obtained a similar version, this time with its tune, in Derbyshire.

The first reflection we might make on comparing these versions is that Richard Hill's refrain seems to be unconnected with the common 'matter'. We might therefore be tempted to think that it was merely an indication of the tune to which the carol was to be sung. That this is not so is shown by the fact that in 1840 the following lines were known to a Scottish mother:

The heron flew east, the heron flew west,
The heron flew to the fair forest;
She flew o'er streams and meadows green,
And a' to see what could be seen:
And when she saw the faithful pair,
Her breast grew sick, her head grew sair;
For there she saw a lovely bower,
Was a'clad o'er wi' lilly-flower;
And in the bower there was a bed
With silken sheets, and weel down spread:
And in the bed there lay a knight,
Whose wounds did bleed both day and night;
And by the bed there stood a stane,
And there was set a leal maiden,
With silver needle and silken thread,
Stemming the wounds when they did bleed.

What remarks can we make on a bare reading of these poems? What do we know for certain about them? It may seem a trivial and crude observation that the poet was not primarily concerned to record a sad case of haemophilia. Nor was he indulging in the *macabre* for its own sake. These versions do not read as if the author were counting on the reader to contrast the unreality of the poem with an utterly alien present civilisation. They are clearly an evocation of a *significant action*. It is possible that the common use of the 'magic' or 'riddle' formula—'in that hall there was a, etc.'— points to an earlier form of the poem than those extant, in which no explicit 'solution' was provided. It may be that the version from Scotland has developed without mutilation from such an original. The Christian significance is most pointed in the 'ballad' form, where we might well think that the poem has been made to illustrate a version of the Grail legend propagated by the monks of Glastonbury Abbey according to which, when Joseph of Arimathea arrived there bearing the Grail, he thrust his staff into the ground, where it took root and still blooms each year on Christmas Day.

What we know for certain, however, is that if there once was a pre-Christian religious poem behind our texts, or if there was a non-religious love poem, the work of the composer of the Christian poem did not resemble that of a Salvation Army hack who would take an old popular tune and 'lyric' and reissue it with the minimum of change. The anthologies of religious poetry from the fourteenth to the sixteenth century are full of such hack work and bowdlerisa-tion. We should reserve the word 'popular' for such uninspired writing-down and writing-for. The important thing about our poem is not the public it was destined for, but the quality that makes it thrilling to present-day readers who have no certain solution of the 'riddle'. This quality is art of a high order and should be defined in accordance with the spirit in which it was composed. We might as well call it 'aristocratic' or 'high art' as anything else. For we must not be misled by the crudity of its transmitters: nothing is more unlikely than that the first shaper of this song resembled its last singer, whether in Derbyshire or Scotland. Nor should we leave the poem to the 'folklorist', for it is a poem and subject to the laws of poetry. What is transmitted to us is the original power of shaping. All our versions are clearly debased: Hill's poem repeats 'bedside', the North Staffordshire version has altered the movement, etc. etc., so that we cannot restore the original shape. But we know that whoever shaped it, and however it was shaped, and whatever it was shaped from, it was done by someone who understood the art of making poetry out of traditional materials. The poem could not be capable of thrilling us unless the original artist had understood the traditional mode in which he was working and had been powerfully moved by what he was doing.

Another example from Hill's commonplace book will reinforce
and extend this impression:

> Ther ys a blossum sprong of a thorn,
> To saue mankynd þat was forlorne,
> As the profettis sayd beforne.
> Deo patri sit gloria!
> þer sprong a well at Maris fote
> That torned all þis world to bote:
> Of her toke Jhesu flesshe & blod:
> Deo patri etc.

Scholars say this resembles:

> At a sprynge wel vunder a þorn
> þer was bote of bale a lytel here a-forn
> þer by-syde stant a mayde
> fulle of loue y-bounde
> Ho so wol seche trwe loue
> yn hyr hut schal be founde.[1]

In the anthology of poems known as the *Carmina Burana* we find
the following:

> Veris dulcis in tempore
> florenti stat sub arbore
> Iuliana cum sorore
> dulcis amor!
> Qui te caret hoc tempore
> fit uilior![2]

To begin with the Latin poem, it would again be a crude and
trivial remark to say that the air and movement of this stanza were
not inspired solely by the thought of an assignation with one or both
of the girls. It is impossible to believe that the poet was not in the
tradition to which we owe

> Cras amet qui nunquam amauit, quique amauit cras amet.

The point of evoking the *Pervigilium Veneris* may be seen by selecting
one stanza:

> Cras amorum copulatrix inter umbras arborum
> Inplicat casas uirentes de flagello myrteo:
> Cras canoris feriatos ducit in siluis choros,
> Cras Dione iura dicit fulta sublimi throno.

The fate of the individual is not distinguished from that of the whole

---

[1] Magdalen Coll. Oxford MS., 60 f. 214a.
[2] Codex Buranus *fol.* 36 *verso.*

body of dancers obeying a social rule or law that has the force of a law of nature, for it, too, is not distinguished from a natural law. The poet projects himself into this ideal, central, position which gives a love song universal significance, since there can be no greater sanctions than God, Nature and Society all pulling the same way.

I do not profess to know quite what is meant by

> Ruris hic erunt puellae uel puellae montium
> Quaeque siluas quaeque lucos quaeque fontes incolunt.

But if we look at the two English pieces in the spirit of Mr Eliot's equivocal

> Blessed sister, holy mother, spirit of the fountain,
> spirit of the garden,

it is hard to say which breathes more of religion or which is historically the older religion. The second piece is more powerful because uncontaminated: the 'spring' and the 'thorn' still work for us as 'natural magic' whereas the 'blossom' and the 'well' are on the way to homiletics—if still nearer to poetry than the usual adaptation of 'pagan' lyrics for godly purposes, or the straightforward exposition in Hill's book beginning:

> There ys a flowr sprong of a tre,
> The rote of it ys called Jesse,
> A flowr of pryce,
> þer ys non such in paradice
> The flowr is fresshe & fayer be hewe,
> Ytt fadis never, but euer ys newe:
> The blessid stoke þat yt on grew
> Ytt was Mary, that bare Jhesu,
> > A flowr of grace:
> > Of all flowers it ys solas . . .

However difficult it may be to define and distinguish in the realm of 'popular' poetry, there is no difficulty in marking it off from

Item 67: A poem by Lydgate

for whatever prove to be the animating spirit behind the successful 'popular' poems, Lydgate has no touch of it. He is the professional Great Man of letters, the self-satisfied representative of literacy, whose tradition is to be found not in these songs, carols and ballads, but in the works on rhetoric in the mediaeval library. We must not, however, deny all merit to the bookish tradition, for we are reminded by Hill in his

Item 88: A treatice of London

by William Dunbar that the professional literate poets were not all decadent.

One entry in the commonplace book, however, defeats classification and makes the literary historian despair:

Item 106: The Nutbrowne Mayde,

for if this poem had not survived we could comfortably record that the art of creating new literature out of the folk tradition had died out somewhere between Chaucer and Wyatt. But this poem presupposes a 'popular' tradition, yet is itself sophisticated. Moreover its merits were recognised: it sold along with other ballads for a penny in 1520, and it was adapted to make a bad religious poem. Nor did it ever lose its popularity altogether. It was preserved by Pepys and taken up by Prior. The disturbing thought aroused by *The Nutbrowne Mayde* is that it is impossible to believe that this was an isolated success. The ease with which the author transforms the simple into the sophisticated forces us to believe that he wrote for a public capable of appreciating both. Yet I know of no poem of this order written in the last remaining years—say, 1480–1520—when an audience could be equally *en rapport* with both sides.

Next in the book comes a section that may have been copied *en bloc* from an old collection of seasonal and processional carols. Here is a specimen that speaks for itself:

> Now haue gud day, now haue gud day
> I am Crystmas and now I go my way.

This clearly was written to be acted (perhaps by minstrels) and as clearly belongs to a far earlier day than Richard's. It would be interesting to know what use he found for it and how he regarded the 'feudal' language. More obviously adaptable—since it is still in use to-day—is the Boar's Head Carol. Hill could very easily have been present at a Mayor's banquet, where such an elaborate meal was no uncommon thing. We need not suppose that he had any inkling of the ancient origins of this custom. Nearer home, no doubt, was the drinking song:

> How, butler, how,
> Bevis a tout

which, we are told, is English-French for *buvez a tous*!

151

> I am so dry, I can not spek
> I am nygh choked with my mete
> I trow þe butler be aslepe . . .

(It would not surprise me to learn that the first line rhymed with the second:

> I am so dry I can not spete . . .

but we shall not want for coarser notes as we turn the pages of this commonplace book.)

One leaf, however (fol. 249 v.), symbolises a situation we must always keep in mind: that the extremes went together. It is always dangerous to study an age through specialised compartments, and particularly dangerous to separate the coarse earthy songs from the unearthly beauty of the best religious songs. In our public behaviour we rarely pass through so great extremes as was common in the Middle Ages. Of course, we do not know how the two extremes came to be copied on the same leaf, but here they are:

> Hogyn cam to bowers dore[1],
> Hogyn cam to bowers dore,
> He tryld vpon þe pyn for love,
>   Hum, ha, trill go bell!
> He tryld vpon þe pyn for love,
>   Hum, ha, trill go bell!
> Vp she rose & lett hym yn . . .

So far it is in the ballad style. Farce ensues:

> When þei were to bed browght (*bis*)
> The olde chorle he cowld do nowght . . .

I must leave the reader to discover the traditional reprisal of the lady, and pass to the rest of the leaf:

> Quene of hevyn, blessyd mot þou be
> For Godis son, born he was of the
> For to make vs fre,
>   Gloria tibi domine! . . .

Intermediate between these extremes comes the world of morality. Richard Hill's book contains a good number of moral poems. Some are clearly grafted on to traditional ballad openings and thus make a piquant contrast between the life of pleasure and the life of moral thought:

> In a tyme of a somers day
> The sune shon full meryly þat tyde,

[1] Lady's chamber.

152

I toke my hawke me for to play,
My spanyellis renyng by my syde.
A fesavnt henne than gan I see,
My howndis put her to flight,
I lett my hawke vnto her fle,
To me yt was a deynte syght.

My fawkon flewe fast vnto her pray,
My hownd gan renne with glad chere,
& sone I spurnyd in my way,
My lege was hent in a breer.
This breer, forsothe, yt dyde me gref,
Ywys yt made me to turn a-ye,
For he bare wrytyn in euery leff,
This latyn word: Revertere.

There could be no greater contrast than this attitude and that of the
Humanists, who regularly attacked this poetry, calling it filthy and
lewd. Incidentally no greater proof could be required of the grip
such ballads must have had on the audience than this habitual re-
source of mediaeval moralists. Hill has many more examples.

The most arresting moral poem in Hill's book—which reminds
me of the interlude *Everyman*—was also recorded in the previous
century:

Farewell this world! I take my leue for euer,
I am arrestid to appere affore Godis face.
O mercyfull God! thow knowest þat I had leuer
Than all this worldis good to haue an owr space
For to make a-seth for my gret trespace.
My harte, alas, is brokyn for that sorow.
Som be this day, that shall not be to-morow.

This world, I see, is but a chery fayre.
All thyngis passith: & so moste I algate . . .

No collection of poetry in a commonplace book would be complete without a section on the abuse of women. Wyatt must have
known the following poem, or one like it:

Women, women, love of women
Maketh bare pursis with sum men

Sum be mery & sum be sade
& sum be besy & sum be bade,
Sum be wilde by seynt Chade,
Yet all be nat so,
For sum be lewed & sum be shrewed,
Go, shrew, whersoeuer ye go.

Sum be wyse & sum be fonde,
Sum be tame I vndrestond,
Sum will take bred at a mannis hond,
    Yet all be nat so,
    For sum be lewde . . .

Ms. Lambeth 306 has a couplet not in Hill:

Some of them be treue of love
Benethe the gerdelle, but nat above . . .

which may have contributed its mite to Lear's

Down from the waist they are Centaurs
Though women all above.

Undoubtedly the oldest form of this type of verse is the-holly-versus-the-ivy carol. The version in Hill's book is a wonderfully lively rehandling of the old theme:

Nay, nay, Ive, it may not be, iwis,
For holy must haue þe mastry as þe maner is.

Holy berith beris, beris rede ynowgh,
þe thristilcok, þe popyngay, dance in euery bowgh,
Welaway, sory ivy, what fowles hast thow
But þe sory howlet þat syngith How how?

Ivy berith beris as blak as any sho,
þer commeth þe woode coluer & fedith her of tho,
She liftith vp her tayll & she cakkis or she go:
She wold not for C.li.[1] serve holy soo.

Holy with his mery men, they can dance in hall:
Ivy & her jentyl women can not dance at all,
but lyke a meyny of bullokkis in a water fall
Or on a whot somers day whan they be mad all . . .

Another feature of the age, as we have seen, the love of proverbs, finds satisfaction in all true commonplace books. Some of Hill's are still in use:

A birde in hond is better than thre in the wode
Pride goth beffore and shame cometh after
Whan the stede is stolen shit the stabill dore
Mani hondis makith light werke
Betwen two stolis the ars goth to grwnd
Better it is late then never
Brente honde fire dredith
Whan Adam delffid & Eve span
Who was than a gentilman?

[1] One hundred pounds.

Lastly, another feature of the commonplace book is a brief chronicle of important contemporary events. Hill reports two items of interest for our argument. Under the year 1535, after recording the horrible execution of the monks of the Charterhouse:

'hangyd, & þer bowellis brent/ þer hedis cut of & quartered & þer hedis & quarters/ som set on London Brigge and þe rest vppon all þe gatis of London/ & at þe Charter howss gate'

he entered the following:

'Item, þe VI day of Julii/ Sir Thomas Mor þat somtym was Chanseler of Ynglond was behedid at þe Towr Hill/ his hed set on þe Brigge and þe body buryed in the Towre.

'Also this yer þe power & auctoryte of þe pope was vtterly made frustrat & of non effecte within þis realme/ & þe Kyng callid suppreme hed vnder God of þe chirch of Ynglond/ & þat was red in þe chirch euery Festyvall day/ & þe popes name was scrapid owt of euery masse bok & oþer bokis/ & was callid Bishop of Rome . . .'

—a reminder that other traditions were passing in England besides the gift of renewing 'popular' poetry.

If we now place over against this summary tableau of the various kinds of poetry that may be called 'popular' a contrasting picture of the poetry that may be styled 'courtly', we must not expect a contrast between artlessness and art. Indeed it would hardly be an exaggeration to reserve 'art' for the best 'popular' poems and award even the best 'courtly' poems the consolatory but depreciatory label 'artifice'. Yet even this would be to simplify and hence to distort the facts. For what is meant by calling the following 'art'?

> Maiden in the mor lay
> in the mor lay
> seuenyst fulle, seuenist fulle
> Maiden in the mor lay
> in the mor lay
> seuenistes fulle ant a day
>
> Welle was hire mete
> wat was hire mete?
> þe primerole ant the
> þe primerole ant the

Welle was hire mete
Wat was hire mete?
the primerole ant the violet . . .[1]

I have deliberately chosen a poem which I cannot 'explain', in order that it may become clear that the claim that this is art of civilised refinement and of an exceptionally high order does not primarily rest on knowledge of what the poem is about. Something is nevertheless sufficiently present to me in my total ignorance of the 'meaning' to assure me that this effect was not got by writing about nothing: it is not an empty, nonsense poem. The 'formula' or structural principle on which the effect so largely depends was clearly not an invention of the poet, it is the common property of a people. But what was done with the formula was the unique secret of the poet. If we see the simplicity of the very greatest poetry in this minimum deviation from what is in itself quite a banal formula, it does not mean that the poet was simple or primitive. Certainly it would be hard to believe that this success could come to a poet who had lost his power of participation in the underlying beliefs that made the old formula an appropriate vehicle for its matter. It cannot be sophisticated in this sense. And if we call it refined and civilised, the refinement is in terms of the civilisation of which the ballads, for instance, are an eminent expression.

When we consider how locked away from us this civilisation is, it is a remarkable tribute to the poet that he makes so strong and so immediate an effect upon us. For I have never met or heard of anyone who did not, after reading a representative selection of good 'popular' poetry, unhesitatingly place this poem among the very best. Its very perfection, however, seems to place it in a category apart; its skill seems to be a secret, but a lost secret. For an effective contrast we need something less unearthly and something which indicates in human terms what the old civilisation did for the primary human impulses. The following may perhaps give us the start we need:

When þe nyhtegale singes þe wodes waxen grene,
Lef ant gras ant blosme springes in aueryl y wene
ant loue is to myn herte gon wiþ one spere so kene
nyht ant day my blod hit drynkes myn herte deþ me tene.

Ich haue loued al þis ȝer, þat y may loue namore
Ich haue siked moni syk, lemmon, for þin ore
Me nis loue neuer·þe ner ant þat me reweth sore.
suete lemmon, þench on me ich haue loued þe ȝore.[2] . . .

---

[1] MS. Rawlinson D. 913.   [2] MS. Harley 2253 f. 80b.

156

Here again we have a fresh song made to an old formula: the ritual salutation of the season coupled with the lover's mood. More than this, if we could have before us every love song written since the first love poem was penned in English, I should expect to find every phrase of this poem in one or other of the preceding poems. To triumph under such conditions is to be an artist indeed. Such a triumph could only come in a civilisation with well-established modes of expressing and refining love. This time, fortunately, we do not have to guess what went before in order that we might have this poem, for one of the phrases was current in the twelfth century. It is recorded that a bishop, known to have been active in the years 1184–1190, had to take disciplinary action against a priest who early one morning went up to the altar to celebrate mass and in a loud voice sang the opening words, or rather, instead of *Dominus vobiscum*, the words that came out were

Swete lamman þin are.

These words came to his lips because he was still half asleep and had spent the whole night either listening to or taking part in the songs and dances round the church.

I should like to think that the point of this story was that the priest was not in love with any particular girl, for I imagine that the 'I' of our earliest love songs was applied to a dramatic figure in a dance, a figure which more than one dancer, or even all, could personate. These communal celebrations of love could, of course, be applied to individual needs, even if they were never written for individuals, as Chaucer's Absolon applied them:

> And Absolon his gyterne hath ytake,
> For paramours he thoghte for to wake.
> And forth he gooth, jolif and amorous,
> Til he cam to the carpenteres hous
> A litel after cokkes hadde ycrowe . . .
> He syngeth in his voys gentil and smal,
> 'Now, deere lady, if thy wille be,
> I praye yow that ye wole rewe on me,'
> Ful wel acordaunt to his gyternynge . . .

and he uses the consecrated phrases:

Lemman, thy grace, and sweete bryd, thyn oore!

If we cannot fully reconstruct the human context—the elaborate patterns of courtship and the play between the individuals' feelings and the established forms—we can, even from the few surviving

157

scraps, detect some of the elements in the literary tradition which made for effective love poems. It is, for instance, striking, how often *alliterative* phrases are worked in: *e.g.*

> Foweles in þe frith
> þe fisses in þe flod
> And i mon waxe wod
> Mulch sorw I walke with
> for beste of bon and blod.

But however hard we may find it to define the quality that pleases so evidently in the best of these 'popular' love poems, we have no difficulty in knowing when it is present and when it is absent, *e.g.*

> So hath myn herte caught in remembraunce
> Your beaute hoole and stidefast governaunce,
> Your vertues alle and your hie noblesse,
> That you to serve is set al my plesaunce.
> So wel me liketh your womanly contenaunce,
> Your fresshe fetures and your comlynesse,
> That whiles I live, myn herte to his maystresse
> You hath ful chose in trewe perseveraunce
> Never to chaunge, for no maner distresse.

Why does this seem dead and the following alive?

> Adoun y fel to hire anon
> ant cried, ledy, þyn ore!
> ledy, ha mercy of þy mon!
> lef þou no false lore,
> ʒef þou dost hit wol me reowe sore.
> Loue dreccheþ me þat y ne may lyue na more ...[1]

The attitude of the lover is equally conventional in both. What is the difference? We can begin to answer by remarking that in Chaucer the *direction of interest has changed*. He appears to be more interested in his pattern of rhymes than in arranging the stock materials into a convincing dramatic representation of the lover's rôle.

Of course, there is more to be said about the difference than this, but as the example from Chaucer was a particularly bad one, let us look at further formal patterns inside Chaucer's longer works. The conventions within which Chaucer's short 'courtly' love poems have their setting can be seen in *The Franklin's Tale*; for example, when Aurelius is in love

> no thyng dorste he seye,
> Save in his songes somwhat wolde he wreye

[1] MS. Harley 2253 f. 128a.

His wo, as in a general compleyning:
He seyde he lovede and was biloved no thyng.
Of swich matere made he manye layes,
Songes, compleintes, roundels, virelayes . . .

These are the forms—the fixed forms—of French poetry which
Chaucer himself wrote in. In this tale he gives us two examples of the
formal love complaint:

For wel I woot my servyce is in vayn:
My gerdon is but brestyng of myn herte.
Madame, reweth upon my peynes smerte,
For with a word ye may me sleen or save.
Heere at youre feet God wolde that I were grave!

'Service' and 'gerdon' are taken straight from the vocabulary of
French courtly love. But the rhymes herte-smerte must have been
worked out long before Chaucer in the adaptation of French modes
into English. 'Sleen or save' is another cliché, which, incidentally,
lasted to Wyatt's day:

And if an Iye may save or sleye . . .

Aurelius makes another formal complaint when the miracle has
been accomplished:

My righte lady . . .
Whom I mooste drede and love as I best kan,
And lothest were of al this world displese,
Nere it that I for yo have swich disese
That I moste dyen heere at youre foot anon,
Noght wolde I telle how me is wo bigon.
But certes outher moste I dye or pleyne:
Ye sle me giltelees for verray peyne.
But of my deeth thogh that ye have no routhe,
Avyseth yow er that ye breke youre trouthe.

. . . .

Nat that I chalange any thyng of right
Of yow, my sovereyn lady, but youre grace . . .

This last remark, like the others, is strictly 'according to the book';
it persisted down to Wyatt's time:

Clayming of you nothing of right, of right
Save of your grace only to stay my liff.

These examples, I take it, illustrate the fact that a literary habit was well established by Chaucer's day: there was a traditional vocabulary, part translation from the French, part native coinage, part borrowed from the 'popular' love conventions, for handling the situations of courtly love. Let us now see what Chaucer could do in his own right. His most formal piece is 'The compleynt of Anelida'. Here, too, the contribution of Chaucer's art is merely artifice, the elaboration of the stanzas into patterns. There is hardly a line here that might not be found in other poems of this type. For instance,

line 214:   That turned is in quakyng al my daunce

occurs in the poem beginning 'The longe nightes . . .'

line 51 :   Whan I shulde daunce for fere, lo, than I quake

A piece of concentrated cliché occurs in the rest of the 'Proem':

> Sith hit availeth not for to ben trewe,
> For whoso trewest is hit shal hir rewe
> That serveth love and doth her observaunce
> Alwey til oon, and chaungeth for no newe.

This last cliché is found in poems good, bad and indifferent from before Chaucer and down to Wyatt; indeed we hardly feel any passage of time in passing from the above passage of Chaucer to this of Wyatt:

> All my poore hart and my love trew,
> Whyle lyff dothe last I gyve yt yow
> And yow to serve with servys dew
> And neuer to change yow for no new.

Since I shall be dwelling on this poem later on in this chapter, it may be as well to note here that another line

> When ye be mery than am I glad

in this poem is also a floating cliché caught up in Anelida's 'compleynt':

line 224:   And when that he was glad then was I blithe . . .

These instances will, I hope, suffice to make the point. If not, as a final example, we might compare

line 346 :   But as the swan I have herd seyd ful yore
              Ayeins his deth shal singen his penaunce,
              So singe I here my destinee or chaunce . . .

with Wyatt:

> Lyke as the Swanne towardis her dethe
>   Doeth strayn her voyse with dolefull note,
> Right so syng I with waste of breth,
>   I dy!

160

We must not, however, suppose that all Chaucer's treatments are artifice and little else. But the distinction between 'popular' and 'courtly' comes out best where Chaucer ie-works traditional 'popular' material. One of the traditions that link us with the *Pervigilium Veneris* is the spring festival that is also a lovers' festival, St. Valentine's Day. Traces of the rite were still known when Ophelia sang:

> To-morrow is Saint Valentine's day . . .

Under the date February 1477, we find in the Paston Letters, 'cosyn, vppon Fryday is Sent Valentynes Daye and every brydde chesyth hym a make'. This was an occasion on which the court poet was expected to shine, and one that suited Chaucer, as we know from *The Parliament of Fowls:*

> For this was on seynt Valentynes day
> Whan every foul cometh there to chese his make . . .

That Chaucer was in full and perfect *rapport* with the spirit of this festival we know even more surely from the prologue to *The Legend of Good Women*:

> And for the newe blisful somers sake
> Upon the braunches ful of blosmes softe
> In hire delyt they turned hem ful ofte
> And songen Blessed be Seynt Valentyn
> For on this day I chees yow to be myn
> Withouten repentyng, myn herte swete!
> And therwithalle hire bekes gonnen meete,
> Yeldyng honour and humble obeysaunces
> To love, and diden hire other observaunces
> That longeth onto love and to nature . . .

But if Chaucer is here *en rapport* with a celebration of Nature and Love, in which immemorial tradition is blended with the ever-new return of season to all and of youth to each successive generation, with what can we say that his songs in these two poems are *en rapport*? For when Chaucer in *The Parliament of Fowls* set himself to dramatise what he described in the passage just quoted, and to show what it meant

> To don to Nature honour and plesaunce

he offered a translation of a French roundel. Here I wish we could compare the song beginning

> Now welcome, somer, with thy sonne softe

with a popular poem beginning

> Vp son and mery wether
> somer draweth nere

but even without the rest of this 'popular' fragment we can see that Chaucer's 'observaunce' is an inferior thing that does not deserve the name. It is more than artifice, of course; in fact it stands to popular poetry in an analogous relation to that discussed in the prologue, where the old May Day rite brought to perfection by centuries of accreted ceremony was transformed by Henry VIII into something neither 'natural' nor yet a mere masquerade.

In both cases the substitution of the new, modish thing for the traditional meant a loss of power, a debilitating breaking-off of communications with the past. The new note is not one of civilisation but of sophistication. Similarly, it is a disappointment in *The Legend of Good Women* when after the promise of a worthy celebration of Love in the lines:

> And after that they wenten in compas
> Daunsynge aboute this flour an esy pas
> And songen as it were in carole wyse

we find Chaucer, after one lovely line

> Hyd, Absalon, thy gilte tresses clere,

offering a catalogue of classical names.

We do not know how much, if anything, had been done by Chaucer's predecessors and senior contemporaries at court to assimilate the French models, but we do know that Chaucer was quite easy with the French modes and by no means their slave. A good example is *The Complaint of Venus*, where we can see Chaucer inserting traditional English phrases into his translation:

> Of him whos I am al while I may dure

is a tag which lasted to Wyatt's day:

> Then in my boke wrote my maystresse:
> I am yowres yow may well be sure
> And shall be whyle my lyff dothe dure.

The line

> As wake abedde and fasten at the table

is in the French, and Wyatt may have borrowed it from Chaucer:

> But faste at borde and wake abed.

If this shows that Chaucer was not aware of any hostility between the new and the old such as we feel in contrasting the 'popular' and the 'courtly', lines such as

Jelosie be hanged be a cable!

show that Chaucer did not feel that the assimilated French manner required very strict decorum.

But the treasure-house for expressions of courtly love is *Troilus and Criseyde*, where we may make the same distinctions between phrases already current by Chaucer's day and formal poems in the French manner, such as Antigone's song in Book II. *Troilus* also provides us with models of other forms of courtly verse, such as the verse letter, one of which begins at line 1317 of Book V. If we abstract the few phrases which attach it to the context, we have here the formula of recommendation that every amateur court poet down to Wyatt was expected to turn out. It is, of course, only a sub-species of the formal complaint and uses all the clichés in vogue, *e.g.*

And graunte it that ye soone upon me rewe
As wisly as in al I am yow trewe.

Chaucer, then, as the author of the courtly love poems discussed above, seems to have taken the first step down the slippery slope that led to the utter banality of most of the similar poems written after him. For, once the forms had been provided, anybody could string together the tags into the semblance of a poem. What happened when the author ceased to be *en rapport* with the civilisation behind the best 'popular' love poems can be estimated from Lydgate. Lydgate professed indeed to be conscious of what made him inferior to Chaucer:

Chaucer is deed, that had suche a name
Of fayre makyng that withouten wene
Fayrest in our tongue as the laurer grene.

We may assay for to countrefete
His gaye style but it wyl not be;
The welle is drie with the lycoure swete . . .

but it may be doubted whether he believed it. At any rate he attempted a 'Balade Symple' which contains the lines that make commentary superfluous:

'With al my might and in my best entent
With al the faythe that mighty God of kynde
Me yaue, syth he me soule and knowyng sent
I chese, and to this bonde euer I me bynde
To loue you best whyle I have lyfe and mynde.'
Thus herde I foules in the dawenyng
Vpon the day of Saynte Valentyne synge.

163

Our only evidence of the habits bequeathed to the court in the fifteenth century by Chaucer is something of a freak. For the only considerable body of surviving court love poetry is a sequence of balades and roundels by a French poet, Charles d'Orléans, who spent twenty-five years in England (compulsorily) after Agincourt. Although he acquired a knowledge of English, he is not an English poet, and we can only use his writings as evidence of the *literary habits* of courtiers in the fifteenth century. It is in fact a penance to have to read through his English works. Yet, judging by the fragments that survive of other courtiers, we have no reason to suppose that he was exceptionally bad.

In saying this, however, I am pronouncing the verdict that the English verses of Charles d'Orléans stand *outside* literature. They are part of a courtly ceremonial—unfortunately, they, the only surviving part, are the deadest part of the ceremonial. These verses would have meaning if we could restore their context, but the meaning would still be sociological, not literary. They would be interesting merely to the extent that they informed us how they fitted into the pattern of ceremonious courtship Charles was able to indulge in, though a prisoner, during his stay in England.

Nevertheless through this collection of verse we can come to understand something of the function of the court poet down to Wyatt's time. For, whatever the place in Charles's love intrigues these verses may have had, they have a second function, as matters addressed to all young people at court. It is quite possible that Charles would not have thought of composing poems addressed to various individuals and on individual occasions in his private life if he had not from the first destined them to the public interested in the upholding of the love conventions of which Charles was such an amiable exponent. Just as Wyatt wrote

> All ye lovers, perde
>   Hathe cawse to blame hys dede,
> Which shall example be
>   To lett yow off yowre spede . . .
> For I vnto my coste
> Am warnyng to yow all . . .

so Charles wrote offering a collection of roundels

> Parde folk sayne that lovers lyue by lokis
> And bi wisshis and othir wanton thought
> Wherfore sum thing y trust in this bok is
> To fede them on . . .
> For with laboure y haue it for hem bought

164

As them to please . . .
Wherfore as this vnto yow louers alle
Here is my fest . . .

The noble poet thus becomes the court entertainer. He would accumulate his occasional poems into his own 'book' and this book would be copied for the entertainment of his friends. (We can see in one of Wyatt's manuscripts this process in action.) Indeed we can imagine the function of most court poetry as analogous to the collection of jazz records kept (the newspapers inform us) by an August Personage. We can imagine the relation Charles's lyrics bore to the emotional needs of his circle as being roughly parallel. The poems are so vague and general they could fit anybody, because they fit nobody, they are so removed from actuality.

These verses have a further interest for us in that they typify the relation of the court poet to Chaucer. For it is clear that Charles wrote his poems out of Chaucer, and notably out of *Troilus* and *The Knight's Tale*. In this he resembled all the court poets we know of down to Wyatt. One example will suffice to bridge the centuries. Charles, like Wyatt, had been especially impressed by the accounts of May Day in *The Knight's Tale*. Now Charles—who had personal reasons for sympathy with the prisoners in Chaucer's tale—wrote a poem on one of his May Days:

This tyme when louers alþermost defie
Eche heuy thought as ferforth as þei may
And rise or phebus in þe morow gray
leiying aside alle slouthe and slogardy
To here the birdis synge so lustily
Ouyr þe spryngyng boddes on þe spray . . .
Thyn waylyng on my pilow thus y ly
For þat as was and now is goon for ay
Wisshyng no more but deth eche howre of day
Saiyng myn hert allas whi nelt þou day . . .

This resembles what might also be a prison poem by Wyatt:

You that in loue finde lucke and habundaunce
    And liue in lust and ioyful iolitie
    Arrise for shame! Do away your sluggardie!
    Arise, I say, do May some obseruaunce!
Let me in bed lye dreming in mischaunce,
    Let me remember the happs most vnhappy
    That me betid in May most comonly,
    As oon whome loue list litil to auaunce . . .

Wyatt has crossed *The Knight's Tale* with *Troilus*: compare this last line with

165

Of hem that Love list febly for to avaunce

from Book I, and in Book II, on May 3rd, Pandarus went to Criseyde and said:

> Do wey youre book, rys up, and lat us daunce
> And lat us don to May som observaunce.

We can find a striking instance of this courtly habit in what is known as the 'Devonshire' manuscript, the source from which we derive many of Wyatt's most admired 'lyrics'.[1] In some ways we might regard it as the aristocratic counterpart of the poetry section of Hill's commonplace book; for, just as the London merchant's book has no courtly poems, so this aristocratic ladies' album has no popular poetry. The striking thing about it is not that it contains so many poems by Wyatt, but that, having a contemporary live poet to hand, the ladies also bothered to copy out passages from Chaucer, who was by then in print, and from 'pseudo-Chaucer'. This may, of course, mean that the ladies were short of contemporary verse, and Wyatt's heavy dependance on the body of 'pseudo-Chaucerian' verse may be due to an absence of more recent models for the young beginner in the early 1520's.

Some entries in this manuscript enable us to come very close to the problem touched upon in discussing the context of Charles's verse, the problem raised by the failure of the love convention to canalise and purify the human feelings. It is a serious matter when the language of love poetry ceases to have a civilising influence on the passions. The passion may then turn hypocritical or brutal. As a notable instance we have the stiff, frigid, love-letters Henry VIII wrote in French to Ann Boleyn. The 'Devonshire' manuscript provides a rather different example. It appears to have accompanied two almost ideal lovers to the Tower of London. For Lord Thomas Howard had secretly married Margaret, niece of Henry VIII—a lady destined for some monarch or at any rate for the marriage market princes conducted to bolster up their foreign policy. The lovers not only braved the wrath of the prince—which usually meant death—but they persisted in their love and thus fulfilled what I take to be the ideal pattern laid down by Chaucer in *The Legend of Good Women*:

> For there hath Eneas ykneled so,
> And told hire al his herte and al his wo,
> And swore so depe to hire to be trewe,
> For wel or wo, and chaunge hire for no newe,

[1] MS. Add. 17492.

> And as a fals lovere so wel can pleyne,
> That sely Dido rewede on his peyne,
> And tok hym for husbonde, and becom his wyf
> For everemo, whil that hem laste lyf.

The interest of the case for us is that here we seem to have a reality behind the verse conventions. For these lovers, faced with such a serious menace, contrived to exchange the most banal and wishy-washy verses in Wyatt's emptiest style—such stuff in fact as, taken by itself, would lead us to talk of their love as a half-hearted game.[1] This is surely proof that the court verse of the period corresponded to a need though it could not fulfil it. Secondly, when Lord Thomas fell seriously ill and was on the point of death, he sent a poem containing the following lines to his dear wife:

> O very lord, O loue! O god, alas!
> That knowest best myn hert and al my thowght,
> What shall my sorowful lyfe donne in thys case,
> Iff I forgo that I so dere haue bought
> Syn ye   and me haue fully brought
> Into your grace and both our hertes sealed,
> Howe may ye suffer, alas, yt be repealed?

The reader of *Troilus* will at once supply the missing name and understand what happened: that, needing some more powerful means of conveying his last message, the dying courtier wrote out a piece of Chaucer suited to his circumstances.

When we ask ourselves what is the relation of Wyatt to these two traditions, which, for want of sufficient information, we must leave rather shadows than realities, we soon find it impossible to separate what looks like an enquiry into 'fact' from a critical estimate, which may appear merely an 'opinion'. At any rate, as soon as we face the question: what is the place of Wyatt in a serious account of our literary history? And the related question: which poems of Wyatt matter to us sufficiently to-day to give them a place in an anthology of the ever-living? we enter the field of controversy. At the risk of seeming impertinent and arrogant—for the claim is made after reading all the available opinions—I would assert that with Wyatt we must start from the beginning. Not because all serious literary enquiry starts *again, as if* the subject had never been looked at before, but because I think that Wyatt never has been looked at,

---

[1] The text of these poems is conveniently reprinted by Professor Kenneth Muir in *Proceedings of the Leeds Philosophical Society* (Literary and Historical Section), vol. VI, Part IV, pages 253–82.

properly looked at, before, or at least, if Wyatt was properly looked at by one or two of his contemporaries, though not by Surrey, he has not been properly looked at since. The reader, who has already condemned the fatuity of such a claim and is ready to apply in the critical domain the moral *maxime*

C'est une grande folie de vouloir être sage tout seul,

is asked to stay judgement for a while and allow the evidence to pile up.

For with Wyatt we are dealing with a reputation very much like Herrick's. Wyatt, as a poet, after his death, enjoyed a long sleep, hardly disturbed by the formal mention of his name in catalogues of our early poets. Even when he was virtually rediscovered in the early years of the nineteenth century and handsomely edited in a huge, heavy volume, the *Edinburgh Review* saw no reason to take notice of the editor's labours. As with Marvell and Herrick, Tennyson was largely responsible for getting a few poems into circulation in Palgrave's *Golden Treasury*. (This does not mean that Palgrave did nothing: we have his annotated copy of Wyatt in the British Museum.) These poems reappear in later anthologies and by and large constitute the claim that is usually made for Wyatt in universities, and the claim that poetry readers generally are ready to acknowledge. That this claim is by and large an endorsement of Tennyson rather than the result of much intensive independent inspection of Wyatt's poems can be shewn by the amusing fact that in the original *Oxford Book of English Verse* two of Wyatt's poems are printed under another poet's name.

This claim does not, of course, mean that nobody beside Tennyson and Palgrave has ever read the whole of Wyatt with a view to assessing his permanent importance, but that the assessors as yet do not constitute a formidable body of opinion which it would be presumptuous in me to question. The reader can obtain a rough idea of the lightweights in critical authority who have pronounced on Wyatt by glancing at those quoted in Professor Muir's edition of Wyatt's poems—and, for a rough idea of present-day opinion, he might turn to the introduction Professor Muir wrote for that edition.

At any rate, I have so far deferred to prevailing opinion as to start with the common verdict that the best poems of Wyatt's are his 'lyrics'. Against this I would assert that most of Wyatt's 'lyrics' are not poems at all. Let us take one at random, that is, a poem not demonstrably the worst of those attributed to Wyatt and one bearing obvious similarities to many others that pass under his name. The following lines are found in the 'Devonshire' manuscript:

Sum tyme I syghe, sumtyme I syng,
Sumtyme I lawghe, sumtyme mornynge,
As one in dowte, thys ys my ssayyng:
Have I dysplesed yow in any thyng?

Alake, what aylythe you to be grevyd?
Ryght sory am I that ye be mevyd:
I am your owne yf trewthe be prevyd
And by your dyspleasure as one myschevyd.

When ye be mery than am I glad,
When ye be sory than am I sad:
Such grace or fortune I wold I had
Yow for to plese howeuer I were bestad.

When ye be mery, why shuld I care?
Ye are my joye and my wellfare.
I wyll you love: I wyll not spare
Into yowre presens as farr as I dare.

All my poore hart and my loue trew
Whyle lyff dothe last I gyue yt yow
And yow to serue with servys dew
And neuer to change yow for no new.

This poem is found in a collection apparently made for or by noble
ladies of the court in the reign of Henry VIII. Let us compare it
with a poem from a collection made for or by ladies sometime in the
fifteenth century—now MS. Ff. 1.6. in the University Library at
Cambridge:

Now wold y fayne sum myrthis make
All oneli ffor my ladys sake
and hit wold be
But now J am so fferre from hir
hit wille nat be
Thoghe J be long out of your sight
J am your man both day & night
And so wille be
Wherfor wold god as J loue hir
that she louid me
When she is mery than am J glad
When she is sory then am J sad
And cause whi
    ffor he leuithe nat that louithe hir
as well as J
She sayth that she hath seene hit wreten

That seldyne sayne is soone for yetene
hit is nat so
ffor in good feithe saue oneli hir
J loue no moo.
Wher-for J pray, both nygth & day
That she may cast [all] care away
And leue in rest
And euer more wher so euer she be
to Loue hir best
And J to hir for to be trew
And neuer chaung for noone new
vn-to myne end
And that J may in hir seruice
for euir Amende.

This poem has been attributed by some editors to a certain A. Godewhen, but I think it more likely that the words under the poem represent the lover's sigh: 'Ah, god, when?'

This comparison makes it clear that Wyatt was not *creating* when he wrote:

When ye be mery than am I glad,
When ye be sory than am I sad

and when he wrote:

All my poore hart and my loue trew
Whyle lyff dothe last I gyue yt yow
And yow to serue with servys dew
And neuer to change yow for no new.

Nor, we may be sure, was Mr Godwin. His poem was merely a cento of all the clichés current on the subject from at least the fourteenth century. Is Wyatt's poem anything else?

Have I dysplesed yow in any thyng?
Alake, what aylythe you to be grevyd?
Ryght sory am I that ye be mevyd:

This constellation—displesyd, greuyd, meued—is also found in another poem of the same fifteenth-century anthology:

ffor if y hadde hure displeased
Jn worde or dede or hire greued
Than if she hadde be sore meued
She hadde cause in dede

We find the rhymes glad-had-bestad of the stanza:

When ye be mery . . .

170

in a song very like

> Now wold J fayne sum myrthis make
> All oneli ffor my ladys sake

which begins

> No wondre thow J murnyng make
> . . . .
> and all is for my lady sake . . .

This song was written down in Wyatt's day,[1] but is clearly of the fourteenth or the fifteenth century. The stanza with Wyatt's rhymes runs:

> Trow ye that J wold be glade
> To seke a thynge þat wyll not be hade
> Saw J neuer man so sore bestad . . .

And an even closer parallel occurs in Gower's *Confessio*:

> Whan they ben glad I shall be glad
> And sory whan they ben bestad

Now these parallels come from the extremely scanty remains left to us. Can we doubt that if we had *all* the songs sung at court between Chaucer and Wyatt we should be able to shew that every word and phrase used by Wyatt was a commonplace and had been used by many of his predecessors?

Secondly, this poem is no better and no worse than many others in the 'Devonshire' collection. By a little application we could compose a dictionary of conventional phrases which would show that many of these poems of Wyatt's are simply strung together from these phrases into set forms. There is not the slightest trace of poetic activity. The reason, I suggest, is that no poetic activity was attempted. Wyatt, like the other court writers, was merely supplying material for social occasions. Consequently, the study of these poems belongs to sociology rather than to literature.

On the other hand, we should not suppose that these poems are merely trivial words for possibly excellent music. No doubt poems like the one chosen were set to music; yet we must not therefore conclude that they would not have been put together if there had been no musical occasion. Even if a poem is known to have been set, we must not conclude that it was written for that purpose, nor must we exclude the possibility that the poem was enjoyed in a non-musical context. After all the song

> Now wold y fayne sum myrthis make

is found in the anthology mentioned above *without* its tune. The

---

[1] P.R.O. MS. Ex^r. Misc. 22/1/1.

171

most certain thing we know about the context of these poems of
Wyatt is that they were collected into a written manuscript by
certain ladies, one at least of whom made marginal notes of appreciation of her reading. In short, many of Wyatt's poems are pieces of
courtly behaviour, and not necessarily contributions to the musical
life of the court.

This behaviour is most obviously literary when it consists in writing for ladies' albums, either in the form of verse epistles or of
discourses on themes proposed by the ladies, such as we may well
imagine Wyatt's poems on 'patience' to be. We may speak of the
activity as literary in the ordinary sense in that it is possible that
Wyatt, like Charles, thought of sending his poems out in a manuscript book—a few copies for court friends. He certainly thought of
the poems as *reading* matter, whether or not they were also matter
for singing.

If we look at the poems in this light, we can see that some of them
were written to be read in company, or by a group of associates.
Some of them do not make sense unless we suppose that Wyatt was
in the poem obliquely reflecting in company on the private behaviour
of a lady in that company. Indeed in one poem he says the company
complained that he was too oblique:

> My songs ware to defuse
> Theye made folke to muse . . .

This does not mean that the readers were bothered about the lack of
condensation in the poems and the conventionality of the style, but
that they could not divine who or what he was alluding to when he
praised or blamed his lady or complained of his sufferings.

Let me therefore break off the argument for a moment to state
what I take to be a possible context for these 'Devonshire' poems.
I suppose that Wyatt's situation was not unlike that of the lover in
Gower's *Confessio Amantis*, who says of himself:

> And also J haue ofte assaied
> Rondeel, balade and virelai
> For hire on whom myn herte lai
> To make and also for to peinte
> Caroles with my wordes queinte
> To sette my purpos alofte
> And thus J song hem forth ful ofte
> Jn halle and ek in chambre aboute.

Wyatt, I take it, indulged in amours with court ladies: Ann Boleyn
may very well have been one of his mistresses. He certainly found

another by frequenting the ladies-in-waiting of Henry's first queen. The way in which private and public life might intermingle is well suggested by the close of Boccaccio's *Decameron*. For though the company there was somewhat special, it would not differ in essentials from the social conditions and opportunities open to Wyatt. I assume that Wyatt with his closest male friends would be able to dine with the Queen and her ladies in semi-informal conditions— say, with less than a hundred persons present. Halle records that the King was able to form small parties and visit the ladies in this semi-informal way. Wyatt therefore might well have been present at such a scene as this from the close of the *Decameron*.

After dinner the company began to sing, to play on instruments or to dance. And while one lady led the dance, the master of ceremonies ordered a lady to recite to music a poem in a fixed form, called a *canzone*. The lady complied and in her poem spoke of her fears that the other ladies of the party might steal from her the love of the man she admired, and thus cause her to fall into a fury of jealousy. When she had finished her song, one of the gentlemen went up to her and said with a smile: 'Lady, you would oblige us if you would tell all the company here who was the man you were alluding to in your poem, in case any one of the ladies through ignorance of the name might gain possession of his love and thus throw you into a rage.' [1]

To return to the argument: my first proposition can now be restated as follows: poems like the one I have been dwelling on can hardly be said to have an author, since they are put together conventionally from conventional materials, without transcending art. Indeed I doubt whether we can even attribute the putting together of this poem to Wyatt.

> Alake, what aylythe you to be grevyd?
> Ryght sory am I that ye be mevyd:
> I am your owne yf trewthe be prevyd
> And by your dyspleasure as one myschevyd.

I must leave it to the experts to decide whether the forms *mevyd* and *prevyd* are found in any court verse after 1500. Certainly in the poems in Wyatt's own handwriting he rhymes these words with *love*. In all the extant verse Wyatt has only four rhymes in -ove: move, prove, love, above. (The scarcity of new rhyme words and rhymes contrasts with the fecundity in metrical forms.) There is one exception: the last stanza of the poem beginning *Ys yt possyble* contains

---

[1] If this is a plausible context, we have a further reason why the poems could not be broadcast indiscriminately.

the rhymes *preve* and *leve*. I conjecture that if the rest of the poem *was* written by Wyatt this stanza was an addition by another hand.

The point, however, is: even if we admit that the poems are by Wyatt, since they have no character as *art*, they do not count. We have not yet found Wyatt the lyric poet. In our search, however, we might continue with rejections. Nobody, for instance, can believe that the poem beginning *Payne of all payne* was written by Wyatt —at least not on internal grounds. For in no other poem does Wyatt 'make rehearsall of old antiquitye'. More striking still, in no other poem does Wyatt invert the adjective and the noun in the phrases, *sighis painefull, lookes Rufull, mynde sensuall*. I conjecture that this is a fifteenth-century translation of a French poem, for it contains a piece of medical terminology that is not English:

> For true love, ons fixid in the cordiall vayne
> Can never be *revoulsid* bye no manner of arte.

And so I could go on throwing doubt on Wyatt's authorship of many of the poems found only in the 'Devonshire' manuscript. The poems that would remain, however, are our real concern. They have a distinctive character, for they are in a convention: but the convention is linguistically bad and bad in sentiment. It is true that the language is a selection from the earlier styles: it rejects 'aureate diction', it rejects the massive use of French words, particularly strings of rhymes in -aunce, but it also rejects the particular and the new, or rather, it does not attempt either. Even if it gains in simplicity from blending 'courtly' vocabulary with 'popular', the blend is stale, flat, and consequently unpalatable:

> The wofull dayes so full of paine
> The werye night all spent in vayne
> The labor lost for so small gayne
> To wryt them all yt will not bee . . .

These words have no more life for me than the words of popular songs to-day: they are banal, if inoffensively banal. The fault of sentiment is also that it is too monotonous. If the lover is complaining, he is all complaint, if he spurns service, he is all scorn. He never departs from, enriches or in any way transcends his conventional rôle. We are aware only of the part he is playing, not of anything behind the words he uses.

So far, about the greater number of Wyatt's 'lyrics' at least, most critics, I take it, are in agreement. We come now to a parting of the ways: those who see Wyatt as the last writer of a dying movement claim that he occasionally strikes the note of true poetry by catching

the manner of the best poems in the 'popular' tradition: others, who
see in Wyatt the first of the Elizabethan song writers, claim that
occasionally he departs from the dead mediaeval convention he
was writing in and brings fresh feeling and melody to English poetry.

Let me take the mediaevalists first. Mr Tillyard[1] was not afraid
to say that a lyric such as that beginning

'What shulde I saye'

'carries on the tradition of' the greatest of mediaeval popular poems:

I syng of a myden   þat is makeles
kyng of alle kynges   to here sone che ches

he cam also stylle   þer his moder was
as dew in aprylle   þat fallyt on þe gras

he cam also stylle   to his moderes bowr
as dew in aprille   þat fallyt on þe flour

he cam also stylle   þer his moder lay
as dew in aprille   þat fallyt on þe spray

moder & mayden   was neuer non but che
wel may swych a lady   godes moder be.[2]

There we have a standard of simplicity—simplicity in great complexity—the kind of thing to evoke when we read Mr Eliot:

A condition of complete simplicity
(Costing not less than everything).

Is Mr Tillyard right in thinking that we have the same simplicity
here?

What shulde I saye
    Sins faithe is dede
And truthe awaye
    From you ys fled?
    Shulde I be led
With doblenesse?
Nay , naye, mistresse!

I promiside you
    [And] you promisid me
To be as true

---

[1] *The Poetry of Sir Thomas Wyatt* (1929), p. 14.
[2] Sloane MS. 2593, f. 10v.

175

                    As I wolde bee,
                    But sins I se
                Your doble herte
                Farewell my perte!

                You for to take
                    [Yt] ys not my minde
                But to forsake
                    [Your cruell kinde]
                And as I finde
                So will I truste
                Farewell, vniuste!

                Can ye saye naye
                    But [that] you saide
                That I allwaye
                    Shulde be obeide
                And thus betraide
                Or that I wiste
                Farewell, vnkiste!

This, to my mind, is another kind of simplicity and belongs to
another tradition, the tradition represented by this:

                O mestres, whye
                owtecaste am I
                all vtterly
                    from your pleasaunce?
                Sythe ye & I
                or thys truly
                famyliarly
                    haue had pastaunce

                And lovyngly
                ye wolde aply
                þy company
                    to my comforte:
                But now, truly,
                vnlovyngly
                ye do deny
                    Me to resorte.

                And me to see
                as strange ye be
                as thowe þat ye
                    shuld nowe deny
                or else possesse
                þat nobylnes
                    176

>   To be dochess
>   of grete Savoy.
>
>   But sythe þat ye
>   So strange wylbe
>   As toward me
>   & wyll not mell,
>   I truste, percase,
>   to fynde some grace
>   to haue free chayse
>   & spede as welle![1]

If we now seek to characterise the simplicity of *this* tradition, we must clearly do so in terms not of plenitude but of absences. It is quite unlike the simplicity of the great popular poems. The sympathy of the natural world with the human is totally absent. Another significant absence can be brought to consciousness by a comparison with the polar opposite (earthy as distinct from unearthly) in the 'popular' tradition, that is, we can define courtly simplicity by contrasting it with 'folk' simplicity at a social level below that of the court. The example I have chosen is a conventional dance song in a fixed form: four lines with the same rhyme and a refrain:

>   Ladd y þe daunce a myssomur day
>   y made smale trippus soþ fore to say
>   iak oure haly watur clerk com be þe way
>   & he lokede me vpon he þout þat y was gay
>   þout yc on no gyle . . .[2]

Here we have simplicity masking a good deal of sophistication. That this type of poem—the poem of seduction, usually by a priest —was sophisticated we may see from another in the same manuscript (p. 210), where the following stanza occurs:

>   he seyde to me he wolde be trewe
>   & change me for non oþur newe
>   now y sykke & am pale of hewe
>   for he is far . . .

My reason for dwelling on this quite different traditional use of simple and direct speech (which Chaucer wove into his *Canterbury Tales*) is to bring home how much less than fully human is the voice of the lover in Wyatt's poem. We are fortunate in possessing many specimens in prose and verse of the vigour of Wyatt's natural speech, which make this poem seem to speak if not in a falsetto voice at

---

[1] Harley MS. 2252 f. 84v.
[2] MS. 383 in the Library of Caius College, Cambridge, p. 41.

any rate with a very restricted range. So that if we praise its technical perfection, we must at the same time stress how drastically limited its perfections are. Certainly the best of Wyatt's 'lyrics' in this tradition of plain speech show more finish than any of the predecessors we happen to have left. But Wyatt soon exhausted the possibilities of this narrow mode, and the tradition, such as it is, comes to an end with him.

For Professor Muir, for example, is surely right in seeing a break between Wyatt and the Elizabethans. There is no continuity between his songs and the songs of those whose verse was set to music by madrigal composers and composers of airs to the lute. I conclude, then, that the Wyatt of the 'Devonshire' manuscript does not offer us any matter when we are seeking to trace the living current of new poetry in the early sixteenth century. The right thing to do with these poems would be to treat them as anonymous matter and to print them along with the surviving songs of Henry VIII's court. We should then see them in their right context. In this context, too, we may understand Ann Boleyn's praise of Wyatt as the chief of the amateur writers of court ballets.

A friendly critic, who had followed me sympathetically so far might here complain if I tried to close the topic and so dismissed the claim that Wyatt's best poems are his 'lyrics', 'if by "lyric" you mean only those poems which are preserved in no other manuscript than the "Devonshire", your account will, perhaps, stand. I might agree that the anthology pieces *And wylt thow leue me thus* or *Fforget not yet* are open to the criticisms you make upon the other anthology piece, *What shulde I saye*. I might grant that these poems can only be highly praised by one who, like Tennyson, overvalues the courtly lyrics of Queen Elizabeth's poets and undervalues the courtly lyrics of, say, Carew. But these are not the lyrics I admire. What have you to say of the others in the Egerton manuscript? What about *They flee from me* and *What rage is this?*'

To this my reply would be, 'granted: these are two fine poems, and if you wish, you may call them lyrics. But they are not in any sense continuous with the "Devonshire" poems. They belong to Wyatt's real activity as a poet. For Wyatt did not become a poet in the true sense until he abandoned the courtly lyric for something I should like to describe as translation.'

WYATT: 'GRANT TRANSLATEUR'

The Relation of Wyatt to the Humanists

Wiat's customary method of recording some personal experience is by means of a translation or imitation of an Italian or French poet, which he finds suitable as expressing his own feelings.
The Poems of Sir Thomas Wiat, ed. by A. K. FOXWELL, vol. II, p. 72

In many cases the poems are translated so closely as to suggest mere literary, or language, exercises; for the most partial enthusiast must admit that Wyatt's genius was chiefly derivative.
Tottel's Miscellany, ed. by H. E. ROLLINS, vol. II, p. 76

The mystery of Wyatt is simply whether he knew what he was doing or whether he did not.
Times Literary Supplement, September 19, 1929

His finest poems are not, as far as we know, translations.
Collected Poems of Sir Thomas Wyatt, ed. by KENNETH MUIR, p. xviii

MY first reason for dwelling both on the songs and similar pieces attributed to Wyatt and on the tradition to which they belong was to put beyond doubt that to be courtly as those poems are courtly was not to exhibit the renewing and reinvigorating power by which civilisation maintains itself in health, and to show once again what is meant by the *waning* of the Middle Ages. In these poems Wyatt is merely one of a clique, perhaps the best of the court amateurs,

179

though we have no means of knowing how seriously his competitors came to rivalling him in any of the exercises expected of the courtier, pen in hand. Such evidence as we have suggests that the court poets who rivalled Wyatt were not concerned with 'making it new'.

My second reason was the desire to create a favourable reception for the search in another direction for signs of genuine creative activity: for I should not like the reader to think that I decided *a priori* that the valuable activity in this period was translation and then automatically gave preference to whatever translations I could find over traditional or home-grown production. As will become apparent, I do not seek to question the verdict that most of Wyatt's translations in the ordinary sense of the word are of little interest to us. They do not figure on my list of the poems of Wyatt that matter. On the other hand, some of the translations are on the short list of Wyatt's interesting poems, and in an attempt to win approval for these hitherto neglected poems, I should like first to borrow the words addressed to the contemporary reader by Wordsworth in defence of 'Poems so materially different from those upon which general approbation is at present bestowed' and make a similar appeal 'which is, that in judging these poems he would decide by his own feelings genuinely, and not by reflection upon what will probably be the judgement of others'.

The main argument I wish to put forward and defend is that *the Wyatt we should attend to is the author of poems that stand in a significant relation to the work of the Humanists.* Wyatt in his lifetime was thought to belong to that company. He translated at least one treatise of Plutarch as a New Year's gift to the Queen. If none of his poems had survived, we should still have the letter in which he recommended to his son, 'the good opinion of moral philosophers, among whom I wold Senek were your studye and Epictetus, bicaus it is litel to be euir in your bosome'. The Wyatt we should attend to is the figure we may discern through the formalities of the epitaph written by Surrey and printed shortly after Wyatt's death:

> Wyat resteth here, that quicke coulde neuer rest,
>   Whose heuenly gyftes, encreased by dysdayne,
> And vertue sanke the deper in his brest,
>   Suche profyte he of enuy could optayne.
>
> A Head where wysdom mysteries dyd frame,
>   Whose hammers beat styll in that lyuely brayne
> As on a stythy, where some worke of fame
>   Was dayly wrought to turn to Brytayns gaine.

180

A Vysage sterne and mylde, where both dyd grow
　Vyce to contempne, in vertues to reioyce,
Amyd great stormes whome grace assured soo
　To lyue vprighte and smyle at fortunes choyse.

A Hand that taught what might be saide in rime,
　That refte Chaucer the glorye of his wytte,
A mark the whiche (vnperfited for tyme)
　Some may approche but neuer none shall hyt.

A Tonge that serued in foraine realmes his king,
　Whose curtoise talke to vertue dyd enflame
Eche noble harte, a worthy guyde to brynge
　Our Englysshe youth by trauayle vnto fame.

An Eye whose iudgement no affect coulde blind
　Frendes to allure and foes to reconcyle,
Whose pearcynge looke dyd represent a mynde
　With vertue fraught, reposed, voyde of gyle.

A Harte where drede yet neuer so imprest
　To hide the thought that might the trouth auaunce,
In neyther fortune lyfte nor so represt
　To swell in welth nor yelde vnto mischaunce.

A valiaunt Corps where force and beautye met,
　Happy, alas, to happy, but for foos,
Lyued and ran the race that nature set
　Of manhodes shape where she the mold did loos.

But to the heauens that symple soule is fled
　Which lefte with such as couet Christe to knowc
Witnes of faith that neuer shal be deade,
　Sent for our welth but not receiued so.

Thus for our gylt this iewell haue we lost.
　The earth his bones, the heuen possesse his goost.
　　　　AMEN.

Here, at any rate, is my first specimen of what I mean by Wyatt's
genuine poetic activity:

Stond who so list vpon the slipper toppe
of court astate, and lett me here reioyce
and vse me quyet without lett or stoppe
vnknowen in courte that hath suche brackishe ioyes:
in hidden place so lett my dayes forthe passe

181

that, when my yeres be done, withouten noyce
J may dy aged after the common trace.
For hym deth grippithe right hard by the croppe
that is moche knowen of other, and of him self, alas,
doth dy vnknowen, dazed with dredfull face.

Even at a first hearing, I think it would be granted that this poem
has an urgency about it that suggests a personal occasion; it reads
as though it were prompted by some personal and pressing experience. It would be convenient if this impression were supported by
external evidence, if we knew, for instance, that the poem was a
record of Wyatt's experience in 1536 when he was imprisoned in
the Tower of London and forced to witness from a window above
the gate the execution of some of his friends. The impression of
urgency, however, is independent of such conjectures. It comes out
in the insistent, onward rhythm and the vivid phrases, such as
brackishe ioyes. If the poet had been only moderately moved, there
were plenty of conventional epithets for this conventional topic.
Again, in the phrase:

For hym deth grippithe right hard by the croppe

every word is active, suggesting the fierceness and the horror of the
summons. It is as dramatic as the episode in *Everyman*, where Death
surprises the hero in the midst of life's pleasures. The phrase

dazed with dredfull face

recreates for us the impression of being an eye-witness of a public
execution.

Nevertheless, powerful as these impressions of personal urgency
are, it is equally clear that the 'I' of the poem, the speaking voice, is a
dramatis persona and that the theme has been generalised and im-
personalised. The poem has become a means of communicating a
judgement, a judgement which bears no doubt primarily on the
court of Henry VIII, but covers our own and earlier times. We can
equally well say of this poem that it is a commonplace which has
been given a personal stamp.

Yet this poem has been dismissed as a mere exercise, a mere
translation, coming under the judgement of Professor Muir: 'Wyatt's
finest poems are not, as far as we know, translations.' A translation
it certainly is, but we have only to compare it with other translations
to see that it is no ordinary translation. We may take for relevant
comparison a translation made some thirty years later by a poet
whom Mr Eliot praised as exhibiting 'flashes of that felicity which is

present in Tudor translation more perhaps than in the translations of any period into any language'.

> Let who so lyst with mighty mace to raygne,
> In tyckle toppe of court delight to stand
> Let mee the sweete and quiet rest obtayne.
> So set in place obscure and lowe degree
> Of pleasaunt rest I shall the sweetnesse knoe.
> My lyfe unknowne to them that noble bee,
> Shall in the steppe of secret sylence goe.
> Thus when my dayes at length are over past,
> And tyme without all troublous tumult spent,
> An aged man I shall depart at last,
> In meane estate, to dye full well content.
> But greevuous is to him the death, that when
> So farre abroade the bruite of him is blowne,
> That knowne hee is to much to other men:
> Departeth yet unto him selfe unknowne.

From this alone we can see what differentiates Wyatt's poem from mere translation. Nevertheless a reference to the original will help us to add further points:

> stet quicunque uolet potens
> aulae culmine lubrico:
> me dulcis saturet quies:
> obscuro positus loco
> leni perfruar otio.
> nullis nota Quiritibus
> aetas per tacitum fluat.
> sic cum transierint mei
> nullo cum strepitu dies,
> plebeius moriar senex.
> illi mors grauis incubat
> qui, notus nimis omnibus,
> ignotus moritur sibi.

But how are we to take the Latin? At one extreme we can allow ourselves to be swayed by the surface movement of smooth, stately diction, and under this influence take the substance at its most general. At the other, we can concentrate upon all that seems to link it to the dangerous situations through which the author had lived, and so see it as a contemporary poem, and under this influence stress each hidden point of *wit*. A true translation would doubtless embrace these two extremes, but as I wish to illustrate Wyatt's bent as a translator, I shall give a paraphrase in which by peppering the target each time with several shots I shall try to see how contemporary the Latin may be made to sound to *us*. The reader may judge to what extent what I squeeze out is actually there in the text:

'you may try to hoist yourself up to the highest position the state can offer, if you like that sort of thing, but I warn you, it is a point without magnitude, the apex of an acute-angled triangle: one false step on either side and down you come. Palace revolutions are certain but unpredictable: as Shakespeare put it:

> the art o' the court
> As hard to leave as keep, or so slippery that
> The fear's as bad as falling.

I prefer to steep myself up to the eyes in the pleasures of political absenteeism. Give me a broad solid base down at the roots of society; let me relax there and enjoy genuine freedom from the "cares of state". I don't want my birthdays made an excuse for civic banquets. I'd have year follow year as smoothly and unobtrusively as the river under the London newspaper offices, and so with no fuss or bother pass my prime and reach a "ripe old age" as a member of what Marx and Engels call the "historically inactive" class. I'd like to learn who I really am before I go. The V.I.P. is surprised to find that excessive notoriety brings sudden death whipping down on his back.'

Wyatt's poem can stand stiffer tests than comparison either with Heywood or with a modern paraphrase. This passage of Seneca has attracted many poets, and each has brought his own context to the poem. How in a general way Wyatt's poem differs from later translations made when the language was more developed, we may see by taking *Cowley's* version:

> Upon the slippery tops of human State,
>   The guilded Pinnacles of Fate,
> Let others proudly stand, and, for a while
>   (The giddy Danger to beguile)
> With Joy and with Disdain look down on all,
>   Till their Heads turn, and so they fall.
> Me, o ye Gods, on Earth, or else so near
>   That I no fall to Earth may fear,
> And, o ye Gods, at a good distance seat
>   From the long Ruins of the Great.
> Here, wrapt in th' Arms of Quiet, let me lie;
>   Quiet, Companion of Obscurity.
> Here let my Life with as much silence slide
>   As Time, that measures it, does glide.
> Nor let the breath of Infamy or Fame
> From Town to Town eccho about my Name.

184

> Nor let my homely Death embroidered be
> With Scutcheon or with Elogie.
> An old *Plebeian* let me die:
> Alas, all then are such as well as I.
> To him, alas, to him, I fear,
> The face of Death will terrible appear,
> Who in his life, flattering his senseless pride,
> By being known to all the World beside,
> Does not himself, when he is Dying, know,
> Nor what he is, nor whither he's to go.

We hardly need the prose context to determine out of what experience this poem was made, but as Cowley has provided it, we may as well draw upon it:

'I account a person who has a moderate Mind and Fortune, and lives in the conversation of two or three agreeable friends, with little commerce in the World besides, who is esteemed well enough by his few neighbours that know him, and is truly irreproachable by any body, and so after a healthful quiet life, before the great inconveniencies of old age, goes more silently out of it than he came in, (for I would not have him so much as cry in the *Exit*.)'

We have only to contrast the comparative security of gentlemen in Restoration England with the perilous situation of Wyatt to understand how he came to turn Seneca's moral commonplaces into a haunting poem.

Having now presented one sample of Wyatt's translation for unprejudiced inspection, I should like to set out my general claim. First, as to his practice as a translator, the following remarks are applicable to all his best translations: Wyatt takes over the general framework and order of ideas from his original. He recasts the foreign idiom into English idiom. For instance, in Wyatt's version of Seneca there is none of the half-digested Latin we find in Heywood's, such as 'set in place obscure' for *obscuro positus loco* or 'greeuuous is to him the death' for *illi mors grauis incubat*. Wyatt transmutes the situation of his original into one relevant to his own times. Wyatt turned to creative translation when he had some urgent personal matter to 'distance'. Secondly, as to the value of Wyatt's best poems and his position in our literature, I would claim that among Wyatt's translations are to be found most, if not all, his more interesting poems, for Wyatt used his original as a Mask or Persona, as a means of finding and creating himself. His best translations, so far from being proof that he was a derivative poet or an unskilled translator, show that he was an independent critic of his sources and rehandled them in a manner similar to Eliot's creative rehandling of Laforgue and Théophile Gautier. Translation represents the point of development in Wyatt's poetical career. His characteristic verse, the verse on which his reputation should rest, is 'moral-reflective' rather than lyrical. This verse is also representative of the best efforts of his period, a period that closed with his life. Wyatt had no successors, and his aims and methods were not understood after his death. He is a very much greater poet than those who came immediately after him. He is not the Father of a school. His poetry represents the culminating and closing achievement of a period in which the first attempt to be modern since Chaucer's comes to an end. He should therefore be considered along with More and Erasmus rather than with Raleigh and Donne. Wyatt expressed in English the sensibility of a period that came to an end during his lifetime. He is the only poet of the first period of Humanism.

This is in effect a claim that Wyatt's poetical career was directed and purposeful. He no doubt first learned to versify by writing court poems and songs; he learned to write *poetry* by applying these gifts to translation. But before I develop this claim directly, I should like to consider two arguments often heard to-day. The contrast between most of Wyatt's songs and his sonnets and epigrams has always struck readers. In the past, the introduction of Petrarchan sonnets into English was thought to constitute Wyatt's chief claim to fame. But when modern critics began to insist on poetic worth as the criterion for poetic fame, a sharp reaction set in, which took two forms, one turning on the handling of metre, the other on the quality of the translations.

To take the former first, when scholars began to look at Wyatt's manuscripts they noticed that, whereas most of the songs never forced Wyatt to blot a line, when he was translating, he made many corrections. But so far from seeing in Wyatt's blotting evidence of poetic activity, they were inclined to see Wyatt as a mere beginner, incapable of handling unfamiliar problems. Professor Muir, for example, writes, 'Wyatt doubtless over-valued his translations because they were more difficult achievements than the songs which came to him as naturally as the leaves to a tree.' And he concluded, 'most of the sonnets, then, are of minor importance'. After what we have seen of the songs, we may perhaps prefer a different account than the organic relation of leaves to a tree. But what of the 'more difficult achievements', the sonnets? Some critics have seen Wyatt's difficulty here as one of passing from one sort of rhythm to another.[1] It is an undoubted fact that in the poems of Wyatt there are lines which seem to be constructed as a single metrical unit, based on a coincidence of accent and syllables. It is also a fact that many lines contain a marked caesura dividing the line into two separate rhythmical units. It is a further fact that when Wyatt's poems came into editor's hands before being printed by Tottel in his Miscellany, some of these lines in so-called pausing rhythm were rewritten to conform to a syllabic metrical pattern. Finally, it is a fact that sometimes Wyatt wrote a line first in the metrical way and then rewrote it in pausing rhythm.

How are we to interpret these facts? If we allow ourselves to be influenced by the consideration that lines in pausing rhythm are the norm of fifteenth-century verse, and lines in metrical syllabic rhythm are the norm of late sixteenth-century verse, we may be tempted to place Wyatt's verses written in pausing rhythm as early, and his metrical lines as late and put in the middle a period of metrical confusion. Although we cannot place all Wyatt's poems in chronological order, some bear external evidence of date, and these confute such a theory. For instance, here are some lines, probably written in 1541, the year before Wyatt died, and they are in marked pausing rhythm:

> Syghes ar my foode,/ drynke are my teares:
> Clynkinge of fetters/ suche musycke wolde crave:
> Stynke and close ayer/ away my lyf wears:
> Innocencie/ is all the hope I have.
> Rayne, wynde, or wether/ I judge by myne eares.
> Mallice assaultes/ that rightiousnes should save:
> Sure I am, Brian,/ this wounde shall heale agayne,
> But yet, alas, the scarre/ shall styll remayne.

Before bringing forward my second specimen of Wyatt's translation, I should like to deal with the second prejudice against Wyatt's sonnets. This, too, can itself be split up into two parts: first, the assumption that Wyatt took up Petrarch and his other Italian originals merely as exercises in the sonnet *form*. The critics here say that Wyatt was incapable of appreciating what every Italian hack writer of Wyatt's time knew; the rules governing the rhymes and the division of the sonnet. Others, ignoring the fact that Wyatt was familiar from his 'lyrical' writing with the demand for several rhymes on one word, suppose that Wyatt was incapable of translating *and* retaining the rhyme scheme of the Petrarchan sonnet. The second form of the prejudice is to suppose that when Wyatt deviates from his

[1] See, for instance, 'The Rhythmical Intention in Wyatt's Poetry', by D. W. Harding in *Scrutiny*, vol. XIV, No. 2. December 1946, pp. 90–102.

original, he either did not understand the Italian or had not the taste to stick to it. This last charge was more popular when Petrarch was thought to be infinitely more civilised than Wyatt and when Petrarch's sonnets were themselves more highly thought of than they are to-day.

Among Wyatt's sonnets there are some so badly translated that we must call them failures. But as against the dictum of Professor Muir: 'None of the sonnets, not even the late ones which are comparatively smooth, can be ranked among Wyatt's best poems', I would advance the view that there is one sonnet, at least, that deserves a place among Wyatt's best poems. Secondly, this sonnet is at the same time a technical triumph of pausing rhythm and is also metrically correct, in that each line has the same number of syllables . . . if we allow two slight emendations. Thirdly, this translation refutes the view that Wyatt was a blundering imitator of Petrarch. I think it is quite clearly a radical criticism of Petrarch's whole attitude to women in his poems.

> Who list to hount/ I know where is an hynde,
>> But as for me/ alas, I may no more,
>> The vain travaill/ hath werid me so sore
> I ame of them/ that farthest commeth behinde.
>
> Yet may I by no means/ my werid mynde
>> Draw from the Dere/ but as she fleeth afore
>> Faynting I folowe/ I leve of therfore
> Since in a nett/ I seke to hold the wynde.
>
> Who list her hount/ I put him owt of dowbt
>> As well as I/ may spend his tyme in vain
>> For grave with Diamonds/ in letters plain
> There is written/ her faier neck rounde abowt:
>> *Noli me tangere* for Cesars I ame
>> And wylde for to holde/ though I seme tame.

Here I should like to put on record that I admired this poem long before I came to formulate this general argument. As I enjoyed it for years without knowing it was in any sense a translation, I should like to dwell on its merits as a poem before trying to use it as a key to unlock the secret of Wyatt's intentions and practice as a translator. For if the reader does not find it impressive as a poem, my general argument can have little weight or interest.

What I am above all anxious to win acceptance for is the delicate poise of the sentiment that the sonnet is an attempt to fix or (really) to define. As I see it, there is a certain tight-rope element in it, an avoidance by a narrow margin of falling into one of two inviting but inferior attitudes: the pretty-pretty or external idealisation of Petrarch and the grossness in popular usage of the animal equation running through the sonnet. Those who are fond of generalisations about the Middle Ages assert that a violent ricochet from one extreme to the other on the subject of women without striking a balance between them is a legacy of (*inter alia*) the Christian Fathers, and they quote the notorious instance of the two parts of the *Roman de la Rose*. The best way (to my mind) of establishing the delicacy of Wyatt's poise is by comparing Wyatt with Skelton, who oscillates almost mathematically from Jane Scroupe's pretty foot:

> It raysed myne hert rote
> To se her treade the grounde
> With heles short and rounde

and Elinour Rumming's:

> She dryueth downe the dewe
> Wyth a payre of heles
> As brode as two wheles.

The poem of Skelton's which is most apposite to this discussion is the one beginning, *The auncient acquaintance*, where we find a ludricous attempt to preserve a courtly tone of politeness while communicating a message as gross as that Wyatt delivered without attempting politeness in *Ye old mule*.

In Wyatt's poem we have an instance of a sixteenth-century attempt to set up ideal forms of behaviour to correct the grossness of the times. If it is one of the claims to greatness of More to have asserted the rights of women as members of a family, and of Vives to have asserted the claims of women to receive a thorough education, and of the Protestant Reformers to have insisted on the respect due to wives from their husbands, it was left to the sensitive courtier such as Wyatt to steer people at court away from the mediaeval, Petrarchan ideal of the amorous relations between the sexes, and from the gross relations actually prevailing at court, to a more human and moral ideal.

What gives tension to Wyatt's poise in this sonnet is the presence of a subdued wit, which crops out once in the pun on deer. The poem is thoroughly dramatic and exists in its own right. We do not need to know whether the occasion for it was a strong intimation from Henry VIII that henceforward Wyatt must cease to pay court to Ann Boleyn. Whatever inner need Wyatt had is perfectly released into the poem. The movement is delicately managed: I know of no passage in Wyatt's verse where pauses are used so effectively.

The reader who may be willing to grant that this is a successful poem, may yet object that it is not a case of successful translation, that it is hardly a translation at all. Certainly it is not representative of Wyatt's translations of Petrarch, and I shall at once therefore attempt to redress the balance. But it may be no accident that Wyatt takes over so little here. He may have rejected so much because he found it distasteful. A literal translation will assist a decision:

'As the sun was rising in the bitter season, a white hind with two golden horns appeared to me in the shade of a laurel on the green grass between two streams. So pleasant-proud was its appearance that I left my work, and, like a miser in whom the pleasure of hunting for treasure mitigates the inherent vexations, I followed the hind. Round its fair neck was written in diamonds and topazes: Let no man touch me, for Caesar's will is that I remain free. The sun had reached midday when, my eyes weary but not satiated with gazing, I fell into the water and the hind disappeared.' [1]

The commentators explain that this was a *post eventum* prophecy of the history of Petrarch and Laura, whom the poet first met when she was young and lost when she was thirty. The hind is white to symbolise chastity, the horns are golden because Laura's hair was fair, and the laurel tree is there to hint at her name. The two poems are clearly worlds apart and it seems to me equally clear that Petrarch's moral world is mediaeval while Wyatt's is Humanist and modern.

My third example points in two apparently opposing directions. For, while it does provide welcome support for the two rather precarious claims I have been making about Wyatt's relation to Petrarchan sentiment and to contemporary sexual ethics, it also exhibits an evident desire to go one better than Petrarch in his worst mannerisms and is written in a style and rhythm which go counter to all legitimate expectations and make it questionable whether in discussing Wyatt's poetical development it is possible to speak of 'intentions' at all. Once the manuscripts had been transcribed faithfully, the literary critics found that they had to hand an instrument for discovering some at least of Wyatt's intentions. For we have a number of poems in Wyatt's own hand and some of these contain Wyatt's second and even third thoughts. These 'corrections', taken by and large, show that, as he worked over them, Wyatt made his lines more 'rugged', 'difficult' and less like Surrey's or the Tottel versions. They show that he took particular care over the eight-line

[1] *Rime*, No. CXC.

epigrams. In fact, all the signs point towards the view that Wyatt in his later years was steadily making his poems tighter and more condensed. I shall continue to present evidence to support this view. But the poem beginning *So feble is the threde*, which we possess in Wyatt's own hand with numerous corrections and which was written, as I hope to show, in 1539, is a loose jog-trot composed of alternate alexandrines and fourteeners, a combination in which it is difficult to write concisely and seriously in English.

It is an ironical observation that whereas Wyatt's best poetical inventions (as I see them) were totally ignored by his own and later generations and were freshly rediscovered by Shakespeare and Donne, this disastrous invention of Wyatt's, this metre which he used only twice in the extant verse, proved a *trouvaille* for his younger contemporaries and successors. I cannot conceive what Wyatt thought he was doing in using this metre, and I shall not disguise from the reader, when I come to comment on the details of the poem, what a sickening lapse I take it to be. But the popularity of the metre suggests that we may have here a case for drawing a distinction that must be made in considering the work of all original poets: I mean the distinction already drawn in discussing the Humanists between the 'Zeitgeist'—what the age is all too ready for—and what the age finds, often to its surprise, was struggling into being, but was literally unimaginable until the original poet found words for it.

Wyatt's poem is a translation of Petrarch's *canzone* 'Si è debile il filo'. Petrarch, the commentators say, composed it when travelling in Spain, and it tells of the hopes, fears and longings he endured while separated from Laura. Wyatt's poem is headed 'In Spayne' and was therefore written some time between March 1537 and May 1539. Two *retouches* suggest that he was working on it in 1539. For Wyatt altered a very good and characteristic line (88)

> my faintyng hope my brytill lyff welling dispaire fulfilles

to

> At othr will my long abode my diepe dispaire fulfilles—

which may have been provoked by the King's letter of January 19th informing Wyatt that the return he had been hoping for was delayed. Wyatt altered the last line but one, in which he is addressing his poem, from

> Then say I come for here I may not tary

to

> Then tell her that I come, she shall me shortly se;

191

which he could not say with confidence until April, when Cromwell gave him permission to return. The poem immediately following in the manuscript, also in Wyatt's handwriting, is his farewell to Spain in May, 1539.

'Wyatt seems so confident', wrote the Rev. G. F. Nott, who had to do all his researching into State Papers himself, 'his strains would be graciously received that it will be pleasing to believe they were addressed to his wife.' Alas, the documents are categorical. Wyatt repudiated his wife for adultery soon after his marriage and refused to support her. I think there is no doubt that his poem is also an epistle to his Laura. From the numerous resemblances of phrase I think she must be the Phyllis of the poem immediately preceding in the Egerton MS. It is also in Wyatt's handwriting and it is also a translation from Petrarch, but here the translation is little more than a pretext for the following confession of love:

> sure sins I did refrayne
> Her that ded set our country in a rore
> Th' unfayned chere of Phillis hath the place
> That Brunet had: she hath and ever shal.

We know that Wyatt had a mistress in these years and that his attachment to Elizabeth Darell lasted down to his sudden death in 1542.

The advantage of being able to anchor the poem in Wyatt's personal life is that when we find him at a certain point deliberately abandoning his original it is hardly possible to avoid the conclusion that he did so under pressure set up by the contrast between Petrarch's ideal of woman and his own.

What the critics have most deplored is that Wyatt has not kept the reverence of the close, where Petrarch tells his song that, when it succeeds in reaching Laura and she reaches out her hand to take it, it must not presume to touch the fair hand but must kneel reverently at Laura's feet and announce that the poet is speeding on his way and will arrive either in the flesh or as a naked spirit. Wyatt's convention is bolder and of his time:

My song, thou shalt ataine to fynd that plesant place
Where she doth lyve by whome I lyve; may chaunce thou have this grace.
When she hath red and seene the dred where in I sterve,
Bytwene her brestes she shall the put, there shall she the reserve.

It is in fact an adult relation that Wyatt is struggling to describe: he is not posing as a *galant*, nor does he indulge in the dubious Platonising of Castiglione's circle. His love is human and therefore moral. Some critics have tried to diminish the weight of the one capital document we have on Wyatt's moral standards: the letter he wrote from Paris on April 15th, 1537, offering advice to his newly married son. No doubt there was a convention in such matters and Polonius is true to type. What has escaped these critics is the presence in this letter alongside the wise saws from the copy book of a homely morality based on family sanctions.

'Think and ymagine alwais that you are in presens of some honist man that you know, as Sir Jhon Russel, your father-in-law, your vnkle, parson, or some other such, and ye shal, if at ony time ye find a plesur in naughtye touchis, remember what shame it were afore thes men to doo naughtily. . . . And consider wel your good grandfathir what things therwer in him, and his end; and they that knew him notid him thus: first and chiefly to haue a great reuerens of god and good opinion of godly things . . .'

Wyatt did not shrink from applying this standard to himself and finding himself wanting. 'And of my self I may be a nere example unto you of my foly and unthriftnes. . . . You therefor, if ye be sure and haue god in your sleue, to cal you to his grase at last, ventur hardily by myne example apon naughty unthriftines in trust of his goodnes, and besides the shame I dare lay ten to one ye shal perisch in the aduentur.' After advising his son how to conduct himself towards his wife: 'Frame wel your self to loue, and rule wel and honestly your wife as your felow, and she shal loue and reuerens you as her hed': Wyatt concludes this section with: 'And the blissing of god for good agrement between the wife and husband is fruyt of many children, which I for the like thinge doe lack, and the faulte is both in your mother and me, but chieflie in her.'

Here then is the passage where Wyatt ceased to follow Petrarch in order to give in his own words an account of what he valued in his mistress:

> The wise and plesaunt talk so rare or elles alone
> That did me gyve the courtese gyfft that suche had neuer none,
> Be ferre from me, alas, and euery other thing
> I myght forbere with better will then that that did me bryng
> With plesant word and chere redresse off lingerd payne,
> And wontyd offt in kendlid will to vertu me to trayne.[1]
> Thus ame I dryven to here and herken affter news,
> My confort skant, my large desire, in dowtfull trust renews.
> And yet with more delyght, to mone my wofull cace,

[1] Cf. *Surrey's poem on Wyatt:*
A toung . . .
Whose courteous talke to vertue did enflame.

I must complaine those handes, those armes that fermely do embrace
Me from my sellff, and rule the sterne of my pore lyff,
The swete disdaynes, the plesant wrathes and eke the lovely stryff
That wontid well to tune in tempre just and mete
The rage that offt did make me erre by furour vndiscrete.

It took me a long time to discover any tolerable way of reading these lines, and unless I fix a way by marking my text I find that I have to begin all over again each time I return to the poem. Reading the lines is a losing fight against the merciless pull of the metre. Again, even if the lines are not a translation of Petrarch, they contain more than two or three phrases that are obviously derivative, if not a caricature of Petrarch at his worst. Both these points cannot be controverted. If we compare the original and the translation, we discover that by choosing this particular metre Wyatt diluted his English to three times the length of the Italian. This was not because he needed so many words to express Petrarch's meaning: he is occasionally more compact, *e.g.*

> Ogni loco m'atrista, ov'io non veggio
> Quei begli occhi soavi
> Che portaron le chiavi
> De' miei dolci pensier

is rendered in fewer syllables, though in a literal 'translationese' which mars the poem throughout, by

> Eche place doth bryng me grieff where I do not behold
> Those lovely Iyes wich off my thowghtes were wont the kays to hold.

It would be tedious to quote all the examples of pure padding: two instances of mere line filling will suffice:

> Che, s'altri non l'aita

becomes

> That but it have elles where *some aide or some socours.*

The worst instance is the rendering of the single word *dicendo* by

> Wych doth perswade such wordes vnto my sory mynd.

More seriously telling against my account of Wyatt's attitude towards Petrarch's conceits are the numerous instances where Wyatt introduces exaggerated conceits into his translation where there are none in the original. Here it would be tempting to refer once again to the *Zeitgeist* were it not that the first English poet to translate a sonnet of Petrarch's chose one abounding in such phrases as

> Allas! what is this wondre maladye?
> For hete of cold, for cold of hete, I dye.

194

which goes one better than

E tremo a mezza state, ardendo il verno.[1]

I had better confess that I am completely in the dark and have no explanation to offer. I merely draw attention to the verbal similarity between Chaucer and Wyatt, who inserted the following about his mistress's eyes:

Wich yet so farr towch me so nere in cold to make me swete:

where Petrarch was content to say that the light of her eyes made him die before his time.

It would not be fair to leave this poem without some mention of the signs of genuine poetic activity. As we have it, the text is by no means a finished poem, and there are signs that Wyatt was attempting to fight the jog-trot rhythm. For instance, he altered

With plesant word and chere redresse of all my payne

to

redresse of lingerd payne.

When trying to translate

E perché pria, tacendo, non m'impetro

Chaucer's 'domb as any stoon' may have occurred to him, for his first attempt reads:

Much better were for me
As dome as stone to think on nowght and absent for to be.

He later changed this to:

As dome as stone, all thing forgott, still absent for to be.

O si sic omnia! one can only murmur.

It is now clear that if Wyatt had a poetical career, his path was a difficult one and success did not come easy. I should therefore like to reinforce this impression with a further example to illustrate Wyatt's difficulties as a poet. They were not difficulties of rhyme or scansion, but difficulties of vocabulary arising from the difficulty of breaking away from the deadening language of courtly love poetry. I have once again chosen a translation from Petrarch to show that for Wyatt Petrarch was an unfortunate model.

[1] *Le Rime* CXXXII, *Troilus and Criseyde*, Book I, lines 419–20.

Once again Wyatt has departed strangely from his original:

> The piller perisht is wherto I lent,
> The strongest stay of mine vnquiet minde:
> The like of it no man again can finde:
> From East to West still seking though he went.
> To mine vnhappe for happe away hath rent,
> Of all my ioy the very rote and rynde:
> And I (alas) by chance am thus assinde
> Daily to moorne till death do it relent.
> But since that thus it is by desteny,
> What can I more but haue a wofull hart,
> My penne in plaint, my voyce in carefull crye:
> My minde in wo, my body full of smart,
> And I my self, my selfe alwaye to hate,
> Till dreadfull death do ease my dolefull state.

One editor wrote, 'We must deem it a proof of bad taste that he omitted the beautiful sentiment in the last three lines of his original.' It is indeed hard to believe that Wyatt would not have been taken with the pathetic sentiment of

> Oh nostra vita ch'è si bella in vista
>   Com' perde agevolmente in un mattino
>   Quel ch'n molti anni a gran pena s'acquista.

Professor Lewis complained, 'Wyatt . . . has, so to speak, turned down the lights of the Petrarch.'

These remarks have no point unless in fact Wyatt was attempting what we ordinarily call a translation, and was trying to give a faithful interpretation in English of what he found in the Italian. They fall to the ground if he was attempting a translation in the sense I have been using the word. I think that this poem, like the others we have considered, arose out of a personal experience, the death of Wyatt's protector and friend, Thomas Cromwell, who was executed in 1540. Under the stress of the sorrow he felt, Wyatt, I suppose, looked into his Petrarch to find an analogy to his own position, and chose the sonnet in which Petrarch was lamenting the death of his protector and friend, the cardinal Giovanni Colonna. Professor Lewis also complained of the absence of the green laurel from Wyatt's poem. The green laurel was needed by Petrarch because he was also lamenting the death of Laura: Wyatt, having no such double loss to record, omitted it.

The historians, however, have been reluctant to accept the evidence of this poem, since they felt that such a monster of efficiency as Cromwell could never have inspired such powerful feelings as we

196

must suppose led Wyatt to substitute for the moving close of the Italian the lines:

> My penne in plaint, my voyce in carefull crye:
> My minde in wo, my body full of smart
> And I my self, my selfe alwayes to hate,
> Till dreadful death do ease my dolefull state.

So reluctant have they been that they have refused to accept the evidence of a manuscript in a Cambridge college (C.C.C.C. No. 168) which gave among the last words of Cromwell on the scaffold:

> farewell Wyat & gentill Wiat praye for me

and they have treated as romance an account of the episode in which Wyatt then burst into tears. Faced with this 'misplaced respect for "fact" and a misplaced distrust of "opinion" ',[1] I once asked a historian what were his objections and what would satisfy them. His reply was that reference to Wyatt does not occur in the two accounts (by Halle and Foxe) recognised by historians. It was known, however, that the government issued a broadsheet after Cromwell's execution. 'Find me that,' he said, 'and I shall be satisfied, but I don't expect that the government shared your interest in the emotional life of Wyatt.' Fortunately for my chances of convincing the historians, it was not difficult to find lying under their noses in the British Museum a transcript of the government proclamation and embedded in Cromwell's speech the affectionate farewell to Wyatt.[2]

This cast-iron proof now makes it respectable to refer to the other contemporary account of Cromwell's last words previously dismissed as a romance. Here is a rough translation of the Spanish original:

'Among the gentlemen around the scaffold Cromwell caught sight of Master Wyatt, and he called to him and said, "Gentle Wyatt, God be with you, and I pray you to pray God for me." There had always been great love between him and this Master Wyatt. And Wyatt could not answer him, for his tears came too fast.'[3]

Although this anecdote will illuminate the claim that Wyatt's translations are more truly autobiographical than his so-called lyrics, in itself it is beside the point of this argument. Our concern is still to find out which are Wyatt's *best* poems, not which are most revealing about his life. And here, I think, we have an example of a failure, and a characteristic failure. For even if we are prepared to grant that

[1] See p. 3.   [2] B.M. MS. Harl. 3362 f. 79r.
[3] Crónica del Rey Enrico Otavo de Ingalaterra, Madrid, 1874.

Wyatt's reason for departing from Petrarch was to enable him to handle strong personal feeling for Cromwell, the fact still remains that Wyatt has here fallen back on the hackneyed conventional language of his love poems to deal with feelings that demanded a new convention. The poem is in fact a cento of Wyatt's familiar jingles. I have not counted the number of times the hap/unhap antithesis had appeared in his verses. Even the striking line

> Of all my ioye the vearye rote and rynde

is modelled on Wyatt's lines in *The wandering gadling:*

> . . . he sawe me sitting by her side
> That of my helth is very croppe and rote.

Both phrases are Chaucerian: cf. *Troilus and Criseyde*:

> IV. 1139: 'The woful Mirra thorugh the bark and rynde.'
> II. 348: 'And ye, that ben of beaute crop and roote.'

As for *by chaunce assynde*, no cliché occurs more often in Wyatt's verse. And so on: illustrations could be provided for almost every word in the poem of previous uses which drag the words into an inferior context in which genuine feeling stifles.

I hope now to have shown that several of Wyatt's translations seem to have been made with a similar if complex purpose: primarily, perhaps in an attempt to create a vehicle for conveying strong private feelings in a public form. With the exception of the line that seems to point too plainly to Anne Boleyn.

> Her that ded set our country in a rore

which Wyatt changed, perhaps with publication in mind, to

> Brunet, that set my welth in such a rore,

there is scarcely a line in these translations that indiscreetly obtrudes the private sources of the inspiration. What I have not sufficiently stressed is Wyatt's technical struggle to find the language for the feelings that compelled him to break away from the Petrarchan convention. I have instead perhaps unduly stressed the unsuitability of Petrarch as a springboard, and the extent to which Wyatt was bogged down in the habits formed in writing within the convention.

An embarrassment I have not been able to overcome is that of needing at the same time to obtain due recognition for Wyatt's *critical* activity and to insist on its lack of drive and power. I do, however, think that Wyatt was consciously attempting something it is not ridiculous to compare with the programme or *apologia* Wordsworth prefixed to the 1800 edition of *Lyrical Ballads*, at least to the extent that we can trace in Wyatt's verse a development from 'inane phraseology' to 'a plainer and emphatic language', from 'false refinement', from a class of Poetry which 'is neither interesting in itself, nor can *lead* to anything interesting; the images neither originate in that sane state of feeling which arises out of thought, nor can excite thought or feeling in the Reader' to one 'well adapted to interest mankind permanently, and not unimportant in the multiplicity and in the quality of its moral relations'. The translations I have next to consider seem to me successful attempts 'to chuse incidents and situations from common life and to relate or describe them, throughout, as far as was possible, in a selection of language really used by men'. I think it would not be inappropriate to prefix to a choice of Wyatt's more interesting poems Wordsworth's phrase: 'I wish to keep my Reader in the company of flesh and blood, persuaded that by doing so I shall interest him.'

Although the element of anachronism in applying these phrases to Wyatt is felt only (I think) in the explicitness, in the number of distinctions drawn by Wordsworth thanks to at least a hundred and fifty years of ethical discussion, I shall attempt to sketch Wyatt's historical task as a poet in more direct terms. What he was called on to do, very much on his own, was to create a focus of consciousness. His abler contemporaries were aware, each according to his lights, of the need in a moral world threatening to break up for the restatement of moral standards in such a way as to revive respect for the bonds which keep society from anarchy. The shift in taste—for 'questionists' were dropped rather than critically weighed and found wanting—from schoolmen to *vulgarisateurs* of the Latin moral classics had not assisted in bringing about the necessary intellectual revolution. On the contrary, the very wealth of examples drawn (chiefly by Erasmus) from these pagan moralists made it impossible to see any object steadily. If you call to mind the most celebrated treatises of the day, from More's *Utopia* to Machiavelli's *Prince* and ask: in what spirit are general principles being brought to bear on particular questions of the day; with what flexibility are the actual complexities of the real world being handled, in short, how much thinking do they contain of the kind that really advances any question, the answer must (I think) be that general principles are applied *a priori*, the particularities of the actual world are either not taken into account or are not brought into fruitful relation with general principles, in short, that there is no genuine thinking, no precision and delicacy of judgement, no real focussing of the mind—no looking steadily at any object.

Nevertheless the examples from the Latin writers did implant in a fresh way the notion of a model type of thinking: the intellectual class in Wyatt's time knew that they should be trying to fuse 'reason' and 'experience' into a single vision. And in one domain we can see the point where the mere humanist and the mere bearer of the traditional culture met: in the cult of the proverb or pithy saying embodying some bit of wisdom in an idiomatic form. I hope that it will not seem a cheap way of putting it to describe the growth of civilisation in the sixteenth century as measurable largely by the gradual assimilation of the classical adage to the homely proverb. What I cannot expect to obtain immediate assent to is the proposition that what was *there* already in English as a body of pithy sayings was far more important than the thousands of Latin phrases collected in Erasmus's *Adagia*. We must not forget that the former were alive and the latter dead. The Latin classics could only be brought to life by being swallowed and digested, i.e. by passing from the status of ornaments or phrases in the head to that of habits of feeling and thinking indistinguishable from native movements of the mind and heart. This can never be accomplished completely, in the nature of things.

Nevertheless just by being exotic, foreign, for ever alien, these importations—and here I would extend the term to all that was not English, 'of the soil', in Wyatt's world—provided a ground plan for the construction of ideal modes of living, generated by a sort of polar attraction between the moral intuitions still current in these late Middle Ages and the suggestions the intuitions could discover (and so really create) in this mass of alien material. Wyatt, like his fellow students, thus sought to derive nutriment from the most easily assimilable parts of the classics, the prose moralists. His verse is strewn with *sententiae*, chiefly borrowed through Erasmus. The poet's task, however, so much harder, began where the Humanists' left off: it was to find modes of bringing about a harmony at deeper levels of the experience derived from books and that obtained from 'life'.

Wyatt's purpose resembled Wordsworth's in a further respect: for it was the discovery of means of informing his verse with prose virtues. Not enough attention has been paid to the virtues of Wyatt's prose, for it is all practical prose: very effective, but except for his two speeches written for his trial in 1541, not of present absorbing interest. Yet it is far more flexible than any other prose of the period. Wyatt only once or twice achieved in verse the blend of tones he could handle in prose. Two features of the prose cannot be passed over, even in this brief reference. Wyatt's value as an ambassador, apart from his mastery of languages, lay in his ability to discern the motives hidden behind the Emperor's 'poker' face and to describe them in novelist's prose. His reports of his interviews with Charles should be in all anthologies. In prose he could look steadily at his subject. (He apparently succeeded in divining the Emperor's intentions.) Secondly, his prose abounds in witty remarks summarising the point of a situation.

This account would be misleading if it suggested that Wyatt's task was merely to incorporate the pith and strength of village talk into his verse. (It is interesting to note that the staple of Wyatt's prose is quite different from that of the Evelyn Waugh of his day.)[1] Wyatt had also

To purify the dialect of the tribe.

To illustrate one of the ways in which his prose required refining, we need go no further than the phrase that nearly cost Wyatt his life— 'By God's blood, ye shall see the king our master let out at the cart's arse.' Or this: whereas Henry couches his instructions in sober terms, ordering Wyatt 'to travail to fish out how th' Emperour is disposed', Cromwell sends an accompanying letter urging Wyatt to 'fishe out the botom of his stomake'.[2]

This, then, is the sense in which I would maintain that Wyatt is a great translator. His originality lay in finding means of making something contemporary out of the alien or dead past. His stature is to be measured both by the comprehensiveness of his comment on the civilisation he had to live in and by the degree to which he created a focus, a poetic mode enabling the strength of the living English tradition to infuse meaning into lost parts of the European tradition or parts that had not previously been assimilated into English culture. It is well known that the early Humanists could make little of Latin poetry: they failed to conceive a worthy function for poetry. Latin poets existed (if it can be called existence) only in so far as they provided models for exercises in verse composition, for the composition of *vers de société*, or quarries for moral tags. If it is a tribute to Wyatt's critical powers that he saw a possibility of doing something serious in poetry by 'imitating' Horace in the form of verse epistles, it is a greater tribute that, as most critics agree, he saw his Horace through Chaucer; for only in this way, I think (judging

[1] See the smart, flippant, man-about-town tone of the letters to Wyatt from Thomas Wriothesley.
[2] L.P. XII(2) 869,870. Diplomatic packet of Oct. 10th, 1537.

by what went before and after) could Wyatt emerge as a whole man in his poetry.

A further comparison with Wordsworth, however, will serve to bring home Wyatt's limitations, and the dangers inherent in these general remarks. For it is only with a Wordsworth cut off before he had produced the *Prelude* that we could compare the Wyatt of these translations. And the public in 1800 would have read the *Preface* with less hopeful expectations if the author had been within a year or two of middle life. What cannot have escaped the present reader's notice is that some of Wyatt's failures to find the right direction as a translator occur at the very end of his life. It is therefore not going to be possible to make a very tidy claim for Wyatt's poetical career. Nevertheless I do think that these occasional pieces prepare our minds for a critical reception of his poems in *terza rima*, which represent Wyatt's only known sustained efforts to reap the harvest of his years of experiment.

It is because of Wyatt's very modest achievement, as distinct from his intentions, as a poet, that, in order to understand what he did, we need to understand what could be done in his line. For this reason it will be necessary to look beyond Wyatt, both to the consequences of failing to advance in his line and to a successful translator who realised fully with Horace what Wyatt only hinted at in his verse epistles. The reader is therefore requested to consider specimens of 'translation' by Ben Jonson[1] after looking at Wyatt's poems in *terza rima* and then to measure how far on the line of Wyatt's intentions his achievement extended.

There are, then, formidable difficulties facing anyone who tries to make out that Wyatt had a poetical career, that as he wrote he acquired a sense of direction, a conception of where his occasional verses were leading him. For he was an occasional poet throughout his life, and we may well suspect that for Wyatt writing poetry was rather a means of whiling away enforced leisure—the inevitable wasted time of any courtier or ambassador dependent on the will of king or emperor—than something that forced itself upon the man of affairs and interrupted his business. Nevertheless, when we examine the poems in *terza rima*, the cultivation of this new metre does seem to have gone hand in hand with a new purpose, which may be loosely described as being to extend the principles and practice of his local and limited translations to a wider range, to a total criticism of man

[1] In the epilogue.

and society. These poems in *terza rima* enable us to place Wyatt in his times as the poet who carried out in verse what the Humanists were attempting in prose, to see life from a central, a truly human point of view.

Such an interpretation of Wyatt's career must, to justify itself, rest on a critical estimate of the poems in *terza rima* as they strike the reader to-day. It would, however, still be desirable if the critical reading could be buttressed by an external chronology, for the value-fact would then have greater explanatory power. The general opinion is that Wyatt's *Psalms* in *terza rima* are inferior to the so-called *Satires*. If then, as is usually supposed, the Psalms were undertaken *after* the Satires, we should have to conclude that Wyatt's powers were declining before he was suddenly cut off in 1542. Even on a superficial reading, it is clear that the Psalms are also occasional poems, that they refer to Wyatt's circumstances at a time when he was threatened by enemies and feared the prospect of death. To make out the sense of the poems is in part to make out what these circumstances were. Here again it is important to know when the Psalms were written. Consequently, although the critical question—the intrinsic worth and significance of the poems in *terza rima*—is our main concern, we must first enquire whether the development of Wyatt's powers can be described as a temporal evolution.

Since one of the 'satires' is virtually a translation of a satire by Luigi Alamanni, and since Alamanni also composed versions of the Seven Psalms, both satires and psalms being in *terza rima*, it is highly probable that the impulse to try out this metre in English came to Wyatt when he discovered Alamanni's *Opere Toscane*, which were first printed at Lyons in 1532. As we shall see when we examine the materials out of which Wyatt's Psalms were composed, an essential ingredient was a prose version by Pietro Aretino, first published in 1534. This gives us two *termini a quo*. We are therefore at least dealing with a mature poet, not with Wyatt's first efforts.

The dating difficulty lies inside the period from 1532 to 1542. One 'satire' appears to refer to a time of confinement to his home that was imposed on Wyatt by order of the king after his imprisonment in 1536. In spite of the fact that the three 'satires' differ in style and each shows pronounced development in skill over its predecessor, some commentators have assumed that they were all written in the years 1536-7. Yet there is one passage in the third 'satire' which suggests that it may have been composed while Wyatt was in prison in 1541. There is a striking resemblance of phrase between words used in the 'satire' to address Wyatt's fellow ambassador and

friend, Sir Francis Brian, and Wyatt's description of his own labours
as an ambassador, as we find it in the speech he prepared for his
defence in 1541:

> To thee, therefore, that trots still up and down
> And never rests, but running day and night
> From realm to realm, from city, street and town . . .

It is hard to resist the suggestion that these lines were written while
the following passage from his defence was still fresh in his mind:

'I, as God judge me, like as I was continually imagining and com-
passing what way I might do best service, so rested I not day nor
night to hunt out for knowledge of those things. I trotted continually
up and down that hell through heat and stink, from councillor to
ambassador, from one friend to another. . . .'

(I have modernised the spelling of both extracts.) This hint supports
the critical finding that the third 'satire' marks a very great advance
on the best previous work of Wyatt in *terza rima* and the consequent
verdict that Wyatt was cut off at the moment when he seemed to be
coming into his own as a poet and exploiting the results of his years
of experiment in this metre.

A similar hint can be used to support a dating for the Psalms. Since
they were clearly written in the midst of the events they allude to,
and those events include imminent death at the hands of political
enemies, there are only two possible dates within the period, those
when Wyatt was imprisoned and in danger of execution, 1536 and
1541. One of the arguments in favour of the later date is that Wyatt
was likely to turn to religion towards the end of his life. This argument would appear stronger if we knew that Wyatt had neglected his
religious duties in his earlier years, or if he had not died unexpectedly
at a time when he was restored to favour at court—for Wyatt died
of a cold caught while on a diplomatic mission. Another argument
for the later date is the apparently late position of these Psalms in
the autograph manuscript book in which Wyatt entered them, for
there is only one poem in that book after the Psalms and that is
unfinished, while the Psalms themselves come after poems that can
be dated to 1537–8. The force of this argument is weakened by two
considerations: we do not find in this book any of the other poems
which seem to refer to Wyatt's stay in prison during 1541 or any of
the other writings we know he composed there. Secondly, the Psalms
are clearly a separate entry: there must have been at least one blank

page before them and there might well have been more when Wyatt made the entry.

Support for the earlier date can be found in the language of the Psalms, but as this evidence is not unambiguous, an external reference may be adduced. It is the similarity of language between passages of the Psalms and three phrases in poems by Surrey, which purport to have been written in 1537, when Surrey was confined to Windsor Castle. Of course, it is possible that the younger poet may have influenced the elder. It will therefore be necessary to show that the common phrases were dictated to Wyatt by the necessities of his translation.

The first apparent borrowing does not carry this external proof. In Surrey's poem beginning *When Windsor walles* he recalls his old friend, the Duke of Richmond:

> Wherwith (alas) the heauy charge of care
> Heapt in my brest breakes forth against my will
> In smoky sighes that ouercast the ayer,
> My vapord eyes such drery teares distil . . .

In Wyatt's prologue to his Second Psalm of the Seven, we find the line

> With vapord iyes he lokythe here and there

The O.E.D. records no other instances of the phrase 'vapoured eyes' than these, save one from Melbancke, who is notorious for purloining from Wyatt and Surrey.[1]

In the other two passages Wyatt's priority is proved by reference to the original from which he was translating. Surrey's poem beginning *So crewell prison* refers to the same feelings of regret for his friend:

> And with this thought the blood forsakes my face,
> The teares berayne my chekes of dedly hewe
> The which, as sone as sobbing sighes, alas
> Vpsupped haue, thus I my playnt renewe . . .

In Wyatt's prologue to the Fourth penitential psalm we find a reference to 'terys'

> Off wyche some part when he vppsuppyd had.

Wyatt was translating here, as in the prologue to the Sixth psalm where he wrote:

> and whilst he ponderd thes thingis in his hert,
> his knee, his arme, his hand, susteind his chyn.

---

[1] The phrase, however, is found in Sackville's *Induction*.

205

This seems to be echoed by Surrey in *When Windsor walles*:

> When Windsor walles susteynd my werid arme
> My hand my chin to ese my restles hed . . .

These are by no means the only places where Surrey borrows from Wyatt's Psalms—indeed we shall see later (p. 243) that he used this very passage of Wyatt on another occasion—but they are the only borrowings which can be placed before 1541.

Further support for the view that the Psalms mark the decisive break into the new metre will be supplied as their inner significance is made out. But before the critical estimate can be attempted, there is a further external preliminary to be cleared up. It has been known for many years that the form chosen by Wyatt of connecting the Seven Psalms by a narrative of David's stages of repentance was taken from *I Sette Salmi* of Pietro Aretino. But it was thought that when Wyatt turned to the psalms themselves, he was no longer translating but paraphrasing and diluting and padding out the Biblical texts. This supposed fact was largely responsible for the neglect under which Wyatt's Psalms have suffered in modern times. For it seemed evidence both of want of taste and want of intensity and power to spin out the verses to such length, and it made it very hard for scholars to account for the admiration expressed by Wyatt's contemporaries, such as we find in Surrey or in Thomas Sackville, who wrote:

> not worthy wiat worthiest of them all
> whom Brittain hath in later yeres furthbrought
> his sacred psalmes wherin he singes the fall
> of David dolling for the guilt he wrought
> and Vries deth which he so dereli bought
> not his hault vers that tainted hath the skie
> for mortall domes to heuenlie and to hie. . . .[1]

Here is the main critical problem: are Wyatt's Psalms what these contemporaries thought they were, or are they what a modern critic once called them: 'academic exercises, penitential not merely in matter, but to those whose task it is to read them'?[2] Fortunately for my claim that Wyatt counts as a translator and as a Christian Humanist, I was able to turn up the work he was translating from. It is a paraphrase of the psalms, in Latin prose, by an up-and-coming Hebrew scholar. The book was an instant success and became a European best-seller as soon as it was printed in 1532. Wyatt

---

[1] From MS. 364 in the Library of St. John's College, Cambridge.
[2] E. M. W. Tillyard: *The Poetry of Sir Thomas Wyatt*, 1929, pp. 48–9.

was therefore responding to the most advanced scholarship open to him in choosing to translate from the *Enchiridion Psalmorum* of Johannes Campensis, in the edition published at Lyons in 1533. This discovery removes a prejudice and makes it possible for us to see what in fact Wyatt was undertaking here. It was a strange, even startling, undertaking, as I hope to make clear, but one preliminary point may be at once made: that Wyatt was here doing in verse what an unknown translator did in prose in 1535,[1] in making available to readers of English the true sense of the Hebrew psalms as interpreted by Johannes Campensis.

But before the specific, unique and modern thing Wyatt was doing in this translation can be appreciated, it must be marked off from a traditional aspect which joins Wyatt with all his contemporaries and with his predecessors for many centuries. The use of the Seven Psalms in exercises of penitence spread from the monasteries to the laity and became well-established during the Middle Ages. So much so that there was a demand for translations into the various vernaculars long before Wyatt wrote. The habit of translating these psalms (Nos. 6, 32, 38, 51, 102, 130, 143 in our Psalter) into verse persisted in England well into the middle of the sixteenth century. We may judge of the place of these Seven Psalms in private devotion from their regular appearance as a special feature of the *Horae* or Books of Hours, which doubtless were among the first books Wyatt would have in his hands as a child.

To judge by what has survived, the chief interest of this group of psalms for the layman was twofold: as a preparation for death and as enacting the drama of penance. Both these interests can be seen at work in Wyatt's translation. He may indeed have been specially stimulated by Alamanni's example, for the Italian poet printed a letter before his penitential hymns describing how he had fallen ill and had 'seen death in the face' and had then realised how ill-prepared he was to come before his Maker. During his convalescence he therefore examined his conscience and used the Seven Psalms as a means of ordering his behaviour under the heads of the Seven Deadly Sins. That this practice was, however, of great antiquity may be seen by comparing Alamanni's hymns with one attributed to Gautier de Châtillon.

What was meant by the phrase 'enacting the drama of penance' is that by reciting these Seven Psalms the sinner brought himself into the proper frame of mind to perform and undergo with understanding the three parts of Catholic penance: contrition, confession and satisfaction. Often the repetition of these seven psalms was itself

[1] The only known copy of this edition is in Lincoln Cathedral Library.

set as a penance. This situation provides the framework of the earliest surviving verse paraphrase in English, written about 1414, attributed to Thomas Brampton. In the prologue the author describes how he rose at midnight and prayed to Jesus for forgiveness of his sins. He went to his confessor, who gave him these instructions:

> And ferthermore, for thi trespace,
> That thou hast don to God of hevene,
> Zif God wille sende the lyif and space,
> Thou shalt sayn thise Psalmes sevene:
> The bettyr with God thou mayst ben evene,
> Or evere thi soule passe fro the,
> Begynne, and seye with mylde stevene
> 'Ne reminiscaris, Domine!' [1]

But in these contexts the drama was not historical: the penitent was not impersonating David. One psalm, however, No. 50 in the Vulgate, *was* connected with David's concupiscence and homicide, as we may see from Caxton's version of the *Golden Legend*.

These two interests are combined in the first of the works which had a direct formative and shaping share in Wyatt's version. For Wyatt must have had before him as he wrote the book containing the sermons on these psalms delivered by *John Fisher* in 1507. In these sermons Fisher not only expounded the meaning of penance and the relevant history of David, but provided a prose version of the Seven Psalms. It is not, however, a work of advanced Humanism, for the revival of the study of Hebrew by Christians had hardly begun to bear fruit when Fisher delivered his sermons. It is, nevertheless, a moving work, and was used for devotional purposes down to the beginning of this century.

Wyatt's concern with this work of genuine piety makes it all the more inexplicable that the final precipitating influence should have been the prose paraphrase of Pietro Aretino. Some critics have found it all too characteristic of Aretino that he should have thrown his paraphrase into the form of a love story—although the love is largely off-stage and in the text is wordily repented of—since he was at the same time composing some of his most celebrated obscenities. Yet in so casting his story, there is reason to believe that he was influenced by a fashion that went back to the earliest days of printing. At least it is a remarkable fact that throughout Europe a change comes over the books in which the psalms as a whole or the Seven Psalms as a group were illustrated by woodcuts. In the years before printing became universal, the illustrations to the psalms had been, generally speaking, uniform. David was shown with his harp while

[1] Printed for the Percy Society, vol. 7, by William Henry Black in 1842.

God or one of His angels looked down on him from the heavens. In hand-painted illustrations and in the first printed Books of Hours this typical scene was superseded and gave place to a picture of Bathsheba being spied on by David. One or two details in Caxton's account suggest that he had either a contemporary tapestry or one such book illustration of the scene in his mind's eye. The *motif* was not confined to worldly productions designed to relieve the boredom of church services by offering the noble worshipper the consolation of seeing his mistress's naked form under the traits of Uriah's wife, for we find Bathsheba in the nude figuring at the head both of John Fisher's sermons on the Seven Psalms and of one edition of Luther's translation of these psalms.

If we turn now to direct inspection of Wyatt's Psalms with his handbooks in easy reach—and it may perhaps be worth noting that both *I Sette Salmi* and the *Enchiridion* could have gone comfortably into the prisoner's smallest pocket—it becomes clear that Wyatt began disastrously with the intention of turning all Aretino's prose into verse. It has been my experience that for many readers, willing enough to test the claim that Wyatt has here created a dramatic poem, the first seventy-two lines (which constitute the first prologue) have proved a final deterrent, since these readers have felt that anything put into the mouth of such a pictorially conceived puppet as the David of this prologue would only sound insincere if not blasphemous. Their feeling is not only that here we have a hopelessly undramatic setting, but that the verse is incapable of expressing conviction. This failure to convince as verse inhibits any attempt to search for an underlying conviction in the poet's mind. It is true that at this point in the poem we cannot say that Wyatt's intention was in any sense dramatic. If Wyatt had carried out his initial intention and had carried on to the end as he had begun in this first prologue and the first eight lines of the First Psalm, he would have produced a shallow, insincere work. What most mars his poem is that, although in the first psalm he broke away from the spirit and letter of his Italian model, in the next three prologues he carried on with Aretino both in spirit and in the letter.

This being so, to set up a sympathetic feeling towards Wyatt's poem, the reader had better take it up where it is generally thought to be convincing. Most commentators pick out the following lines from what they consider a dreary waste of mismetered verbiage: the opening lines of Psalm 130. Here it would be preferable to hear rather than see, not only because Wyatt's spelling is unfamiliar to the ordinary reader, but chiefly because Wyatt's rhythms are lost if the

reader is a strict prosodist and used to applying the rules of 'strict'
terza rima. One of these difficulties can be overcome by modernising
the spelling:

> From depth of sin and from a deep despair,
> > From depth of death, from depth of heart's[1] sorrow,
> > From this deep cave, of darkness deep repair,
> Thee have I called, O Lord, to be my borrow,
> > Thou in my voice, O Lord, perceive and hear
> > My heart, my hope, my plaint, my overthrow,
> My will to rise; and let by grant appear
> > That to my voice Thine ears do well entend.
> > No place so far that to Thee is not near,
> No depth so deep that Thou ne mayest extend
> > Thine ear thereto: hear then my woeful plaint;
> > For, Lord, if Thou do observe what men offend
> And put Thy native mercy in restraint,
> > If just exaction demand recompense
> > Who may endure, O Lord? Who shall not faint
> At such account? Dread, and not reverence
> > Should so reign large. But Thou seekest rather love
> > For in Thy hand is mercy's residence
> By hope whereof Thou dost our hearts move.

The pleasing quality of these lines is one of supple strength, the
strength that has subdued the rhetorical changes on 'deep despair'.
In discussion of these lines it often comes out that recognition that
the banal potentialities of the opening have been quenched is not
reached until we come to the felicitously placed half line

> My will to rise;

It is also a strength (of poetry, if not of piety) that after the solemn
declamatory opening, Wyatt modulates into the tone of argument
or of effective pleading. We hear a living voice.

Even if admiration for these lines is tempered, it must at once be
granted that they establish a dramatic contrast with earlier passages.
David is made to speak as one who has 'come through' when in this
penultimate psalm he says

> > Dread, and not reverence
> > Should so reign large.

The point of the phrase depends on our recalling where he started
from:

> > O Lord, I dread, and that I did not dread
> > I me repent and evermore desire
> Thee, Thee to dread: I open here and spread

---

[1] A dissyllable.

210

My fault to Thee, but Thou for Thy goodness
Measure it not in largeness nor in breadth:
Punish it not as asketh the greatness
Of Thy fury, provoked by my offence.
Temper, O Lord, the harm of my excess
With mending will that I for recompense
Prepare again, and rather pity me,
For I am weak and clean without defence.
More is the need I have of remedy,
For of the whole the leech taketh no cure:
The sheep that strays the shepherd seeks to see.
I, Lord, am strayed, I, sick without recure,
Feel all my limbs that have rebelled for fear
Shake—in despair unless Thou me assure.
My flesh is troubled, my heart doth fear the spear:
The dread of death, of death that ever lasts,
Threateth of right and draweth nearer and nearer.
Much more my soul is troubled by the blasts
Of these assaults that come as thick as hail
Of worldly vanities that temptation casts
Against the weak bulwark of the flesh frail:
Wherein the soul in great perplexity
Feeleth the senses with them that assail
Conspire, corrupt by vice and vanity,
Whereby the wretch doth to the shade resort
Of hope in Thee in this extremity.
But Thou, O Lord, how long after this sort
Forbearest Thou to see my misery?
Suffer me yet in hope of some comfort
Fear and not feel that Thou forgettest me.
Return, O Lord, O Lord, I Thee beseech,
Unto Thine old, wonted benignity,
Reduce, revive my soul, be Thou the leech
And reconcile the great hatred and strife
That it hath ta'en against the flesh, the wretch
That stirred hath Thy wrath by filthy life:
See how my soul doth fret it to the bones,
Inward remorse so sharpeth it like a knife,
That, but Thou help the caitiff that bemoans
His great offence, it turneth anon to dust.

There is already here a rudimentary *drama of penitence*. I hope to
go on to show that it is a fully-worked-out drama, but for the
moment we may content ourselves with a preliminary observation:
the poems *are* related: that is, at the very lowest, they differ from
Alamanni's static plan of expounding one of the seven deadly sins
in each of the seven psalms.

211

Here, then, is a *prima facie* case for supposing that there is in spite of all an underlying unity to be found in the poems and that some of the passages at least can give an account of themselves and show why they occur as they do and where they do. It remains true, however, that the poems contain an element of incoherence, and the rightness of the passages that are right cannot be grasped until this incoherence is clearly seen to constitute a drastic limitation. If we return for a moment to the opening lines of Psalm 130, and, in particular, to the line

> From this deep cave of darkness deep repair

we can say at once that if this cave had not been previously established in the poem as the place where David was situated, if David had not been geographically as well as spiritually crying out *de profundis*, we should not feel so confident about using the word *strength* to describe these lines. In a word, here the dramatic setting provided in the prologues is functional in that it supports the dramatic situation: a remark which immediately provokes the counter-judgement, that elsewhere, or at least in the first four prologues, this is just what does *not* occur.

If we now turn to the powerful passage quoted above from Psalm 6, we can see in what spirit Wyatt handled Aretino. There is no doubt that a full and faithful translation of Aretino would seem to us a sickening performance, offensive alike to literary and religious taste. Nevertheless Aretino occasionally speaks in the accents of piety, even if of rhetorical piety. (In the seventeenth century a pious Catholic translated him into English on his religious merits and his work received the *imprimatur* on those merits.) What Wyatt did in his First Psalm was to reject wholesale a mass of extravagance and to select carefully some of the more telling phrases from Aretino. More than this, Wyatt occasionally transmuted these phrases into convincing poetry. The strength of the First Psalm lies in the vivid presentation of the sinner's state, and the possibility of a developing drama is wholly bound up with the success of this first scene. Now the strokes which convince do not come from Campensis, but in suggestions taken from Aretino. For instance,

> O Lord, I dread, and that I did not dread
> I me repent and evermore desire
> Thee, Thee to dread. . . .

is an almost literal translation. The momentum, however, which is obtained by reduplicating *Thee* is Wyatt's own. Again, the account of Temptation's assault on the citadel of the soul with the assistance of an inner fifth column is taken in part from Aretino.

212

> Much more my soul is troubled by the blasts
>   Of these assaults that come as thick as hail
>   Of worldly vanities that Temptation casts
> Against the weak bulwark of the flesh frail
>   Wherein the Soul in great perplexity
>   Feeleth the senses with them that assail
> Conspire . . .

Here, however, Wyatt has, characteristically, strengthened the Italian by borrowing an expression from Chaucer:

> strokes, whiche that wente as thikke as hayl.[1]

On the other hand, our sense that Wyatt is really exploring the troubled conscience, the first condition of receiving pardon, is weakened by his adopting rhetorical developments from Aretino, as here, in a passage of almost literal translation:

> Some do present to my weeping eyes, lo,
> The cheer, the manner, beauty and countenance
> Of her whose look, alas, did make me blind:
> Some other offer to my remembrance
> Those pleasant words, now bitter to my mind,
>   And some shew me the power of my armour,
>   Triumph and conquest, and to my head assigned
> Double diadem: some shew the favour
>   Of people frail, palace, pomp and riches:
>   To these mermaids and their baits of error
> I stop mine ears. . . .

It is now possible to introduce more careful language in defining Wyatt's poem as 'drama'. There cannot be a drama of penitence unless it is recognised that penitence is a process, a progress through definite and publicly acknowledged stages. Wyatt's first scene establishes the moment when recognition and admission of sin occur: the predominant feeling is dread. The second prologue makes the point that such recognition is merely the initial step:

> Eased, not yet healed, he feeleth his disease.

The Second Psalm brings in (very obscurely, I must confess) what I take to be the unifying principle of the drama: that the stages are those of repentance rather than of penance. Negatively, it is quite clear, that though Wyatt had a detailed exposition before him in Fisher of the stages of penance, he avoids all that is characteristic of the Catholic account. The distinction Wyatt seems to be working towards—as we see from the later psalms—is one which More seized

---

[1] *The Legend of Good Women: Legenda Cleopatre*, line 655.

on in his attacks on Tyndale. In More's *Dialogue*, for instance, the substitution of repentance for penance is quoted as an instance of the heretical tendencies of Tyndale's translation of the New Testament. Two quotations will suffice to make the point. The first is from Book Three, Chapter Eight: 'Confession he translateth into knowleging. Penance into repentance. A contrite heart he chaungeth into a troubled heart. And many moe thinges lyke, and many textes vntruely translated for the maintenance of heresie . . .' The second is taken from Book Four, Chapter Two: 'doth it not playnly appere that this fonde felowe so playeth with thys holy sacrament of penaunce, that he goeth aboute vtterlye to distroy it?'

More was not inventing the charge, as we can see from Tyndale himself:

'Penaunce is a worde of their awne forginge to disceaue vs with all, as many other are. In the scripture we fynde penitentia, repentaunce, Agite penitentiam, do repente, Peniteat vos, let it repente you. Metanoyte in greke, forthinke ye, or let it forthinke you. Of repentaunce, they have made penaunce, to blynde the people and to make them thinke that they must take payne and doo some holy deades to make satisfaction for their synnes, namely soch as they enioyne them." [1]

And in replying to More, he wrote:

'And in lyke maner, by this word penaunce, they make the people vnderstonde holy dedes of their enioynynge, with which they must make satisfaccion vnto godwarde for their synnes. When al the scripture preacheth that christ hath made full satisfaccyon for oure synnes to godwarde, and we must now be thankefull to god agayne and kyll the lustes of oure flesh wyth holy workes of gods enioynynge and to take pacientlye all that god layeth on my back. And if I haue hurte my neyboure, I am bounde to shriue my selfe vnto hym and to make hym a mendes, yf I haue where with, or if not then to axe him forgeuenesse, and he is bounde to forgeue me. And as for their penaunce the scripture knoweth not of. The greke hath Metanoia and metanoite, repentaunce and repente.' [2]

In this Second Psalm it is a delicate matter to decide whether Wyatt, who is clearly reading the text with St. Paul in mind, is also

[1] From *The Obedience of a Christen man*, etc. (1535 ed., f. xciv verso).
[2] From *An answere vnto Sir Thomas Mores dialoge made by Willyam Tindalle*, f. xii recto.

reading it with Luther's commentary on Paul. Wyatt is less specific when he writes:

> Oh happy are they that have forgiveness got
> Of their offence, not by their penitence
> As by merit which recompenseth not—
> Although that yet pardon hath none offence
> Without the same—but by the goodness
> Of Him that hath perfect intelligence
> Of heart contrite

than Tyndale when he thus translates Luther:

'Here with nowe stablyssheth Saynct Paul his doctryne of fayth afore rehersed in the .iij. Chapter, and bringeth also testimony of Dauid in the .xiij. Psalme which calleth a man blessed not of workes, but in that his synne is not rekened & in that fayth is imputed for ryghteousnes, though he abyde not afterwarde with out good workes, when he is once iustifyed. For we are iustifyed and receaue the spryte for to do good workes, nether were it other wyse possible to do good workes, excepte we had fyrst the spryte. . . . Goddes mercy in promysinge, and trueth in fulfyllynge his promyses saueth vs & not we oure selues. And therfore is all laude, prayse and glory, to be geuen vnto God for his mercy and trueth, & not vnto vs for oure merites and deseruinges.'[1]

Similarly, we must note that though Wyatt uses the tell-tale words 'impute' and 'knowleging' (see More) in

> And happy is he to whom God doth impute
> No more his fault by knowledging his sin

he could have taken the word 'impute' from Aretino. Nor in the following fine passage is it apparent that we *must* think of Luther's doctrine of justification:

> Oh diverse are the chastisings of sin,
> In meat, in drink, in breath that man doth blow,
> In sleep, in wake, in fretting still within,
> That never suffer rest unto the mind
> Filed with offence, that new and new begin
> With thousand fears the heart to strain and bind.
> But for all this, he that in God doth trust
> With mercy shall himself defended find.
> Joy and rejoice, I say, ye that be just,
> In Him that maketh and holdeth you so still . . .

[1] *A prologe vpon the Epistle of Saynct Paul to the Romayns*, 1536, sig. A v.

especially when we note that Wyatt is building here on two passages from Fisher: 'these enemyes laye awayte bothe daye and nyght, they spare vs neyther slepynge nor wakynge, etynge or drynkynge, in labour, or ony other study, but always besy them selfe to catche our soules in theyr snares' and 'The lyf of man is here but for a whyle, shortly it shal perysshe & be at an ende, no space, no voyde tyme no leyser can be had but alway it draweth to an ende, it can not be at a point, it is neuer at rest truly one mynyte of an houre, whether we ete or drynke, wake or slepe, laugh or wepe, euer our lyfe here draweth to an ende.'

The Third Psalm is the most personal. Although doctrinally it may rest on the argument that if justification delivers the spirit from the fear of destruction, it nevertheless leaves the flesh a perpetual prey to temptation, yet the verses are formed out of personal experience. It is not merely an attempt to reword a theological doctrine in general human terms, but it tries to find language to express the feeling behind expletives such as 'filthy' when applied to sin. It is worth noting how close one of these attempts is to the language of Wyatt's best love poem. It is hard not to see a significant relation between

> And of my flesh each not well cured wound
> That festered is by folly and negligence
> By secret lust hath rankled under skin,
> Not duly cured by my penitence

and

> What power, what plague doth weary thus my mind?
> Within my bones to rankle is assigned
> What poison pleasant sweet?

and between this from the same poem (*What rage is this?*)

> In deep wide wound the deadly stroke doth turn
> To cured scar that never shall return

and Wyatt's first thoughts in line twenty of this Psalm:

> By force whereof the evil cured scars . . .

If it was possible to suppose that the Jacobean period was haunted by the horror of syphilis, surely it is reasonable to suppose that the imagery here reflects the feelings of those who saw the disease in its first deadly onslaughts—particularly when we note the prominence of the theme in the primers and other prayer books of the period and the popularity of Fracastorius' poem *Syphilis siue morbus gallicus* (1530)?

We have seen that throughout the history of Christendom Psalm

51 (Psalm 50 in the Vulgate) was taken to be the psalm of penitence *par excellence*. It might almost be said to be the one point where Catholic and Protestant could meet. At any rate, Savonarola's fine meditation upon this psalm was reprinted in English primers of a Protestant tinge and Luther re-issued it along with his own meditation on the psalm. Luther, however, read into it all the distinctive tenets of his faith:

'Est autem multis modis huius Psalmi cognitio tum necessaria tum utilis: Continet enim doctrinam de praecipuis nostrae Religionis capitibus, de Poenitentia, de Peccato, de Gratia, et Justificatione, Item de Cultu quem nos Deo praestare debemus.' [1]

It is the heart of Wyatt's drama of repentance: here the sense in which Wyatt's religious attitude is Protestant is clearly manifest. Wyatt's poem is a Hym to Justification:

> My tongue shall praise Thy Justification

he writes, where his sources offered him justice or righteousness.

This is also the point where the personal 'break-through' occurs. Wyatt's tone is now broader and more confident as he makes his triumphant confession:

> My tongue shall praise Thy Justification,
> My mouth shall spread Thy glorious praises true.
> But of Thyself, O God, this operation
> It must proceed, by purging me from blood
> Among the Just that I may have relation,
> And of Thy lauds for to let out the flood
> Thou must, O Lord, my lips first unloose.
> For if Thou hadst esteemed pleasant good
> The outward deeds that outward men disclose
> I would have offered unto Thee sacrifice,
> But Thou delightest not in no such glose
> Of outward deed as men dream and devisc.
> The sacrifice that the Lord liketh most
> Is sprite contrite. Low heart in humble wise
> Thou dost accept, O God, for pleasant host.
> Make Sion, Lord, according to Thy will
> Inward Sion, the Sion of the ghost,
> Of heart's Jerusalem strength the walls still.
> *Then* shalt Thou take for good these outward deeds
> As sacrifice Thy pleasure to fulfil.
> Of Thee alone thus all our good proceeds.

---

[1] *Enarratio Psalmorum LI. Miserere mei Deus*, etc., 1538. W. A. 40², 315, 27–30.

The feeling that here a break-through has occurred is further strengthened when we notice that for the first time the lines that come after the Psalm—which form the prologue to the next Psalm—actually carry on from this Psalm and do not, as elsewhere, provide a merely formal link between the Psalms. Wyatt, still staggered by the daring of the phrases

> Make Sion, Lord, according to Thy will
> Inward Sion, the Sion of the ghost,
> Of heart's Jerusalem strength the walls still

—which go a long way beyond what Luther would have sanctioned—exclaims:

> Of deep secrets that David here did sing,
> Of mercy, of faith, of frailty, of grace,
> Of God's goodness and of Justifying
> The greatness did so astound himself a space,
> As who might say: 'Who hath expressed this thing?
> I, sinner, I, what have I said, alas?'

This is very much in the spirit of Luther, who remarked: 'Quis enim hominum sic posset loqui de Poenitentia et Remissione peccatorum, sicut Spiritus sanctus in hoc Psalmo loquitur?' [1]

The point is taken up again in the next prologue, which, to my mind, together with the end of Psalm 51, represents the dramatic core of Wyatt's conception of the process of repentance. It is the moment when David is tempted to complacency or, as Wyatt puts it, he 'ginneth to allow', that is, to praise, 'his pain and penitence':

> But when he weigheth the fault and recompense,
> He damns his deed, and findeth plain
> Atween them two no whit equivalence,
> Whereby he takes all outward deed in vain
> To bear the name of rightful penitence,
> Which is alone the heart returned again
> And sore contrite, that doth his fault bemoan,
> And outward deed the sign or fruit alone.
>
> With this he doth defend the sly assault
> Of vain allowance of his void desert,
> And all the glory of his forgiven fault
> To God alone he doth it whole convert;
> His own merit he findeth in default . . .

There is surely more than a chance resemblance of phrase between the line

> And outward deed the sign or fruit alone

[1] *Ibid.*

and Tyndale's:

> euen so are all other good workes outewarde signs and
> outewarde frutes of fayth[1]

which he derived from Luther's *Praefatio in Epistolam Pauli ad
Romanos*: '. . . sic bona opera, solum externa signa sunt, non quae
hominem iustificant, sed quae hominem intus coram Deo iustificatum
et fidem uiuentem et agentem, ceu signa quaedam et fructus
probant.'

The survey has now come round to its starting point, the opening
lines of Psalm 130. It is now clear that this translation is also the
creation of an original statement of faith. It would be a delicate
matter to find a label for the animating faith in these poems. 'The
life of a Christian man is inward between himself and God,' wrote
Tyndale. Wyatt's stress is almost wholly on the individual, and we
might think that his came dangerously near to being a private religion. Yet, if we look, not at the bold formulators of new creeds, but
at the far greater number of Wyatt's unattached contemporaries
who were trying for a living and working faith, I think it is fair to
say that much of Wyatt's faith as expressed in these Psalms would
have been as acceptable to 'reformists' inside the Catholic church as
50 'reformers' outside it, even if the converse is true, namely, that it
would have been as unacceptable to traditionalists inside the church
as to extreme Protestants outside it. It is therefore a valuable document showing us what 'making it new' was like from the inside as
the new religion made its first impact on the old.

It is characteristic of this process of 'making it new' that it should
draw its strength as much from tradition as from the opposition to
that tradition. Many of Wyatt's best passages are based on dramatic
conceptions of the plight of the sinner which persisted from well
before *Everyman* down to *The Pilgrim's Progress*:

> Perceiving thus the tyranny of sin
>   That with his weight hath humbled and depressed
>   My pride, by grudging of the worm within
> That never dieth, I live withouten rest.
>   So are mine entrails infect with fervent sore
>   Feeding the harm that hath my wealth oppressed,
> That in my flesh is left no health therefore.
>   So wondrous great hath been my vexation
>   That it hath forced my heart to cry and roar:
> O Lord, Thou knowest the inward contemplation
>   Of my desire, Thou knowest my sighs and plaints,
>   Thou knowest the tears of my lamentation

[1] *A Prologe*, etc., A v recto.

Cannot express my heart's inward restraints.
My heart panteth, my force I feel it quail,
My sight, mine eyes, my look, decays and faints:
And when my enemies did me most assail,
My friends most sure, wherein I set most trust,
Mine own vertues, soonest then did fail
And stand apart. Reason and Wit unjust,
As kin unkind were farthest gone at need . . .

An elaborate commentary would be needed to define completely
in what sense this poem is a translation. The framework is supplied
to Wyatt by his originals, and he has in the main followed the
order of his matter. His Psalms are still paraphrases of the Biblical
psalms, but they have been completely adapted to the poet's inner
needs.

The aim of this enquiry was to discover the significance as a
moment in Wyatt's poetical career of his translation of the Seven
Psalms. It is unfortunate for such a purpose that Wyatt left this poem
virtually unfinished. It contains lines that can hardly be called written: though Wyatt corrected some weak passages, he left many more,
just as weak, uncorrected. When he did find his theme and began to
fulfil it in what I have described as the heart of the poem, he did not
go back and rewrite the earlier part and so construct a properly unified poem. There is thus an immense gap between intention and
execution. Although the theme of this poem was central, for it
turns on the restatement of man's relation to God, its universal significance is lost or so clouded as only to emerge in patches. Nevertheless Wyatt's plan of dramatising the issue was a good one: the psalms
were thought to pre-figure this issue as it presented itself to his
contemporaries. And we have the most formal proof that the autobiographical form suited Wyatt and roused his poetic powers, for
his translation of Psalm 37 into *terza rima*, and also taken from
Campensis and Zwingli, remains a mere translation.

Nevertheless, for the reasons given, we cannot call Wyatt's version
of the Seven Psalms, this drama of repentance, a great poem. We
cannot see it as focussing the aspirations of those of his contemporaries who were seeking to restate the old faith in living terms.
Nevertheless in places Wyatt wrote as well as he was ever to write.
These good parts deserve to be known and retained since they
stand comparison with and indeed surpass the paraphrases of the
psalms by later poets. If the reader will turn back to page 211 and
compare the extract given there from Wyatt's version of Psalm 6
with this:

> Pity me, Lord, for I am much deject,
> And very weak and faint; heal and amend me:
> For all my bones, that even with anguish ache,
>   Are troubled: yea, my soul is troubled sore;
> And Thou, O Lord, how long? Turn, Lord; restore
> My soul . . .

he will surely have to admit that Wyatt's movement is more eloquent and carries the mind to the things he is speaking of, and that Milton by comparison seems stale and feeble.

Finally, the evidence of the Psalms reinforces the impression that the moral epistles in *terza rima* which followed owe part of their strength to their Christian basis. With these poems behind us we can read Wyatt's two prose epistles of 1537—cardinal documents for us in our attempt to discover in what sense Wyatt was a Christian Humanist—with a proper appreciation of the spiritual atmosphere in which Wyatt composed his best work.

It is easier to make out the case that Wyatt was performing a task the earlier Humanists were unable to carry out, that is, to show how to make poetry a serious pursuit, and how to write poems bearing a serious relation to life, when we turn to the three remaining poems in *terza rima*, which, as we have seen, he probably wrote in the years 1536–41, for in them, if anywhere, Wyatt found himself and fulfilled the functions of the true Humanist. It is seriously misleading to call them 'satires', for they are verse epistles and in them we can see a significant development from the verse letter to dialogue and drama, a development which is at the same time one of progressive mastery of the possibilities of the metre. Just as More's *Utopia* required the framework of dialogue to 'place' the central mass of critical observations, so Wyatt's three translations gain their power from being cast in the form of familiar letters or of talk with a friend. This was the indispensable preliminary for any effective assimilation of the Classics.

Secondly, in these poems Wyatt turned to the central subject for the Humanists; criticism of the court civilisation. Here was a subject where the courtier who wished to make pointed criticism had to tread carefully. We shall never know the volume and intensity of dislike aroused by the habits of the king and his powerful favourites: it was far too dangerous to put pen to paper. Wyatt, however, has one short poem on the court:

> In court to serue decked with freshe aray,
> Of sugred meates felyng the swete repast,
> The life in bankets and sundry kindes of play
> Amid the presse of lordly lokes to waste

Hath with it ioynde oft times such bitter taste,
That who so ioyes such kinde of life to holde
In prison ioyes, fettred with cheines of gold.

I assume that Wyatt was not satisfied with this minor triumph, and that he wanted a form that would allow him to be both more personal and to make a more telling comment in dramatic terms on the position of all those in his class, obliged to pass their lives in the only cultural centre the country provided. I assume, too, that once again Wyatt wanted a literary model offering a close parallel to his actual situation in 1536, for Wyatt's epistle is not merely 'observations on life at court' but a passionate protest against the shabby treatment to which he felt he had been subjected there. For in that year he had been suddenly arrested, carried secretly to the Tower, kept there *incomunicado*, then released, to be confined to his father's estates in Kent, and later given various positions of trust, and finally in the next year made ambassador to the Emperor. I assume that this desire for a parallel was one of the determining reasons why Wyatt turned to the satires of Alamanni, for he found there a poem which mirrored his situation while masking it.

Nevertheless there are reasons for regretting that Wyatt chose this model rather than Horace or Juvenal: for Alamanni has all the weaknesses of his Italian culture. Since he did not feel Juvenal's Rome as sufficiently remote, he was unable to see it in contemporary Paris. His epistle is a string of commonplaces. He describes himself to his friend as withdrawn from court and seeking true peace among the *rusé*, but not too troublesome peasantry of Provence. He himself was an exile from Florence and had spent many years at the court of Francis I. His theme is that of Juvenal's third satire: *quid Romae faciam? mentiri nescio:* what can a man do who tells the truth in the capital? It is the farewell to city life of its last honest inhabitant. Unfortunately, instead of dramatic episodes Alamanni gives us moral rhetoric, and in this Wyatt has to some extent followed the Italian.

Alamanni develops his theme by the simple device of cataloguing the falsities required of the courtier; the author claims that he (literally) 'would not know how' to endure them and so justifies his retirement from court to country. This mechanical application of the rhetorical figure 'amplificatio' by enumeration excludes passion and requires the introduction of points of merely formal antithesis. Wyatt, for all his passionate interest, retained the formal disposition of the matter as he found it in Alamanni. A short prose paraphrase of both epistles would differ only in saying that the speaker in one poem is in Provence and the other in Kent. But although Wyatt accepts the catalogue form, he is more skilful than the Italian in

222

varying the repetitive elements: thus he repeats 'I cannot' only seven times to Alamanni's sixteen. For all this, when we look closely at Wyatt's poem, there is hardly a phrase that has not been completely transformed and subdued to his purpose. No one, judging solely by the English text, could detect the point where Wyatt introduces his own matter. There are not many poems in which Wyatt appears to be so much himself.

Wyatt's problem was to find some means of converting abstract moral statements into convincing concrete presentation of the moral facts. He did this by substituting the tone of conversation for Alamanni's consistent declamation. One of Wyatt's methods was to clinch his points by homely proverbial expressions. He says, for example, 'I cannot dye the colour black a liar' and speaks of courtiers 'who weigh a chip of chance more than a pound of wit.' Another example of the assimilative or digestive power of popular speech may be seen in the passage where Wyatt translates the following lines of Alamanni:

> Non saprei piu ch'a gli immortali Dei
> Rendere honor con le ginocchia inchine
> A piu ingiusti che sian, fallaci, & rei.
> (I could not go on my knees and honour more
> than the immortal gods those that are as unjust,
> deceitful and criminal as it is possible to be.)

by

> I cannot crowche nor knelle to do soche wrong,
> To worship them lyke gode on erthe alone,
> That ar as wollffes thes sely lambes among.

This is the very language of Wyatt's peasant contemporaries in Norfolk, who in 1549 asserted, 'As sheep or lambs are a prey to the wolf or lion, so are the poor men to the rich men.' Here we see the assimilation of the biblical phrase: 'Behold I send you forth as sheep in the midst of wolves.'

Wyatt slips with equal ease into the morality habit:

> And say that Favell hath a goodly grace
> In eloquence;

Favell is a personage in Skelton's *The Bouge of Court:*

> The fyrste was Fauell, full of flatery,
> Wyth fables false that well coude fayne a tale;

Puttenham has a passage which throws light on the whole context in Wyatt's poem:

'But if such moderation of words tend to flattery, or soothing, or

223

excusing, it is by the figure *Paradiastole*, which therefore nothing improperly we call the *Curry-fauell*, as when we make the best of a bad thing, or turne a signification to the more plausible sence: as, to call an vnthrift, a liberall Gentleman: the foolish-hardy, valiant or couragious: the niggard, thriftie: a great riot, or outrage, an youthfull pranke, and such like termes: moderating and abating the force of the matter by craft, and for a pleasing purpose. . . .' [1]

That Wyatt was conscious of the effects obtained by the use of homely illustration is shown by his modification of the passages where Alamanni draws on classical instances. For example, where Alamanni, who wished to protest against the corrupt literary taste of his time, which preferred the second-rate poet to the original genius, takes for his example the Maevius mentioned by Horace and Virgil as their contemporary bugbear, Wyatt draws his example from Chaucer, and says that he cannot:

> Praysse Syr Thopas for a nobyll talle
> And skorne the story that the knyght tolld.

It is, however, far easier to show Wyatt's superiority to his Italian model than to state plausibly a case for regarding the epistle as a major triumph on a scale on which the epigram *In court to serue* would be only a minor success. At least it can be said that Wyatt has found means to catch the note of indignant honesty reproduced in Johnson's *London*. Yet I cannot help thinking that in this respect the verse letter is inferior to one of Wyatt's prose letters to his son, which has 'honesty' as its theme:

'I haue nothing to crye and cal apon you for but honestye, honestye. It may be diuersly namid, but alway it tendith to one end. And as I wrate to you last, I meane not that honestye that the comen sort callith an honist man: Trust me that honist man is as comen a name as the name of a good felow, that is to say, a dronkerd, a tauerne hanter, a riotter, a gamer, a waster: so are among the comen sort al men honist men that are not knowin for manifest naughtye knaues. Seke not, I pray the, my son, that honesty which aperith and is not in dead. Be wel assured it is no comen thing nor no comen mans iugement to iuge wel of honestye, nor is it no comen thing to come by: but so mitch it is the more goodlye for that it is so rare and strang. Folow not therfor the comen reputation of honestye; if you wil seme honist, be honist, or els seame as you are. Seke not the name without the thing, nor let not the name be the only mark

---

[1] *The Arte of English Poesie*, 1589, p. 154.

you shote at: that wil folow tho you regard it not, ye, and the more you regard it the lesse. I meane not by regard it not, esteme it not; for wel I wot honist name is goodly, but he that huntith only for that is like him that had rathir seame warme then be warme, and edgith a single cote about with a furre. Honist name is to be kept preseruid and defendid; and not to employ al a mans wit about the study of it for that smellith of a glorious and ambitious fole. I say as I wrote unto you in my last lettirs, get the thing and the other must of necessite folow as the shadow foloweth the thing that it is of. And euin so mitch is the verye honeste bettir then the name as the thing is bettir then the shadow.'

In striking contrast with this prose, the defect of the verse epistle is a certain stiffness and monotony of tone. This can be expressed in a judgement which is at the same time of the content and the style. Wyatt's plain honesty is blunt and over-emphatic. The talk degenerates into the declamation of the original because the scorn expressed is too much of one kind. Nor are the moral discriminations either clearly or subtly drawn. The situation is not sharply focused on, that is, it is not sufficiently *dramatic* in conception, so that the epistle becomes too much like a sermon, and relies too much on saying and not enough on doing. Here Wyatt has not mastered the metre: I do not mean that he has broken its rules, but that the closes of the sense groups and the pauses within the lines impose a certain rigidity upon the speaking voice. The next two epistles, as we shall see, mark a great advance in flexibility. Nevertheless, Wyatt *is* using the *terza rima*, as the following passage shows, which is real speech:

> The frendly ffoo with his dowble face
> Say he is gentill and courtois thcrcwithall;
> And say that Favell hath a goodly grace
> In eloquence; and crueltie to name
> Zele of justice and chaunge in tyme and place,
> And he that sufferth offence withoute blame
> Call him pitefull; and him true and playn
> That raileth rekles to every mans shame.
> Say he is rude that cannot lye and fayn;
> The letcher a lover; and tirannye
> To be the right of a prynces reigne.
> I cannot, I. No, no, it will not be.
> This is the cause that I could never yet
> Hang on their slevis that way as thou maist se
> A chippe of chaunce more then a pownde of witt.

Wyatt's second letter to his best friend, John Poyntz, the brother of the man who befriended Tyndale, whose sympathetic features can still be seen in Holbein's drawing, is of all Wyatt's poems the one I should choose first both to define English Humanism and to show the point where Humanism and Poetry meet. For the ideal aspiration of the period was to bring philosophy and religion down to the human level and into touch with Nature. This aspiration marks the closest point of contact between the Roman and the Renaissance ideal, for its ultimate source is what I have called the archetypal poem of Horace, the sixth 'sermo' of his second book.

It is from this *sermo* that Wyatt drew. Here, however, it is a case of translation and recreation of the *spirit* rather than of the word. Wyatt takes his start at the end of the passage quoted on page 117. Once again I give a rough paraphrase:

'While we philosophise round the table, the man from next door chips in with the sort of yarn old women tell each other: If one of my guests starts to talk big about a millionaire, forgetting that money troubles those who have no money troubles, he interrupts with "Once upon a time, there was, they say, a country mouse who had to put up a town mouse in his agricultural hovel. It was a case of old friends meeting, and the need to show hospitality forced the country mouse, for once, to break his parsimonious habits and bring all his hoarded food out of the larder. He became a generous and attentive host and served a dried raisin for dessert and a piece of half-nibbled bacon for a savoury—anything to get the pampered town mouse to eat. But *he* hardly touched a single course, even with his front teeth. He found the whole thing too nauseating, even though his host had put down fresh straw, and was letting him have the best bits and keeping the coarser items for his own plate. The town mouse tried to remain urbane, but came out in the end with, "I can't see the point of your struggle for existence on this frontier. Can you honestly say you prefer the backwoods and their fauna to the town and civilised people? My dear old friend, haven't you made an . . . unfortunate choice? You had better come with me. Can you get away from the fact that we mice, unlike cats, have only one life, and, as Solomon says, 'What hath man of all his labour . . . there is nothing better for a man than that he should eat, drink and be merry.'" These biblical quotations made such a deep impression on the country mouse that he at once decided to leave home and he found his way to the city through a hole in the walls. The moon was overhead as the two friends broke into the town mouse's flat in, shall we say, Roman Mayfair. There, in a Hollywood-like setting, they found the leavings of a sumptuous five-course dinner still on the table. The

226

town mouse offered his friend a plush-covered chair while he bustled around him like a well-trained waiter tasting each dish first to see if it was fit for his guest to eat. The country mouse lolled back and was congratulating himself on his decision to leave home and trying to live up to his "posh" surroundings, when a tremendous banging on the outer doors shot him out of his chair. Both mice lost their heads and scuttled down the enormous length of the dining-room. When they heard the barking of dogs echoing through the high-ceilinged set of rooms, they were as good as dead. "Good-bye," said the country mouse, "this is no life for me. My meals may be on the thin side, but at least I can eat them without this sort of interruption." '

I hope it will not sound far-fetched to distinguish between the sterile and fruitful forms of this Humanist ideal according as the setting included or excluded all that is symbolised by Horace's *uernae procaces* and the learned conversation was or was not enriched with folk wit.

We cannot now identify the song or ballad Wyatt drew on for his version of the fable. (He does not seem to owe anything of importance to Henryson.) But we do know a little of the songs that may have been sung by Wyatt's

> mothers maydes when they did sowe and spynne.

In their discussion of 'A frog he would a-wooing go' Mr and Mrs Opie refer to a ballad about a frog and a mouse which was current in Wyatt's time. A version of it, orally alive in 1824, has a refrain common to spinning songs, echoing the humming of the wheel and the twiddling and twining of the thread. (Even in the current nursery rhyme the mouse was 'sitting to spin' when 'a cat and her kittens came tumbling in'.) The following lines, taken from the oral tradition, are suggestive: the cat and the kittens attacked 'Lord Ratton':

> But Lady Mouse baith jimp and sma'
> Crept into a hole beneath the wa'
> 'Squeak!' qho' she, 'I'm weel awa'!' [1]

This epistle shows Wyatt to be the heir of Erasmus and More. What More attempted in his Latin epigrams, Wyatt performed in his English poems. Although Wyatt was, as we have seen, a Lutheran, his aim was essentially similar to More's: to discover a secular way of handling a religious point of view. Wyatt, through Poyntz, as it

---

[1] *The Oxford Dictionary of Nursery Rhymes*, ed. Iona and Peter Opie, pp. 179–80.

were, over his shoulder, is reproving his other fellow-courtiers. The epistle is in fact a lay sermon. It passes easily from the Horatian:

> O wretched myndes, there is no gold that may
> Graunt that ye seke! No warr, no peace, no stryff,
> No, no, all tho thy hed were howpt with gold;
> Sergeaunt with mace, hawbert, sword nor knyff
> Cannot repulse the care that folowe should.

to the Christian, if not very charitable, prayer:

> These wretched fooles shall have nought els of me
> But to the great god and to his high dome
> None othre pain pray I for theim to be
> But when the rage doeth led them from the right
> That lowking backwards vertue they may se
> Evyn as she is so goodly fayre and bright:
> And whilst they claspe their lustes in armes a crosse,
> Graunt theim, goode lorde, as thou maist of thy myght,
> To frete inwards for losing such a losse.

Consequently, it is not surprising to find among contemporary tributes to Wyatt praise from the rhetorician, Sherry (in the dedication to *A treatise of Schemes and Tropes*, 1550); the Humanist scholar, Leland (in his *Naeniae in mortem Thomae Viati equitis incomparabilis*, 1542) and the Protestant divine, Becon (in the dedication to *The Pollecy of warre*).

One of the sharpest points of difference between Erasmus and More was over nationalism: More, it is no exaggeration to say, was a thorough-going jingo, but, although attempts have been made to show that Erasmus felt a certain *pietas* towards his fatherland, it is hard to see in what respects his sensibility was distinctively Dutch. The English Humanists were highly conscious of being English and of the virtues of plain English: it is impossible to distinguish between their national and their literary sense. The *ethos* was one of robust simplicity: it was naturally favourable to the virtual re-discovery of Chaucer. This point was well made by Professor Hallett Smith, who quoted appositely from Peter Betham's *Preceptes of Warre*, written in December, 1543:

'Yet lette no man thyncke, that I doo damne all usuall termes borowed of other tounges, whan I doo well knowe that one tougue is interlaced with an other. But nowe to be shorte, I take them beste englyshe men, which folowe Chaucer, and other olde wryters, in whyche studye the nobles and gentle men of Englande, are worthye to be praysed, whan they endevoure to bryng agayne to his owne

clennes oure englysshe tounge, & playnelye to speake wyth our
owne termes as our mothers dyd before us.' [1]

Wyatt is clearly of this company: to make a trivial observation,
the strength of his hold upon his language is shown by the absence
of French, Spanish, Italian and Latin locutions in his everyday prose.
Few Englishmen living so much abroad as Wyatt did and speaking
at least two of these languages, succeed in retaining their native
tongue in its idiomatic purity. But far more important than this, I
think that Wyatt owes to his study of Chaucer the success he obtained
in this epistle in freeing himself from the rigidity of the preceding
epistle. The influence of Chaucer in the following passage is
unmistakable:

> And to the dore now is she come by stelth,
> And with her foote anon she scrapeth full fast.
> Thothre for fere durst not well scarse appere,
> Of every noyse so was the wretche agast.
> At last she asked softly who was there,
> And in her langage as well as she cowd,
> 'Pepe', quoth the other syster, 'I am here.'
> 'Peace,' quoth the towny mowse, 'why spekest thou so lowde?'
> And by the hand she toke her fayer and well.
> 'Welcome', quoth she, 'my sister, by the Roode!'
> She fested her, that joy it was to tell
> The fare they had: they drancke the wyne so clere,
> And as to pourpose now and then it fell
> She chered her with, 'How, syster, what chiere?'
> Amyddes this ioye befell a sory chaunce
> That, welawaye, the straunger bought full dere
> The fare she had: for as she loked askaunce,
> Vnder a stole she spied two stemyng ise
> In a rownde hed with sherp erys. In Fraunce
> Was never mowse so ferd. For tho thvnwise
> Had not ysene suche a beest before,
> Yet had Nature taught her after her gyse
> To knowe her foo and dred him evermore.
> The towny mowse fled: she knewe whither to goo.
> Thothre had no shift, but wonderus sore
> Fferd of her liff: at home she wyshed her tho:
> And to the dore, alas, as she did skippe—
> Thevyn it would, lo, and eke her chaunce was so—
> At the threshold her sely fote did trippe,
> And ere she myght recover it again
> The traytor Catt had caught her by the hippe

And made her there against her will remain,
That had forgotten her poure suretie and rest
For semyng welth wherin she thought to rayne.

Yet even if it is true that Wyatt has succeeded in writing in a more
fluid narrative style thanks to his drawing on Chaucer, it is equally
true that Wyatt here has been indulging in a good deal of archaic
borrowing. This is not the way to succeed in what I have called the
first attempt to be modern since Chaucer's. Wyatt's success must not
be measured by the number of his borrowings from Chaucer, but
by the degree to which we can apply to Wyatt the characteristic
account of Chaucer's genius: for there is all the difference in the
world between having a taste for Chaucer and doing for one's time
something like what Chaucer did for his.

At the close of this chapter I shall consider in what ways Wyatt
differs from Chaucer. In the meantime it is striking to note the
applicability to Wyatt—if we ignore the question of scale—of the
terms used, for instance, by Mr Speirs in his book on Chaucer, in
describing what Chaucer did for his time. Of particular interest here
are the phrases Mr Speirs used to establish the relation between
Chaucer's civilised simplicity—the sophisticated element—and his
colloquial strength—the popular element. 'Chaucer's English is unmistakably the English of cultivated people; it is, as unmistakably
rooted in the speech of an agricultural folk.' This speech Mr Speirs
characterises as 'concrete, figurative, proverbial'. Of closer application is the following remark on the function of translation in
Chaucer: 'Chaucer, as the development of his poetry shows, became
consciously an English poet—consciously a master of English—
through his work of translating, paraphrasing, and adapting from
other European languages (French, Italian and Latin)'. Mr Speirs
admirably insists that it was thanks to his English language that
Chaucer was able to draw on and assimilate what the other languages
had to offer.

Another remark by Mr Speirs in his *Chaucer the Maker* will serve
to introduce my last example of Wyatt's translations. 'The Court
itself must have been a more sophisticated kind of small town community and the talk there a cultivated version of small-town gossip;
we seem, in listening to Chaucer's poetry, to hear that talk organized
into a poetic art that is the nearest thing to dramatic art.' Wyatt's
third epistle seems to me to mark his nearest approach to drama and
the extreme point reached by his art. Upon our judgement of this
epistle will depend our right to speak of Wyatt's 'untimely' death

as a poet, of his anticipation of Donne, and of his fundamentally mediaeval attitude.

Horace in the fifth *sermo* of his second book was writing in a traditional comic mode: burlesque of epic situations. He brings on the stage a mock continuation of a solemn episode in the *Odyssey*, where the hero calls Tiresias from the dead to predict his future. Ulysses, having heard that he is going to be in reduced circumstances when he gets home, asks the prophet how he can best restore his finances. The humour of the piece consists in 'ragging' the epic tone and in putting into Tiresias' mouth an extremely knowing and cynical account of the quickest way of making money in contemporary Rome, which was to get one's name put down in the will of a rich old man or woman. Against this Ulysses makes merely formal protests: Horace's tone is easy and morally neutral.

For Wyatt the question was urgent, a genuine problem, and one that could only be handled with self-regarding irony. Although Wyatt in this epistle is nominally addressing his fellow-ambassador and boon companion, the poet Sir Francis Bryan, the 'vicar of Hell' as he was known to Henry and Cromwell, and ironically advising *him* how to get rich quick, it is worth noting that, as set out above on p. 204, Wyatt uses to him language that in 1541 he applied with equal heat to his own case. Wyatt, too, was notoriously careless with money, if not a spendthrift, and in money troubles all his life. His protector, Cromwell, wrote to him on Jan. 19th, 1539, 'I thinke your gentil franck hert doth moche empovrishe you: whan ye have money ye are content to departe with it and lende it . . .'—and this because Wyatt had lent money to Sir Francis Bryan!

The personal urgency behind and expressed in this epistle makes it the most fully contemporary of Wyatt's poems and the most dramatic. Yet it is constructed on a traditional scheme, as an illustration of a proverb:

> A spending hand that alway powreth owte
> Had nede to have a bringer in as fast,
> And on the stone that still doeth tourne abowte
> There groweth no mosse: these proverbes yet do last.
> Reason hath set theim in so sure a place
> That lenght of yeres their force can never wast.

To show to what extent Wyatt is now master of his metre and the metre helps his speech and gives it a higher charge than could be obtained in prose, we may consider the following passage, which is a recreation and transposition into contemporary England of:

> *scortator erit: caue te roget: ultro*
> *Penelopam facilis potiori trade.*

231

(Suppose your man is given to whoring: don't wait
until he suggest it, but make it easy for him by
getting in first with the offer of your chaste, devoted
wife—since he's your better.)

'In this also se that thow be not Idell:
   Thy nece, thy cosyn, thy sister[1] or thy doghter,
   If she be faire, if handsom be her mydell,
Yf thy better hath for her love besoght her,
   Avaunce his cause and he shall help thy nede.
   It is but love: turne it to a lawghter.
But ware, I say, so gold the helpe and spede,
   That in this case thow be not so vnwise
   As Pandare was in such a like dede:
Ffor he, the ffooll, of conscience was so nyse
   That he no gayne would have for all his payne.
   Be next thy self, for frendshipp beres no prise.
Laughst thow at me? Why, do I speke in vayne?'
'No, not at the, but at thy thrifty gest.

   Wouldest thow I should for any losse or gayne
Chaunge that for gold that I have tan for best
   Next godly thinges, to have an honest name?
   Should I leve that, then take me for a best!'
'Nay then, farewell!'

Bryan's rejoinder is performing by poetic means what we do when
we rise to our·full height and throw off an offensive insinuation.
After working up to the climax of 'honest name' the following line
is a dramatic gesture of spurning.

It is pleasant to record the enthusiasm for these poems of Wyatt's
first editor, the Rev. G. F. Nott:

'The fate which has awaited Wyatt's Satires is somewhat remarkable, and deserves to be noticed. They are unquestionably his
happiest and most finished productions. They may be ranked among
the best satires in our language; and yet they never seem to have
obtained either admirers or imitators: at least I do not recollect that
any of our early writers have spoken of them in particular with
commendation. This, I apprehend, may be easily accounted for.
Wyatt had outstripped, as it were, his times.'

As for outstripping his times, there is no—or at least I know of

---

[1] Wyatt may have been thinking of Ann Boleyn or his own sister-in-law here:
cf. L. & P. XVII, App. B, p. 717, entry 6 (Huyet), 9, Feb. 1542: Chapuys to
Charles V: 'She to whom, for the time, he (Henry) showed most favour and
affection was the sister of Lord Coban and of the wife whom Mr Huyet repudiated
for adultery.'

none—parallel use of language in the poems written by Wyatt's contemporaries or immediate successors. It is tempting to consider this poem as an anticipation of Donne, at least to the extent of claiming that Wyatt was doing with the language of his day something strikingly similar to what Donne did with the language of his. But though this and the other parallels I have suggested are ways of indicating what I take to be Wyatt's function in the tradition of English poetry, they can, and should, be used to define the limitations as well as to secure proper recognition of Wyatt's genius.

For the question remains: how fine are the poems I have selected for consideration? 'Intentions' do not exist for the critic apart from 'realizations'. It is one thing to claim to be appreciating Wyatt more soundly by restating in modern terminology the grounds of admiration felt by Wyatt's contemporaries. It is another thing to claim to be revaluing the poetry. Anxious as I am to establish a proper taste for this group of poems, I think it would be doing Wyatt a disservice to claim too much for them. It is time, therefore, to mention the great differences between Wyatt and Chaucer: they may all be summed up in the differences in their relation to society, to nature and to the universe.

If Chaucer's unfinished 'œuvre' could provoke the exclamation, 'Here is God's plenty!', Wyatt's 'œuvre'—if we may use the word—strikes me as thin, and not only in bulk. Indeed, to define this adjective is to become conscious of the qualities Wyatt does not exhibit in his verse. If Wyatt's poetical substance is thin, it is not (with the exceptions mentioned in this essay) dilute. Nor is it thin for want of experience: at least, Wyatt saw as much of the world, we may presume, as Chaucer, and he probably understood his world as well. But he was not imaginatively one with his world as Chaucer was. Great areas of his known experience were not brought to bear on the experiences he worked up into poetry.

Nor can we suppose that the poetry is thin because the personality was thin. We know that Wyatt impressed his contemporaries as a 'personality' even more than as a poet. Yet here we may take a phrase from Surrey's tribute to that personality, where he said that Wyatt's

> persing loke did represent a mynde
> With vertue fraught, reposed, voyd of gyle . . .

if it provokes the judgement that Wyatt belongs with those poets who start from personality and achieve greatness by escaping into impersonality, but whose drama never wholly frees itself from self-dramatisation.

233

But it is not only that Wyatt found no way to focus his whole personality in his poetry: he did not draw on the extra-personal resources that Chaucer knew how to tap. Indeed, if we had to describe Wyatt's society solely from what is implied in his poetry, we might well have argued that the distinctive gifts of mediaeval civilisation had been lost in the early sixteenth century. Wyatt had no roots in the regions from which the best popular poems drew their virtues. His strength is in a limiting sense, Protestant. Wyatt could send out currents of energy to vivify the concepts that rally the individual to his social tasks: he had positive convictions to set against contemporary corruptions—what he called

> vertue as it goeth now a dayes—

convictions grounded on a faith robust enough to inspire the best parts of his Psalms: but he has no rich and glowing contact with the conception of a divinely sanctioned order of society, such as can be found in Erasmus, More, and . . . Shakespeare.

This thinness is also a sign of Wyatt's isolation. 'Chaucer is no isolated genius', Mr Speirs remarked, 'there were other cultivated poets among his contemporaries.' We know the names of some of Wyatt's poetical contemporaries: it may well be that good verse has perished. It would, for example, be interesting to learn whether Drayton had read poems by Bryan not in Tottel's *Songes and Sonettes* when he wrote:

> And sweet-tongu'd *Bryon* (whom the Muses kept
> And in his cradle rockt him whilst he slept)
> In sacred verses (so diuinely pend)
> Vpon thy praises euer shall attend.

But, judging by all that is extant, Wyatt appears to be a case of Isolated Superiority. I choose the phrase deliberately to recall Mr Eliot's tribute to Ezra Pound, for Wyatt's poems stand out in *Songes and Sonettes* very much as Pound's would in an anthology of Imagism. Wyatt had to do too much for himself: consequently he had to do too much from himself. Wyatt focussed the consciousness of his age in terms of his own consciousness in a way that aligns him with Donne rather than with Chaucer or Shakespeare.

If this quality makes the poetry thin, it also confers a rare distinction. We may test this by returning to the first translation chosen in this chapter and putting it to the further test of comparison with a minor Augustan and a major seventeenth-century poet:

> Whom worldly Luxury and Pomps allure,
> They tread on Ice, and find no Footing sure.

234

> Place me, ye Pow'rs! in some obscure Retreat,
> O! keep me innocent, make others great:
> In quiet Shades, content with rural Sports,
> Give me a Life remote from guilty Courts,
> Where free from Hopes or Fears, in humble Ease
> Unheard of, I may live and die in Peace.
> Happy the Man who thus retir'd from Sight,
> Studies himself and seeks no other Light;
> But most unhappy he, who sits on high,
> Expos'd to ev'ry Tongue and ev'ry Eye;
> Whose Follies blaz'd about, to all are known,
> But are a Secret to himself alone:
> Worse is an evil Fame, much worse than none.

That was taken from *The Genuine Works in Verse and Prose* of the Right Honourable George Granville, Lord Lansdowne.

> Climb at *Court* for me that will
> Tottering favors Pinacle;
> All I seek is to lye still.
> Settled in some secret Nest
> In calm Leisure let me rest;
> And far of the publick Stage
> Pass away my silent Age.
> Thus when without noise, unknown,
> I have liv'd out all my span,
> I shall dye, without a groan,
> An old honest Country man.
> Who expos'd to others Ey's,
> Into his own Heart ne'r pry's,
> Death to him's a Strange surprise.

If Wyatt's version can stand up to comparison with Marvell's, is it not because its distinctive qualities were obtained by giving the Latin a personal reference, by the peculiar form I have tried to sketch of Wyatt's 'translation'?

ISOLATED SUPERIORITY
The Relation of Surrey
to Wyatt

THAT Surrey 'comes in' merely as a foil to Wyatt, as a supplementary demonstration of Wyatt's isolated superiority, is a verdict that will astonish nobody to-day, though fifty years ago the 'voice of history' seemed to have spoken finally in giving the preference to Surrey as *the* early Tudor poet with some condescending mention of Wyatt as a precursor. This voice, however, was little more than an echo of the opinions of critics *circa* 1580, at a time when Surrey himself had ceased to matter and Wyatt had been forgotten. It has not and never had the authority that comes from vital concern: no life-decisions were involved in the relative placing of the two poets.

The claim, however, that Surrey stood in a significant relation to Wyatt goes back to Leland, who no doubt thought that he was saying something pleasing to Surrey in proclaiming in his *Naeniae* (1542) that Wyatt had thought of the younger poet as his heir. That Wyatt meant *something* to Surrey is clear from the comparative success of Surrey's epitaph beginning *Wyat resteth here.* The reader who comes upon this poem fresh from reading, say, Carew's elegy on

Donne, may find it a poor, all-too-formal tribute. But comparison with a poem written to a similar formula, Raleigh's epitaph 'vpon the right Honorable sir Philip Sidney knight', enforces the opinion that Surrey's is the better poem and indeed the best he wrote. On the other hand, a comparison of Surrey's and Wyatt's extant poems yields an almost totally negative result: Surrey nowhere seems to have penetrated Wyatt's poetical intentions or to have carried on (much less extended) his practice. We are thus faced with a paradox: the literary evidence seems to point to the existence of a bond between the poets but refutes the claim that Surrey was Wyatt's literary heir. The exact nature of this bond has never, to my knowledge, been properly clarified. The explanation I have to offer is a concern of history rather than part of a significant literary history. I shall therefore defer it until I have surveyed the facts which make it unnecessary to give prolonged attention to the poems of Surrey and shall then attempt to convert the historical relation between Wyatt and Surrey into a supporting comment to the conclusions reached in the previous chapter.

We have no poems of Surrey to set alongside the traditional short-line lyrics which figure so prominently in the Devonshire MS. The scarcity of contemporary poetry warns us against a hasty conclusion that this absence implies a *critical* decision on Surrey's part. It may be that Wyatt's conventional court poems belong to the 'twenties rather than to the 'thirties and that by the time Surrey was old enough to take part in the social life of the court, he was no longer expected to provide the ladies with complaints, etc., in the moribund mediaeval style. The courtly love poems of Surrey are rather in the mode of the poem beginning *For want of will*, which Tottel's editors attributed to Wyatt. This poem is a representative of a number of poems which may or may not have been written by Wyatt. They are so lacking in character that nothing else attaches them to Wyatt's name than their preservation in collections containing poems undoubtedly written by Wyatt. The three chief characteristics of this poem are commonplace sentiments, smooth metre and the lack of any commanding idiom. It is a poem without obvious antecedents, in that the phrases are *not* the time-honoured clichés, but its novelties do not arise from any grip on the world or the word: in fact, parts are written in no recognised language:

> I dye, though not incontinent,
> By processe, yet consumingly . . .

it blunders about a meaning, as if it were a translation made by a foreigner, some latter-day Charles d'Orléans.

The poem where Surrey comes closest to this mode is the one beginning *As ofte as I behold,* a poem which was acceptable to the Elizabethans and must have circulated in a manuscript version alongside the printed text of Tottel. It will also serve as a notable instance of the misuse and abuse of Petrarch and of the continuation of the worst faults of Wyatt. The points are lifted from various sonnets and other poems of Petrarch, but, so abstracted and re-assembled, they refuse to cohere or suggest a limiting form. A poem like this could go on for ever or at least until the whole Petrarchan stock were exhausted. It might have been put together by a committee, each member contributing a borrowed comparison: 'as flame dothe quenche', 'like as the fle', 'as cruell waues', 'as he that beares flame', 'and as the spyder', etc. To illustrate at one stroke the coarsening of Petrarch, the imprecision of the language and the debt to Wyatt, let me instance the following stanza:

> Like as the flee that seethe the flame
> And thinks to plaie her in the fier,
> That found her woe and sowght her game,
> Whose grief did growe by her desire.

How blunted the original point has become we may see by turning up the original (*No. 19 in vita*):

> Et altri, col desio folle che spera
> Gioir forse nel foco perché splende,
> Provan l'altra vertú, quella ch'incende.

In fact, it is possible that Surrey derived the thought from Wyatt's translation rather than from Petrarch:

> Other reioyse that se the fyer bright
> And wene to play in it as they pretend,
> And fynde the contrary of it[1] that they intend. . . .

This suggestion is strengthened by a suspicion that Surrey had only a very rough-and-ready grasp of Italian. The truth, however, may be that Surrey felt no obligation to translate strictly or that his deviations were instances of wilful play, such as Ezra Pound has indulged in. For example, if Surrey had before him

> Amor mi guida e scorge

he may very well have known that 'scourge' was not the true equivalent and have thought that 'guides and points out the way' was too tautologous, and therefore have written

> Blynde Cupide dyd me whipp & guyde . . .

---

[1] Possibly 'that'.

Similarly, he may have known that *fallire* did not mean 'fall' when with

> io fallo e veggio il mio fallire

before him, he wrote

> I fall and see my none decaye.

Nevertheless, these, and other examples arouse suspicion.

Surrey's sonnets are so few and so different that it is impossible to see any definite promise. There are occasional lines with a cadence which seems to look forward to Shakespeare, such as,

> For my swete thoughts sometyme do pleasure bring.

Yet, in the one instance where Surrey translates a sonnet of Petrarch attempted by Wyatt, he strikes me as feeble and unpromising. He seems to have chosen to write the sonnet beginning *Set me whereas* for the reason Puttenham gave: 'Then haue ye a figure very meete for Orators or eloquent perswaders such as our maker or Poet must in some cases shew him selfe to be',[1] yet he and Puttenham fail to appreciate the *finesse* of this artifice, which, as we can see by going back to Petrarch's original, the twenty-second Ode of Horace's First Book, depends on the contrast between the vast panorama and the pointed, precise close:

> dulce ridentem Lalagen amabo
> dulce loquentem.

The sonnet beginning *The soote season* shows us Surrey rejecting the classical allusions of Petrarch for the traditional schema and phraseology of 'Nou sprinkes the sprai' or 'Bytuene mersh & aueril' or 'Lenten ys come'. Yet if Surrey was consciously linked with this non-Chaucerian tradition, he felt the link, as it were, through Chaucer, as we may see by looking up the context in *The Parliament of Fowls* of the line

> The swalwe, mortherere of the foules smale.

This relation, however, does not give Surrey's feeling any profundity. The items in the poem do not coalesce, nor is there any poignancy in the personal reflection. It is an alarming symptom of incapacity to find in the small number of Surrey's poems so many instances of verbal repetition, such as the variations on the phrase,

> With grene hath clad the hill.

A more alarming sign of incapacity is Surrey's resort to what is known as Poulter's measure as a hold-all for any kind of content.

[1] *The Arte of English Poesie*, p. 185.

Here, alas, the model was Wyatt, as we can see by comparing two translations from Petrarch, Wyatt's *So feble is the thred* and Surrey's *Such wayward wais hath loue*. The point may be made by saying that Surrey derives from Wyatt's first thoughts before he had begun to correct the infernal jog-trot of the metre. We find the same padding and prolixity, such as the expansion of

> So com' Amor saetta

to

> He cawseth hertes to rage with golden burninge darte.

The measure leads Surrey away from the language of passion into an artifice that makes only for banality and monotony. We occasionally find Surrey once again reading his Petrarch through Wyatt. The line

> The hammer of the restles forge I knowe eke how yt wurkes

seems to have only a faint connection with Petrarch's lines on the lover's inability to sleep and to have been derived from Wyatt:

> Suche hammers worke within my hed
> That sounde nought els vnto my eris
> But faste at borde and wake abed. . . .

lines which Surrey worked up into a stanza of his epitaph on Wyatt.

There is no need to push the enquiry further into this department of Surrey's work, for he is clearly not a translator in the sense I have tried to define. If we pursue the relationship of Wyatt and Surrey into the further departments of Wyatt's translation and seek to compare their religious poems, there does not at first sight appear to be a more significant connection than has been discovered so far. The critics have not expressed surprise that the Catholic Surrey should have laid so much stress in the poems he wrote on the Protestant Wyatt's death on Wyatt as a religious example and inspiration, or that Surrey should have written a dedicatory poem for Wyatt's Psalms. So sure, for example, was F. M. Padelford that there was no religious heritage passing from Wyatt to Surrey that in his edition of Surrey's poems he could write:

'Surrey as a matter of course shared in that opposition to the protestant wing of the Church which was consistently maintained by the older families. Protestantism was perforce associated in their minds with the pushing middle class whom the Tudors were constantly encouraging at the expense of a long-established nobility.

However little any early religious training may have shown in the conduct of the lad, it was grandly vindicated in the closing days of his life when, for solace in the dark hours, he made translations from the Psalms that breathe the whole spirit of Christian and Catholic faith.'

The discovery that in his versions of the Psalms—with the exception of Psalm 8—and in his *Ecclesiastes* Surrey was working from the same edition of the *Enchiridion Psalmorum* that Wyatt used does not at first sight compel a reversal of this judgement. It does, however, enable us to do one thing previously impossible. We can now see in what spirit Surrey was translating from Campensis, and since he keeps consistently close to the general sense of the Latin, we are bound to find significant the passages where Surrey uncharacteristically throws his original overboard and substitutes something of his own. One such departure can be found where Surrey is rendering the last verse of Chapter IV and the first verse of Chapter V of *Ecclesiastes* (the first two verses of the fifth chapter in the Authorised Version). Here, first, is the passage in the English version of Campensis, in the edition of 1535:

17. Take hede diligently what is to be done when thou shalt enter into the house of god: that is to saye, that thou prayest, and vnderstonde thou this thinge that, whom thou prayest vnto, hym to be present and here al thinges. Beware therefore lest thou makest many wordes wyth him after the maner of foles, all whose thynges that they do ar vnto god not accepte.

The .v. Chapiter.

Be not ouer hasty of tongue when thou shalt praie vnto god nether let not thy herte be to swifte in powering forth wordys in the syght of God: for god is in heuen, from whence he seeth all thy thingis which lyuest in the erthe; wherfore vse thou but fewe wordes before him.

Surrey clearly owes nothing either to Campensis or the Vulgate:

In humble sprite is set the temple of the Lord
   where if thou enter look thy mouth and conscience may accord:
whose church is built of love and decked with hot desire
   and simple faith the yolden host His mercy doth require:
where perfectly for aye He in His word doth rest
   with gentle ear to hear thy suit and grant to thy request.
In boast of outward works He taketh no delight
   nor waste of words: such sacrifice unsavoureth in His sight.

When that repentant tears hath cleansed clear from ill
  the charged breast, and grace hath wrought therein a mending will,
with bold demands *then* may His mercy well assail
  the speech man sayeth, without the which request may none prevail.
More shall thy penitent sighs His endless mercy please
  than their importune suits which dream that *words* God's wrath
    appease,
for heart contrite of fault is gladsome recompence
  and prayer fruit of faith whereby God doth with sin dispense.

It will not be immediately clear to the modern reader that Surrey is here using the language of Tyndale and his followers, and that the doctrine of this passage would have smelt of heresy at the time when it was written, nor that, where this language seems purely Biblical or reminiscent of St. Augustine, the texts alluded to were slogans on the Protestant side. As it is, one example out of many must serve to indicate the relation between the verse and Protestant argument. Tyndale argued from Psalm 51 that David was also a believer in *sola fide*:

'And afterward he knowlegeth that God delyteth not in sacrifices for synnes, but that a troubled spirite and a broken herte is that whych god requireth. And when the peace was made, he prayeth boldly and familiarly to god, that he wold be good to Sion, and Jerusalem, and sayth that then last of all when god hath forgeuen us of mercy and hath done vs good for our euell, we shall offer sacrifice of thankes to him agayne.' [1]

However, I shall not substantiate the case here, for I am more concerned to argue that, whatever his debt to Tyndale and others, Surrey wrote this passage because of Wyatt and could not have written it without Wyatt. I do not mean merely that Surrey had Wyatt's Psalms before him, but that he had in mind what I have called the dramatic core of Wyatt's conception of the process of repentance, the two passages quoted on pages 217–18. Thus Surrey may be adduced to support the interpretation there offered of the significance of Wyatt's Psalms. Any doubts that Surrey was impressed by these central passages will be settled by examining another departure from Campensis a few lines further down, where Surrey by quoting a line from Wyatt makes the connection clear:

With feigned works and oaths contract with God no guile:
  Such craft returns to thine own harm and doth thyself defile.
And though the mist of sin persuade such error light,

[1] *An answere*, etc., f. C. xxvij recto.

> Thereby yet are thy outward works all damned in His sight.
> As sundry broken dreams us diversely abuse,
> So are his errors manifold that many words doth use.
> With humble secret plaint, few words of hot affect
> Honour thy Lord: allowance vain of void desert neglect.

If we now enquire into the consequences of this discovery, and ask how radical a change in our picture of Surrey it forces us to make, it may appear something of an anti-climax to begin by replying that it now seems likely that the commentators down to Professor C. S. Lewis have been mistaken in their reading of the poem beginning *London hast thow*. Misled by some amusing, and indeed piquant, police-court revelations from the State Papers, the critics have supposed that here we have an early instance of the phenomenon once beloved of Evelyn Waugh—drunken aristocracy baying for broken glass—and that the poem is a 'waggish satire' on the would-be reformers. These critics neglected to make anything of the fact that according to this police-court evidence Surrey was a familiar of young Wyatt and George Blage, both men, to say the least of it, closer to Luther and Zwingli than to the religion of their King. More serious was their neglect of the import of their observation that Surrey's poem could not have been organised without a borrowing from Petrarch's four anti-papal sonnets. For these sonnets were taken up and reinterpreted by the reformers, as we may see from a virulent pamphlet in the British Museum, the *Stanze del Berna con tre sonetti del Petrarca*, and from the biased translation into English of these three sonnets in one of the manuscripts in which Surrey's religious poems are found (MSS. Add. 36529).

A more conclusive argument against the current reading of the poem is that if Surrey were mocking the Protestants in this poem he must have been mocking his own beliefs expounded solemnly in his Biblical paraphrases. One instance must suffice: in the third chapter of his *Ecclesiastes* Surrey abandons Campensis and substitutes the following lines:

> Lo thus his carfull skourge dothe stele on vs vnware
> which when the fleshe hath clene forgott, he dothe againe repayre.
> When J in this uaine serch had wanderyd fore my witt,
> J saw a royall throne wheras that iustice should haue sitt,
> Jn stede of whom J saw with fyerce and crewell mode
> wher wrong was set, that blody beast that drounke the giltles blode.
> Then thought J thus: one day the lord shall sitt in dome
> to vewe his flock and chose the pure: the spotted haue no rome:
> Yet be suche skourges sent that eache agreuid mynde,
> lyke the brute beasts that swell in rage and fury by ther kynd,
> his erroure may confesse. . . .

Here Surrey is stating solemnly what his commentators thought he was saying waggishly in his poem to London:

> A fygure of the lordes behest
> whose scourge for synn the screptures shew
> that as the fearfull thonder clapp
> by soddayne flame at hand we knowe
> of peoble stone the sowndles rapp
> the dreadfull plage might mak the se
> of goddes wrath . . .
> Jn lothsome vyce eche dronken wight
> to styrr to godd this was my mynd. . . .

Now, as far as I know, it has not been noticed that these lines of *Ecclesiastes* were in the hands of a Protestant martyr in 1546, who, while awaiting execution wrote a ballad of which the following is part:

> Not oft vse I to wryght
>   In prose nor yet in ryme,
> Yet wyll I shewe one syght,
>   That I sawe in my tyme.
> I sawe a ryall trone,
>   Where Justyce shuld haue sytt,
> But in her stede was one,
>   Of modye cruell wytt.
> Absorpt was ryghtwysenesse,
>   As of the ragynge floude,
> Sathan in hys excesse,
>   Sucte vp the gyltelesse bloude.
> Then thought I, Jesus lorde,
>   Whan thu shalt iuge vs all,
> Harde is it to recorde,
>   On these men what wyll fall.[1]

As this can hardly be a coincidence, I take it as highly probable that Surrey's *Ecclesiastes* came into Protestant hands and was read with sympathetic interest. (We know that Archbishop Parker took a copy with him when he went into exile during the reign of Mary.) I conjecture that the link between Surrey and Anne Askew was the Denny to whom Surrey dedicated one of his paraphrases of the Psalms.

An objection may here be made that if Surrey were not joking in his poem to London, he must have been both singularly lacking in humour and writing in execrable taste in claiming to impersonate

---

[1] From 'The Balade whych Anne Askewe made and sange when she was in Newgate', printed in Bale's *The lattre examinacion of Anne Askewe* (1547) ff. 63v. and 64r.

the Divine Avenger. Yet we find something similar in the poem beginning *Eache beast*. I am therefore inclined to think that just as this Lion and Wolf poem shows us Surrey trying to put a noble face on a discreditable occurrence, so the London poem may have been an attempt to present in a wholly favourable light what may in fact have been a reprehensible, irresponsible piece of hooliganism, or at best, a pathetically silly and impotent outburst of misguided religious zeal.

This latter reproach may have been made to Surrey by George Blage. At any rate Surrey's paraphrase of Psalm 73 reads like the converse of the London poem. Just as the latter represents a mood of overwhelming confidence and self-assertion, so the former is an exaggerated expression of deflation—the wind has gone out of his sails—and depression. The apology to Blage reads remarkably like parts of the Lion and Wolf poem. The paraphrase of Psalm 73 was clearly being used by Surrey as a means of relieving his feelings. Whether or not in the London escapade the attack on Sir Richard Gresham's windows had been deliberate, Surrey's religious poems reveal as one of their main themes an almost hysterical hatred of the vices of the money-getters. In the poem to London Surrey had written:

> Thy windows had done me no spite
> But proud people that dread no fall
> Clothed with falsehood and unright.

and in the Psalm he wrote:

> As garments clothe the naked man thus are they clad in vice.

If we look at all the places in these religious poems where Surrey abandons Campensis, we find that his most passionate outbursts are reserved for the injustice done to the *elect* and to himself as one of them. Surrey comes nearest to Wyatt in harmonising translating with the expression of personal needs in his version of Psalm 88, where the Protestant note is clearest. Yet though the evidence puts it beyond doubt that here we have the true historic bond between Wyatt and Surrey, the bond is not of poetic interest. Surrey's relation to Wyatt is poetically the same as we observed in the other poems. Where Surrey derives from Wyatt he does so in the following mode. The reader will find it hard to say which of these passages is by Wyatt and which by Surrey:

> When that the restles sonne westwarde his course hathe ronne
> Towards the east he hasts as fast to ryse where he begonne . . .

> Westward the sonne from owt thest skant doth shew his lyght

When in the west he hyds him straite with in the darke of nyght
  And rons as fast wher he began his path a wrye
From est to west from west to thest so dothe his jornei ly . . .

The former is from Surrey's *Ecclesiastes*, the latter from Wyatt's
So feble is the threde.

How profound an error the choice of this metre was and how
destructive of all dignity of movement and tone we can see by a
cruel comparison with Coverdale. It is indeed striking that Surrey's
verse should be such a failure, where Coverdale's prose was so great
a success. To explore the question fully, a second essay 'Humanism
and Prose in the Early Tudor Period' would be needed. Nevertheless
when we think of the two media competing for the contemporary
reader's interest, it makes the success of Tyndale and Coverdale
more inexplicable than ever, for the general prose of this period is
clumsy and inelegant, as we may see from this snippet of the translation of Campensis:

'Of al thyngis there is a change nether is there any thinge stable
vnder the sonne. They that ar nowe begotten shall dye in tyme to
come, the thingis nowe planted shall at a nother tyme be plucked
vp agene. Now we cut of which sometime we labored that they
shulde growe: nowe we destroye that thinge which some tyme we
buylded. . . .'

Surrey can overmatch this:

    Like to the steerless boat that swerves with every wind,
  The slipper top of worldly wealth by cruel proof I find.
    Scarce hath the seed whereof that Nature formeth man
  Received life, when Death him yields to earth where he began.
    The grafted plants with pain whereof we hoped fruit
  To root them up with blossoms spread then is our chief pursuit.
    That erst we reared up, we undermine again. . . .

But we move into another dimension with Coverdale:

'Euery thinge hath a tyme, yee all that is vnder the heauen, hath
is conuenient season. There is a tyme to be borne, and a tyme to
dye. There is a tyme to plante, and a tyme to plucke vp the thing
that is planted: a tyme to slaye, and a tyme to make whole. . . .'

The contrast between Wyatt and Surrey is therefore extreme
wherever Wyatt strikes the characteristic note of the best parts of his

Psalms. Here is a fair sample, since both poets are at their best and are developing the same topic: *the dead praise not the Lord*:

> Wherefore dost Thou forbear in the defence of Thine
> To shew such tokens of Thy power in sight of Adam's line
> Wherby each feeble heart with faith might so be fed
> That in the mouth of Thy elect Thy mercies might be spread?
> The flesh that feedeth worms cannot Thy love declare,
> Nor such set forth Thy faith as dwell in the land of despair.
> In blind endured hearts light of Thy lively name
> Cannot appear, as cannot judge the brightness of the same,
> Nor blasted may Thy name be by the mouth of those
> Whom Death hath shut in silence so as they may not disclose.
> The lively voice of them that in Thy word delight
> Must be the trump that must resound the glory of Thy might.

Over against this we may set the lines from Wyatt's First Penitential Psalm beginning

> But Thou, O Lord, how long after this sort
> Forbearest Thou to see my misery?

quoted in the previous chapter. But to complete the parallel the quotation must be continued from

> Here hath Thy mercy matter for the nonce,
> For if Thy rightwise hand, that is so just,
> Suffer no sin or strike with damnation,
> Thy infinite mercy want needs it must
> Subject matter for his operation:
> For that in death there is no memory
> Among the damned, nor yet no mention
> Of Thy great name, ground of all glory.
> Then if I die, and go whereas I fear
> To think thereon, how shall Thy great mercy
> Sound in my mouth unto the world's ear?
> For *there* is none that can Thee laud and love,
> For that Thou nilt no love among them there . . .

In the great tradition of English poetry this may seem, and is, meagre and clumsy, but at least, unlike the passage from Surrey, it is *in* the tradition, if at the extreme edge. When we come to

> Then if I die, and go whereas I fear
> To think thereon

and recall Claudio's

> Ay, but to die, and go we know not where

we recognise both the immense distance that separates them and,

however distant, a genuine kinship of accent. And if we allow Surrey
to continue:

> Wherefore I shall not cease in chief of my distress
> To call on Thee till that the sleep my wearied limbs oppress,
> And in the morning eke when that the sleep is fled
> With floods of salt repentant tears to wash my restless bed

and place this alongside the corresponding passage in Wyatt's First
Psalm:

> How oft have I called up with diligence
> This slothful flesh long afore the day
> For to confess his fault and negligence,
> That to the down, for aught that I could say,
> Hath still returned to shroud itself from cold:
> Whereby it suffers now for such delay.
> By nightly plaints, instead of pleasures old,
> I wash my bed with tears continual
> To dull my sight that it be never bold
> To stir my heart again to such a fall . . .

while we see a certain affinity, we also become aware of sufficient
difference between Wyatt and Surrey to make it proper to stress in
any account of the beginning of modern verse the isolation of Wyatt
among his contemporaries.

While the relation between Wyatt and Surrey was close enough to
be called a community of ideas on religious matters, Surrey does not
stand in the line of development of Wyatt's best verse. There remains
the further argument to be considered that Surrey nevertheless
deserves prominence in that he is in the line of development of the
best Humanist thinking. That, as a translator of *secular* Latin verse,
Surrey is an important figure in early Tudor humanism, and, in
particular, that as the 'father of English blank verse' he deserves
to be approached with respect, are propositions that come to us
almost with the force of tradition. Yet it is remarkable that a dis-
proportionately small degree of interest has been shown in what is
apparently so valuable. There is no reliable edition of Surrey's
translations and some of the very first questions of an unprejudiced
enquirer have still to be answered.

Here, then, is a case where scholarly work is required before a
critical judgement can be made, or rather, before the last touches
can be given to the irresistible critical judgement. For all the scholarship in the world could not affect the verdict that whatever these
translations are they are not poems. This proposition, though not
traditional, can be brought home by the old-fashioned method of

relevant comparison and contrast. It will, I suppose, be granted that
the following extract is at least poetry:

> The herde of hertes founden is anon
> With 'Hay! go bet! pryke thow! lat gon, lat gon!
> Why nyl the leoun comen, or the bere,
> That I myghte ones mete hym with this spere?'
> Thus sey these yonge folk, and up they kylle
> These bestes wilde, and han hem at here wille.
> Among al this to rumbelen gan the hevene:
> The thunder rored with a grisely stevene:
> Doun cam the reyn, with hayl and slet, so faste,
> With hevenes fyr, that it so sore agaste
> This noble queen, and also hire meyne,
> That ech of them was glad awey to fle.
> And shortly, from the tempest hire to save,
> She fledde hireself into a litel cave,
> And with hire wente this Eneas also.
>
> . . . .
>
> And here began the depe affeccioun
> Betwixe hem two: this was the firste morwe
> Of hire gladnesse, and gynning of hire sorwe.[1]

This, clearly, is *written*; a genuine recreation has occurred, and we
can read it for its own sake without reference to the originals from
which it is translated. It thus provides us with a touchstone when
we seek to establish what is meant by a translation that is poetry.
It also serves as a means of testing for poetry a passage clearly
written under its influence.

> Ane othir part, syne ȝondyr mycht thou se
> The herd of hartis with thar hedis hie,
> Ourspynnerand with swyft cours the plane vaill,
> The hepe of duste vpstowryng at thair taill,
> Fleand the hundis, levand the hie montanys.
> And Ascanyus, the child, amyd the planys,
> Joyus and blith hys startling steid to assay,
> Now makis his rynk ȝondir and now this way,
> Now prekis furth by thir, and now by thame:
> Langyng, amang faynt frayt beistis ontame,
> The fomy bair, doun from the hyllis hycht,
> Or the dun lyoun discend, rencontyr be mycht.
> In the meyn quhile, the heuynnys al about
> With fellon noys gan to rummyll and rowt.
> A bub of weddir followyt in the tayll,
> Thik schour of rayn myddillit ful of haill.
>
> . . . .

[1] Chaucer, *Legenda Didonis*, 1212–1231.

> This wes the formaste day of hir glaidnes,
> And first morrow of hir wofull distres.[1]

The second passage errs on the side of fulness as much as the first on the side of economy. But the hunting scene is vivid, full of varied life. The author was clearly concerned to make the reader *see* what Virgil was writing about. Compared with this second passage, the following is a clumsy effort:

> The hartes lykewyse, in troupes takyng theyr flyght,
> Raysing the dust, the mountayne fast forsake.
> The chyld, Iulus, blythe of hys swyft steede,
> Amyds the playne now pryckes by them, now thes:
> And to encounter wisheth oft in minde
> The fomyng bore instedd of ferefull beastes,
> Or lyon browne myght from the hyll discend.
> In the meane whyle the heauens gan romble sore
> In tayle wherof a myngled showre with hayle.
>
> . . . .
>
> Aye me! this was the formost daye of myrthe
> And of myshappe the fyrst occasion eke.

It is as if the author of this third passage had taken the words of the second and redistributed them on a mechanical principle of ten syllables to a line, regardless of word order or natural movement, or, occasionally, of sense. In the process all idiom has been eliminated and awkward novelties introduced in their place.

To the proposition that Surrey has produced an awkward version, whereas Douglas has made a poem, I would add that Surrey's version is made as much from Douglas as from Virgil. Surrey's debt to Douglas in the creation of pentameter lines is great. On the rare occasions when Surrey attempts more than chopped-up ten-syllable lengths and the verse becomes faintly memorable, we almost invariably find that the feeling behind the passage was supplied from Douglas:

> Before thie flyght a chylde had I conceyued
> Or sene a yong Aeneas in my courte
> To play vp and downe, that dyd present thy face,
> All vtterlie I coold not seme forsaken.

Here Surrey's word order corresponds to something, and the last line plays against the piled-up movement of the first three, so that we can imagine the words being spoken. The passage is, however, a pale version of Douglas:

> Bot, at the leist, tofor thi wayfleyng,
> Had I a child consavyt of thyne ofspryng,

---

[1] Gawin Douglas, *Twelf Bukis of Eneados*, *The Ferd Buke*, Cap. IV.

> Gif I had ony ʒong Eneas small
> Befor me forto play within my hall,
> Quhilk representit by symylitude thi face,
> Then semyt I nocht thus wys, allace! allace!
> Aluterly dissauyt nor dissolate.

Douglas, I take it, is here once again following *his* author:

> But let us speke of Eneas,
> How he betrayed hir, allas!
> And lefte hir ful unkyndely,
> So when she saw al utterly. . . .[1]

—and not only in verbal reminiscence. The impression of Virgil we gain from Douglas is more Chaucerian than modern. In following Douglas Surrey reveals that he has had no new perception of the Roman author. His Latin scholarship was elementary and in no sense the product of up-to-date humanist teaching. But what rules Surrey out as a Humanist is rather his inability to produce a poem of any sort when faced with his Virgil. He was not writing from the heart, but almost from the fingers.

The task of translation set Surrey back rather than drew out undeveloped poetic powers. After so many examples of too easy flow in the poulter's measure, it may seem unfair to complain that Surrey's translation of Virgil is too static. This failure to make the lines move, however, is not merely a question of skill in handling the 'straunge metre'. Surrey's *vocabulary* is itself a dead and dreary selection from the language. It is not quite fair to compare the poverty of his vocabulary with the riches of Douglas, but, taken with tact, a point can be made by observing how both deal with a passage expressive of movement. Surrey's translation runs:

> like as when the flame
> Lightes in the corne by drift of boisteous winde,
> Or the swift stream that driueth from the hill
> Rootes vp the feldes and presseth the ripe corne
> And plowed ground and ouer whelmes the groue,
> The silly herdman all astonnied standes
> From the hye rock while he doth here the sound.

When we place this alongside Douglas:

> Lyke quhen the fyre be fellon wyndis blast
> Is drevyn amyd the flat of cornys rank,
> Or quhen the burn on spait hurlys down the bank,
> Owder throu a watir brek, or spait of flude,
> Ryvand vp rede erd, as it war wod,
> Down dyngand cornys, all the pleuch labour atanys,

[1] Chaucer, *The House of Fame*, 293–296.

251

And dryvis on swyftly stokkis, treis and stanys:
The sylly hyrd, seand this grysly syght,
Set on a pynnakill of sum cragis hycht,
Al abasit, nocht knawand quhat this may meyn,
Wondris of the sovnd and ferly at he has seyn.

it is hard to resist the temptation to place Wyatt and Surrey in the opposite camps of Donne and Spenser or of Jonson the translator of Horace's *Art of Poetry* and Jonson the 'translator' of Catullus. In the light of what was to come in Milton and the so-called neo-classic writers of the eighteenth century who read their classics through Milton, we can hardly resist calling it a fateful decision to reject

And dryuis on swyftly stokkis, treis and stanys

as the English way of rendering *praecipitesque trahit siluas* in favour of the 'chaste diction'

and ouer whelmes the groue.

In any case, it is far more enlightening and explanatory of Surrey's translations to see them as a criticism of Douglas and his methods of translation, than to attempt to find in them Surrey's feelings towards the Classics, or, specifically, for the Virgilian hexameter.

Surrey is much more at home in his two translations from Roman poets on the topic of the golden mean. Here he stands in the broad tradition of those who assimilated from the Classics only what suited their moral preoccupations. Martial's description of the happy life[1] lent itself without much change to the contemporary love of pithy sayings and mottoes. Surrey, however, seems to have had his eye as much on his translations of *Ecclesiastes* as on Martial. Of the items of peculiar interest to Martial, such as *toga rara*, we shall look in vain for a trace in Surrey's translation. Horace's ode on the golden mean[2] is treated in a similar spirit, but this poem is more conveniently discussed along with the other translations in Tottel's Miscellany.

Before doing this, however, I should like to halt and take a glance at the general course of the argument. I have been attempting throughout to show how much of the essential literary history of the period can be extracted from a few, and very short, works. For the reader, anxious to know where this period 'comes in', what it has to offer in the pattern that makes up the English tradition, this exclusion of irrelevant matter, this concentration on the revealing moments, will, I hope, have been welcome. Now such a reader might suppose me to be arguing that for the study of this period, beside the little volume of More's *Lucubrationes*, all he needs is Tottel's Miscellany.

[1] *Ep.* X, 47.   [2] *Carm.* II, 10.

The fact is, however, that he needs only some pages in this anthology, the pages where the better poems of Wyatt are printed. There is no good reason for reviewing the rest of Tottel. It would be a case of *délectation morose* to dwell on the various ways in which Surrey was further diluted or Wyatt's 'lyrics' sewn together into 'complaints' of unconscionable humourlessness and monotony. One question, however, may rightly be put to the anthology: to what extent and in what spirit did the poets flourishing in and before 1550 continue the work of the times, that of transmuting the needed vitality from the Classics into vigorous native English? For the answer to this question will bring out the significance of the collection: that it marked a downward turn to sterility, and, though the first in time of the series of anthologies that became such a feature of the second half of the century, it is in fact the grave of Early Tudor poetry.

Tottel's anthology, however, must itself be treated with tact. It is not, nor was it intended to be, a representative collection of the verse of the 1550's. Fear of censorship was only one of the factors which limited its range. Consequently, if we pick on *Grimald*, who in the original collection comes next after Wyatt and Surrey, we must not assume that there were many Grimalds. He is significant for the present argument in that most of his verse is in fact translation. But his chief significance lies in his offering us a parallel to Leland— his contemporary who, writing in Latin, preferred contemporary Latin poetry to the classical. Grimald is in fact an *academic* poet, and his translations give us some insight into the place of the Latin scholars of the day in the development of our poetry.

Even Grimald cannot be treated with too sweeping a stroke: for, though most of his poems are translations from a contemporary Latin poet—the Protestant Beza—yet one of the most curious, a piece of blank verse, is a translation taken from a Latin poem by Gautier de Châtillon, who flourished in the twelfth century. The taste for horrific bloodshed combined with verbal tricks survived down to *Macbeth*, and in fact Grimald seems to have provided more than one phrase in the second scene of that play. The point for us, however, is that Grimald was translating into English in the spirit in which men wrote verse in Latin, i.e. he was writing what we may call *metrical prose*, e.g.

> But of the Macedonian cheftanes knights/ one, Meleager,
> could not bear this sight/ but ran vpon the sayd
> Egyptian renk/ and cut him in both kneez. Hee fell
> to ground/ wherewith a hole route came of souldiours
> stern/ and all in pieces hewed the silly seg.

Negative proof that these were the congenial sources for the academic poet may be found in Grimald's failure to make good use of the great Roman poets. One notable exception in Tottel—a translation of the opening lines of Lucretius' Second Book—was discussed in an earlier chapter. The versions of Horace's ode on *aurea mediocritas* do not constitute further exceptions, for they are so thoroughly assimilated to the mode of the other poems in Tottel on 'the mean estate' that they can hardly be said to have any classical substratum. They retain, however, one advantage from the original: a vestige of form. This is the chronic deficiency of the anthology, that everything goes on too long, nothing has a significant shape. In comparison with these, Surrey appears almost a modern. He has at least cast his poem in the form of an address to a contemporary—perhaps to the poet Wyatt's son. But Surrey is one with his age in converting the poem into a series of pithy maxims—the kind of thing gentlemen entered into their commonplace books.

EPILOGUE
The Humanist Heritage

The third requisite in our Poet, *or* Maker, *is* Imitation, *to bee able
to convert the substance, or Riches of another* Poet, *to his owne
use. To make choise of one excellent man above the rest, and so to
follow him, till he grow very* Hee: *or, so like him, as the Copie may
be mistaken for the Principall. Not, as a Creature, that swallowes,
what it takes in, crude, raw, or indigested; but, that feedes with an
Appetite, and hath a Stomacke to concoct, divide, and turne all
into nourishment. Not, to imitate servilely, as* Horace *saith, and
catch at vices, for vertue: but, to draw forth out of the best, and
choisest flowers, with the Bee, and turne all into Honey.* . . .

BEN JONSON, Timber

*Apes imitari pręcepit Seneca, (Epist. lxxxiv. 3–6) quas videmus
volitare per florea rura, & succos ad mellificandum idoneos quaerere.
Nos similiter, quae ex diuersa, seu multa vnius lectione congessimus,
separare debemus: deinde adhibita ingenij cura, & facultate in
vnum saporem varia illa libamenta confundere.* . . .

BUCHLER, Institutio Poetica, 1633.

*Amicissimo & meritissimo
   Ben: Ionson.
Quod arte ausus es hic tua,* POETA,
*Si auderent hominum Deique iuris
Consulti sequi aemularierque,
O omnes saperemus ad salutem.
His sed sunt ueteres araneosi,
Tam nemo ueterum est sequutor ut tu
Illos quos sequeris nouator audis.* . . .

JOHN DONNE

THE Tottel Miscellany may not be fully representative, but even if
we include in our survey all the contemporary verse extant in print
or in manuscript, we still do not find a single outstanding poem. It
is therefore clear that a period has come to an end, whether we mark

255

the limit at the death of Wyatt or at the death of Surrey. Humanism in poetry and prose, the wave of More and the wave of Wyatt, is in itself barely a ripple when we compare it with the later movement in the second half of the century. Nor can it be said that the great development during the lifetimes of Shakespeare and Donne is the latter end of the small beginnings in the first half of the century. Everything had virtually to be done all over again in poetry. The poets who owe anything to the verse of Tottel's anthology constitute the backwater of the Elizabethan-Jacobean stream.

It is therefore easy to belittle the actual achievement of this first period and anyone who wishes to make an accurate measurement is bound to extend his view beyond the temporal limits of the first fifty years of the sixteenth century. The Humanist movement was arrested, rather than exhausted: its principal concern—what I have broadly designated translation—was a central activity and it was only a matter of time before promise would be converted into fulfilment. In fact it is only when we see the Humanist programme fulfilled that we can look back and declare that there was a valuable moment in the early years of the century. It is only in retrospect that we can see that Humanism bore the fruit it was in its nature to bear. Milton is commonly thought to be the last full inheritor of the movement that begins with Erasmus and More. Yet if we wish to isolate and see at its finest this central activity of the Humanists, we must look rather to Ben Jonson. For Jonson's Humanism (to which Marvell's was closely related) not only shows us what was potentially there in the writings of More and Wyatt, it is also the finest possible test for assessing the Humanism of Milton. As we have seen, the Humanist heritage contained much that was bad, habits of mind that precluded ideal participation in a timeless civilisation. But we are sufficiently prejudiced against 'classicising' not to need further elaboration of the case against the worst side of Humanism. Moreover, as we shall see, the distinction is clear enough in Jonson's own work.

A further argument in favour of Jonson is the practical one that the relation of Jonson to the writings hitherto discussed is plain and direct and does not require any extension of the framework set up in this essay. We may illustrate this relation from a remark made by Mr Eliot in his Harvard lectures, published under the title: *The Use of Poetry and the Use of Criticism* (p. 48).

'A greater critic than Sidney, the greatest critic of his time, Ben Jonson, says wisely:

" 'I know nothing can conduce more to letters, than to examine the writings of the Ancients, and not to rest in their sole authority, or take all upon trust from them; provided the plagues of judging, and pronouncing against them, be away; such as envy, bitterness, precipitation, impudence, and scurrile scoffing. For to all the observations of the Ancients, we have our own experience; which, if we will use and apply, we have better means to pronounce. It is true they opened the gates, and made the way that went before us; but as guides, not commanders.' "

'And further:

' "Let Aristotle and others have their dues; but if we can make farther discoveries of truth and fitness than they, why are we envied?" '

In selecting this passage from *Timber* for special praise, Mr Eliot had been anticipated by Swinburne, who in *A Study of Ben Jonson* wrote:

'at the very opening of these *Explorata*, or *Discoveries*, we find ourselves in so high and so pure an atmosphere of feeling and of thought that we cannot but recognize and rejoice in the presence and the influence of one of the noblest, manliest, most honest and most helpful natures that ever dignified and glorified a powerful intelligence and an admirable genius.'

Swinburne justified this high praise by a selection of passages, from which I extract one:

'how grand is this:

' "I cannot think nature is so spent and decayed that she can bring forth nothing worth her former years. She is always the same, like herself; and when she collects her strength, is abler still. *Men are decayed, and studies: she is not.*"

'Jonson never wrote a finer verse than that; and very probably he never observed that it was a verse.

'The next note is one of special interest to all students of the great writer who has so often been described as a blind worshipper and a servile disciple of classical antiquity.'

Swinburne then gives us the first of Mr Eliot's quotations, but continues to the end:

' ". . . *Non domini nostri sed duces fuere.* Truth lies open to all; it is no man's several. *Patet omnibus veritas: nondum est occupata. Multum ex illa etiam futuris relictum est.*"

'Time and space would fail me to transcribe all that is worth transcription, to comment on everything that deserves commentary, in this treasure-house of art and wisdom, eloquence and good sense. But the following extract could be passed over by no eye but a mole's or a bat's.

' "I do not desire to be equal with those that went before; but to have my reason examined with theirs, and so much faith to be given them, or me, as those shall evict . . . I am neither author nor fautor of any sect. I will have no man addict himself to me; but if I have anything right, defend it as Truth's, not mine, save as it conduceth to a common good. It profits not me to have any man fence or fight for me, to flourish, or take my side. Stand for Truth, and 'tis enough." '

The testimony of these two poets is valuable in that both were probably unaware (Swinburne certainly) that they were singling out for praise, not the work of Jonson, but of Erasmus' disciple, *J. L. Vives*. This unconscious tribute makes it unnecessary to insist on the grandeur of conception of this early Chistian Humanist.

The scholars who discovered that *Timber* was almost entirely a collection of remarks by other people, selected, condensed, and sometimes admirably translated by Jonson, have not been able to explain why Vives figures so prominently in these pages. Certainly, if we go through all the passages which Jonson has taken from Vives, it is puzzling to find Jonson bothering to translate parts which repeat topics from Jonson's favourite classical authors or which give advice on matters where Jonson had every right to consider himself more of an authority than Vives. Yet if we look at the passages praised by Swinburne and Eliot, the reason why they appealed to Jonson is clear, for they come from a document which is a classic statement of the Christian Humanist position. In his preface to his *De Disciplinis* (1531) Vives redefined for his age what should be the relation of modern writers to the classics and of the Christian scholar to the learning of the pagans. In these pages Jonson could find the justification for his greatest work. Their intrinsic importance and their significance for my argument call for an extensive quotation:

'What prompted me to do my best to write this book was the belief that life has no finer and more worthy task than the training of the intelligence in the various disciplines, as they are called. This is what draws our life from the ways and habits of animals and puts us back into the human condition and lifts us up to God himself.

'Unless I am deceiving myself, the method I have chosen is quite different from that we have grown accustomed to for generations.

My first object has been to write plainly and clearly, so as to present no difficulty to the reader, and to enable my meaning to be grasped at once and easily retained. Secondly, I have tried to be adequate to what I take to be the true facts as they occur in nature and in our nature. I want to make it a pleasure to recognise these facts. To enable the student to derive profit from this study, I have constantly kept in mind the needs of the finer spirits who may be drawn to the pursuit of it. I have done my best to write in a polished and attractive style, and for two reasons: it is not right to dress what are beautiful topics in filthy and slovenly clothing. It is a wicked waste of time to compel students of literature to spend all their time deciphering obscure phraseology, as they have to do with most contemporary text-books. I can hardly exaggerate the boredom of swallowing down the beastly jargon and mastering the unnecessary linguistic difficulties with which the subject has been made to bristle.

'My chief aim is to bring the student gradually to see what use Latin and Greek can have. Why do we devote so much of our energies to learning these languages? They are mainly useful to us because the subjects we wish to study are best dealt with in books written in these languages. Latin and Greek are also the best languages for writing our own books in.

'I have departed from my chief classical authorities in two directions. I have purged them of all that made for impiety and dragged them out of pagan darkness into Christian daylight. Secondly, I shall show that these authors made mistakes and that these mistakes are their own fault and not, as is sometimes said, the results of ineradicable and insuperable defects in the human intelligence. On the other hand, I have grounded all my arguments on Nature and make no appeal to religious authority. I have been scrupulous not to confuse rational enquiry with theology.

'If I have succeeded in any of these objects, I have my reward, I am amply satisfied. For I can conceive of no more useful rôle than to lead people out of darkness to see a light, which if we never reach we shall end in everlasting misery, or to bring people who have a dim perception of the light to get a clearer view and to give them the means to achieve a perfect sight of it. There is a real danger that, if we begin our education with the study of classical authors, we may find that insensibly our Christianity has become tainted with paganism. But if we get the student accustomed to thinking soundly and correctly on religion from his earliest years, these views will grow slowly with him as he grows and so become part of him.

'A great difficulty I have had to face is at the same time to demonstrate the rightness of the views of our classical authorities and to expose their errors. Students are only too inclined to accept blindly some author or critic as an infallible guide. So I thought it best to speak out plainly about matters in which I think our authorities are mistaken. I have not dealt with all their errors, for that would take too long, but I have dealt with those which form part of received opinion and have always been supposed to be right. In doing this, I have been conscious of some impertinence and presumption in daring to attack writers who have been admired for centuries. I admire Aristotle and revere him above all other writers for his great industry, critical sense, and genius in all branches of learning. But I beg you not to think me ungrateful or over-bold if I attack him. We owe an immense debt to those authors who did not keep back from posterity the discoveries they won from Nature. If we find that they have gone wrong occasionally, we must remember that they were only human. If we wish to educate ourselves, it is more profitable to form our own judgement about the works of famous authors, than to accept them passively as authorities, and to believe everything because others say it is so. There are, however, dangers to be avoided in fostering a critical spirit: jealousy, spite, bitterness, an over-readiness to pronounce our verdict, irreverence and mere cleverness.

'But we have reason to look to Nature with confidence. Nature is not worn out and done for: she can still produce as much and of as good quality as in the past. Nature does not change: and what is more, it often happens that in some generations she gathers all her strength up and produces richer and more powerful geniuses than before. And there is every reason to suppose that in this age Nature is stronger than ever, thanks to the slow accretions of knowledge made over the last centuries. This is certainly true in the domain of human knowledge. The discoveries of previous centuries and long ages of experience have opened the way for us and facilitated our mastery of all arts and sciences. Consequently, if we apply ourselves to knowledge in the spirit of the old authors, there is no reason why we should not find truer things to say about life and nature than Aristotle, Plato or any other classical author. The study of Nature was such a novelty to them that their contribution consisted more of wonderment than actual knowledge. Again, what was Aristotle doing but rooting up and destroying the received opinion of his day? If he could do this without censure, why should it be thought a crime for us merely to subject his works to critical examination? Did not Seneca long ago make the sensible observation that our predecessors in the study of life and nature are not our masters, but our guides? Truth is a virgin prairie: it is common property, it is not all in private preserve yet or colonised. There is much left for future generations to discover.

'I do not put myself on an equal footing with the classics in saying all this. I ask you merely to place what I say alongside their remarks and to compare. If you prefer my account of things, give me credit for that and no more. If you think our arguments though contrary are of equal weight, I am not so impudent as to complain if you prefer the older authors to me or any other modern writer. Their opinions have stood the test of time: ours are new and unknown.

'As for my own position, I have no desire for blind disciples. I have founded no clique; nor should I do so even if people swore formally to obey me. My friends, if you think that anything I say is right, stick to it because it is right, not because I said it. This attitude will be beneficial to you, personally, and to all your intellectual pursuits. You won't be doing *me* any good by taking up the cudgels on my behalf, and the resulting squabbles and side-takings would only do *you* harm. If you must form a militant sect, fight for truth wherever you find it. Leave me while I'm still alive and after my death to the one Critic my conscience has to face and satisfy.

'I have no doubt that in my book I have made many mistakes: it is to be expected of any author who points out the faults of others incomparably superior to him in intelligence, application, knowledge and experience. Aristotle asked his readers to show gratitude for the discoveries he brought them, and a willingness to pardon his errors and omissions. So I ask you to be charitable and recognise my will to do well, and to pardon and look kindly on my lapses— for my enterprise in one never undertaken before. The pioneer in any branch of enquiry can never hope to round it off. If anyone condescends to put a polish on my rough beginnings and to supply my deficiencies, he may be able to produce a book that will be worth studying.'

If we wish for a touchstone by which to try any work claiming to be animated by the Humanist spirit, we can find it here. If we wish to define the sense in which Humanism is alive to-day, I should say: in so far as it is on the lines of this preface. The affinity between the critical spirit as defined by Vives and the classic formulation by Matthew Arnold is clear. More than this, in these pages Vives has raised himself above time and thus enabled us to see the affinity between the humanism of the sixteenth century and that of the twelfth. In every age the task of the humanist is different, but the spirit is the same, for it is an aspect of all civilisation to struggle for renewal by attacking inert ideas. It has also been the practice of all renewers of values to seek for an ally in the past. A manifesto of humanism which bears striking resemblance to this of Vives has been published recently by Miss Smalley in her book *The Study of the Bible in the Middle Ages*. In a chapter on the Victorines, Miss Smalley describes various attempts to set a critical spirit in motion at the abbey of St Victor in Paris, founded in 1110. Her researches have brought to light a previously little-known figure, Andrew of St Victor, who may have been English or Anglo-Norman. The criticism of his group was concerned with the interpretation of the Bible and the attempt to restore the right to interpret the literal sense—which, as we have seen was one of the chief tasks of the Humanists of the sixteenth century. This was pioneer work, for there was only one Father to support them. 'Andrew realised that he was taking up the work of scholarship where St Jerome had left it.' Wishing to vindicate his right to make independent comments on the Books of the Old Testament, Andrew projected his own feelings on to Jerome and wrote a passage that deserves to become a *locus classicus*: its spirit is almost identical with that of Vives and Jonson: 'patet omnibus veritas: nondum est occupata. Multum ex illa etiam futuris relictum est.'

'Jerome knew, the man was learned and knew very well—who better?—that truth is hidden, hidden deep down, plunged in the depths—*loin des pioches et des sondes*—and how few there be that find her, how hard they have to work to get near her, so that hardly any—even of the select few who are fit to try—ever do quarry her, and then, after immense difficulties, all they get is a speck, a minute fragment. But although truth is hidden, it is not so deeply hid as to be completely unattainable. The very fact that bits of the truth *have* been found proves that bits can again be found. No one ever had the luck to get the whole truth for himself. Truth is dug up bit by bit—it comes up, as the saying is, a crumb at a time. Our parents, our forefathers found some of it, but they left some for their children and descendants to discover for themselves. Truth is ever to seek—there will never come a day when there is no more to find. For these reasons, there is nothing disrespectful or presumptuous, it is not a mere waste of time, for us decadent moderns to sit up at night in the search for the true meaning of the Scriptures. We have a right to follow in Jerome's footsteps. The man deserves our veneration and his commentary our respect. The reader is left to decide whether our utmost efforts have resulted in any advance being made in the discovery of truth.' [1]

[1] For the original see *op. cit.*, pp. 378-9.

Vives was one of the greatest, most distinguished minds among the Humanists, and it is regrettable that, whereas he is still remembered for his work on St Augustine and on the education of women, his transformation of literary studies is now disregarded. He was, however, instantly noted and taken up by Erasmus and More when he published his first important work—an attack on the schoolmen among the theologians of Paris—at the age of twenty-eight. More recognised the affinity between the author of *Utopia* and the author of *In Pseudodialecticos*: Erasmus prophesied that he was one of those who would one day put his own name in the shade. Yet at this date Vives was merely following in the footsteps of his elders. His negative, polemical work, in which he swept aside the *débris* of the Middle Ages, belongs to history. Where he surpassed all other Humanists is in the development of a positive programme. He was well aware that he was a pioneer: he constantly claimed that he was doing something original, defining a critical field and introducing a critical discipline unknown and hostile to that of the mediaeval tradition. His principles, however, are of all time; their formulation and emphasis vary only as the inertia to be overcome takes different forms at different times.

Although he is as much a part of the English scene as Erasmus, in that he was physically present in England while at the height of his powers, I shall not attempt to set out the detail of his programme for founding a humane education, but confine myself to his leading principles, for in this way I can best illustrate how he was useful to Jonson. These principles are now the commonplaces of humanism. First, Vives' main concern was to assert the supreme importance of literature as an element in the good life. To obtain a sense of what good literature was, Vives thought that the first step was to understand and distinguish what was wise and useful in the Roman conception of literature. His task was to clear away mediaeval misunderstandings and to demonstrate that Roman literary theory was securely based on the facts of human nature and universal experience and conformed to the demands of reason. After the debauch of Italian humanism, Vives had to dwell with to us tiresome insistence on the fact that literature has no value as mere manner, that Style cultivated for its own sake is valueless. His second chief concern was to show that literature is a moral force. He held to the conviction that the worth of a piece of literature depended on the worth of the mind that conceived it. The only kind of matter he thought valuable in literature was such as promoted moral action and favoured the growth of wisdom. Thirdly, he thought the study of literature indispensable for the conduct of life and business, particularly for those who on leaving the university would enter politics or government administration.

We may see from *Timber* that Jonson found some of these points worth keeping in Vives' formulation. Here, for example:

'In all speech, [Vives is speaking of literature] words and sense, are as the body, and the soule. The sense is as the life and soule of Language, without which all words are dead. Sense is wrought out of experience, the knowledge of humane life and actions, or of the liberall Arts. . . .'

These phrases, thus taken out of their life-giving context, may appear the flattest commonplace. They are, however, fighting phrases whenever a literature has to be recalled from the cultivation of verbal conceits and flourishes, whenever it is necessary to combat the conception of poetry as purely musical or as an Art that exists for its own sake. There will always be times when the right thing to say is: more matter and less art. Another suggestive phrase picked up by Jonson was:

'*Language* most shewes a man: speake that I may see thee. It springs out of the most retired and inmost parts of us, and is the Image of the Parent of it, the mind.'

This time the profundity of Vives' remark is best appreciated by reference to the original: *quippe oratio ex intimis nostri pectoris recessibus oritur, ubi uerus ille ac purus homo habitat*. Without an extensive commentary this may seem a long way from, say, Mr Leavis, when he makes the distinction between 'that which has been willed and put there, or represents no profound integration, and that which grows from a deep centre of life' or from Mr Eliot's phrase, 'Their words have often a network of tentacular roots reaching down to the deepest terrors and desires.'

But even if the parallel between Vives and the best critics of our own age could be brought closer—and I think it would not be hard to do so—there would be one great reason inhibiting the attempt: Vives, like his best contemporaries, had not formed a worthy conception of the function of poetry. The following quotation alone should suffice to prevent our straining to make Vives seem a modern:

'You must never allow yourself to forget that poetry is to be cultivated only in the time left over after the serious business of the day is finished, and that poetry is to be taken, not as nourishment, but as a sauce.' [1]

A further reason—if any be needed—is that, even if Vives had come to a worthier conception of the proper function of poetry, his teaching could never have had any beneficial results so long as he advocated writing in Latin. For, although poetry in Latin might be better than the poetry in English being written while Vives was professing his views, Latin words could not come from and penetrate to 'the most retired and inward parts of us'. The odd thing is that Vives himself saw this difficulty. Unlike those of his contemporaries who preferred some contemporary Latin verse even to the classics from which it was derived, Vives saw that it was one thing to hope to surpass the Ancients in the sciences, but to think of writing better Latin verse than the Roman poets was absurd:

'To claim to be superior to the Roman poets in style and diction, or even to equal them, is not only a bad thing, deserving severe rebuke, but a danger, in that it leads us to over-estimate our own powers and causes us to make a laughing-stock of ourselves. For how can we, who do not know even what the Latin words sounded like, pretend to judge their quality? It is a quite different matter in a modern language. *There* the people are the forgers of their own words: they are in supreme possession and can judge of words with authority.' [2]

From this alone it becomes clear that if Jonson is the true heir of the Humanists, they left him everything to do. It was one thing to provide the formula, but quite another to apply it to the creation of new English poetry by study of the Roman classics. Nevertheless, in taking leave of Vives, it is only fair to quote his words to prove that he did indeed have the right and fruitful conception of the proper way to set about the translation that is creation:

'. . . That is not imitating, it is downright pilfering, an all-too-common practice nowadays. But if the student adopt my method he will gradually find himself imitating in a truly creative way. I mean that he will be transmuting the suggestions of his model to his own purposes and not stealing the best bits of his original and stringing them together and passing *that* off as a new and original composition. I want the would-be writer to take a long, careful and steady look at his model; and, if he is to produce work to rival it, he must give a

[1] *De Tradendis Disciplinis*, Lib. III, Caput VI.   [2] *Ibid.*, Lib. IV, Caput IV.

great deal of thought and attention to what he takes to be the spirit
and intention of his model and the means there used to obtain the
effects. When he has grasped them, the pupil should try to execute
in a similar spirit something he wants to say for himself.[1]

Before I give examples to show that Jonson was the first poet fully
to realise this programme and justify Vives, there is an objection to
be met that, so far from taking this excellent advice, Jonson was
doing the very thing Vives is here condemning. In his edition of
Volpone, an American scholar with great industry unearthed the
passages from Renaissance books (chiefly Erasmus) that Jonson
made use of when composing his play. Professor Rea there claimed
that 'it is possible to state definitely not merely the source from which
the suggestion for the work as a whole was obtained, but also the
sources of almost all the important parts. . . . Its author must have
kept careful notes, jotting down passages that struck him in his
reading, and sometimes his own reflections on them; such a note-
book we evidently still have in *Discoveries*.' The scholar then argues
that because what he calls the sources form a mosaic, the play
Volpone is a mosaic: 'The play is a patchwork, or mosaic, rather than
a work produced by the imagination, or by observation of life.'
Against this view of the play we may set Donne's view, as given in the
verses quoted at the head of this epilogue:

> To my very great and very worthy friend,
> Ben Jonson.

O POET, if our lawyers and theologians, students of human and
divine law, had the courage you showed in your art in *Volpone*, in
your method of both following and yet rivalling the classical writers
you drew on, we should all of us be in possession of the wisdom we
need to save our souls. But for them the classics are dead and
covered with cobwebs. None of them knows how to make use of the
classics as you do, who treat the authors you translate in a creative,
revolutionary way, making new art out of old. . . .

Since I am here merely making use of Jonson to provide justification for my comments on the translating activities of the Humanists,
I cannot do more than quote opinions, and add my own, which is
that, if recent scholarship has done anything for Jonson, it has been
to rid us of the burdensome image of Jonson the Scholar, the textual
critic *manqué*, the master of an erudition it was not profitable for
a poet to possess. Jonson knew at first hand the authors he found

---

[1] *Op. cit.*, Lib. IV, Caput IV.

useful: Quintilian, both Senecas, Martial, Catullus, Horace, Juvenal, but he knew them as a professional writer, as a poet. His interest in the classics is not qualitatively different from Shakespeare's. He may have read more authors, he may have needed more. He certainly knew how to use parts of the classical tradition which Shakespeare did not tap.

Nor in making Jonson the heir of the Humanists must we overlook Jonson's own activity. To be able to take Vives' advice, Jonson had to discover for himself what Quintilian was talking about. He had to submit himself to his classical models—to give them the steady scrutiny Vives recommended—to penetrate through the manner to the spirit. But it would be misleading to think of a wise passivity as the phrase for Jonson's relation to the classics. His success depended on what he could bring to the classics and what he could make the classics do for him. It is our gain that Jonson was not truly classical or that he was not merely classical. Nevertheless, though it is no paradox to say that Jonson's task was as much to free his successors from the burden of useless classical models and useless forms of imitation, as to open for them fruitful new veins, it must be admitted that he had on occasion a pedantic, slavish interest, which severely qualifies our admiration of, for instance, *Sejanus*.

We cannot too often remind ourselves of the extent to which successful translation is as much a matter of living as of writing. We have only the texts left to us, and it is far too easy to reduce the living process to what literary remains survive and to think of the translating poet as a man with a classic propped open in front of him. For this reason I should like to interrupt the argument for a moment to illustrate by a hint how Jonson lived with one of his authorities.

In an earlier chapter I made a translation of excerpts from Erasmus' classic statement of the permanent grounds of defence open to the satirist who criticises society. I might instead have gone to Jonson's *Timber*, where we find:

'*Whilst* I name no persons, but deride follies; why should any man confesse, or betray himselfe? why doth not that of S. *Hierome* come into their minde; *Vbi generalis est de vitiis disputatio, ibi nullius esse personae injuriam*? Is it such an inexpiable crime in *Poets*, to taxe vices generally; and no offence in them who, by their exception, confesse they have committed them particularly? Are wee fal'ne into those times that wee must not
'*Auriculas teneras mordaci rodere vero*? . . .'

That this transcript from the *Epistola . . . ad . . . Dorpium* was more than a random jotting we may see from an episode in Jonson's life, his imprisonment along with Chapman for some lines in *Eastward Ho*. The episode has become memorable for us because of Drummond's anecdote that Jonson's mother was prepared to smuggle poison into the prison to spare her son the shame of a public execution, and that she had decided, if her son were executed, to kill herself by the same means. Some of the letters Jonson wrote at this time to people who might be moved to get him released are extant, and in one, to the Earl of Salisbury, we find Jonson quoting this article by Erasmus.

'. . . I protest to your Honor, and call God to Testemony . . . I haue so attempred my stile, that I haue giuen no cause to any good Man of Greife, and, if to any ill, by touching at any generall vice, it hath alwayes bene with a reguard and sparing of perticuler persons . . . let Mee be examind . . . whether I haue euer (in any thing I haue written priuate or publique) giuen offence to a Nation, to any publique order or state, or any person of honor, or Authority. . . .'

This last sentence, Jonson's rendering of Erasmus: 'In all the many books I have written, have I ever attacked the reputation of any individual or his slightest failing? What nation, what order of society, what type of man have I ever attacked by naming individuals?' was in Jonson's mind while he was composing the dedicatory address to the two Universities, printed as a preface to *Volpone*:

'. . . and, howsoever I cannot escape from some the imputation of sharpness, but that they will say, I have taken a pride or lust to be bitter, and not my youngest infant but hath come into the world with all his teeth: I would ask of these supercilious politics, what nation, society, or general order or state, I haue prouoked? What public person? Whether I haue not in all these preserued their dignity, as mine own person, safe? My works are read, allowed . . . look into them, what broad reproffs haue I used? where haue I been particular? where personal? except to a mimic, cheater, bawd, or buffoon, creatures for their insolencies worthy to be taxed? yet to which of these so pointingly, as he might not either ingenuously haue confest, or wisely dissembled his disease?'

Here Jonson is not merely quoting an authority: the quotation is fully assimilated: it is Jonson speaking throughout. But the 'I' of the passage is extended, strengthened and defined in its fulness by means of Erasmus. This is a characteristic procedure, as we may see from the pages of *Timber*, where Jonson, like Wyatt, searched his classics for a parallel to his own case and by translation produced something which is more Jonson than Jonson himself. There is an admirable piece of self-defence beginning, 'It is true, I haue beene accus'd to the Lords, to the *King*; and by great ones . . .' which appears to be pure autobiography, for Jonson is here calling up the memory of painful experiences, such as his imprisonment for his share in *The Isle of Dogs* in 1597, his summons to appear before the Privy Council for *Sejanus* in 1603 and several similar brushes with Authority. Yet if we examine the whole passage carefully, we can see that Jonson is once again adopting the classic procedure of the great man on his defence: he is assimilating his experience to that of another great man of the past and using the language and arguments this illustrious predecessor used when *he* was on trial. How closely this resembles translation can be seen by placing a portion of the speech by Jonson alongside an English translation of his model:

'At last they upbraided my pouerty; I confesse, shee is my Domestick; sober of diet, simple of habit; frugall, painefull; a good Counsellor to me; that keepes me from Cruelty, Pride, or other more delicate impertinences, which are the Nurse-children of Riches. But let them looke ouer all the great, and monstruous wickednesses, they shall neuer find those in poore families. They are the issue of the wealthy Giants, and the mighty Hunters: Whereas no greate worke, or worthy of praise, or memory, but came out of poore cradles. It was the ancient pouerty, that founded Common-weales; built Cities, inuented Arts . . .'

Here Jonson has woven himself into the position of the author of the *Golden Ass* in one of the most celebrated trial speeches in antiquity: his defence against the charge of being a sorcerer:

'Pudens actually reproached me with being poor, a charge which is welcome to a philosopher and one that he may glory in. For poverty has long been the handmaid of philosophy; frugal and sober, she is strong in her weakness and is greedy for naught save honour; the possession of her is a prophylactic against wealth, her mien is free from care, and her adornment simple; her counsels are beneficient, she puffs no man up with pride, she corrupts no man with passions beyond his control, she maddens no man with the lust for power, she neither desires nor can indulge in the pleasures of feasting and of love. These sins and their like are usually the nurslings of wealth. Count over all the greatest crimes recorded in the history of mankind, you will find no poor man among their guilty authors. On the other hand, it is rare to find wealthy men among the great figures of history. All those at whom we marvel for their great deeds were the nurslings of poverty from their very cradles, poverty that founded all cities in the days of old, poverty, mother of all the arts. . . .'

(*Apologia*, tr. H. E. Butler, pp. 45–6)

When we seek to carry this process a step further and examine the conversion of prose translation from the classics into English verse, we find that Jonson, unlike Wyatt, rearranged his matter into an order dictated by himself. Here, indeed, Jonson resembles the worker in mosaic. The evidence can be found in the Oxford editors' notes on *Timber*, from which we can see that a long passage was concocted from Seneca's Moral Epistles. Out of this mosaic of Senecan passages Jonson composed the following speech for *The Staple of News*:

> Who can endure to see
> The fury of mens gullets, and their groines?
> What fires, what cookes, what kitchins might be spar'd?
> What Stewes, Ponds, Parks, Coopes, Garners, Magazines?
> What veluets, tissues, scarfes, embroyderies,
> And laces they might lacke? They couet things
> Superfluous still: when it were much more honour
> They could want necessary: what need hath Nature
> Of siluer dishes, or gold chamber pots?
> Of perfum'd napkins, or a numerous family
> To see her eate? poore, and wise, she requires
> Meate only: hunger is not ambitious.
> Say that you were the *Emperour* of pleasures,
> The great *Dictator* of fashions for all *Europe*,
> And had the pompe of all the Courts and Kingdomes
> Laid forth unto the shew to make your self
> Gaz'd and admir'd at: you must goe to bed
> And take your naturall rest: then all this vanisheth.
> Your brauery was but showen: 'twas not possest:
> While it did boast it selfe it was then perishing.

The natural objection here is not against the mosaic, for, after all, a similar piece of mosaic gave us *Drink to me only*, but that Jonson has not succeeded in assimilating his original. Even without the Latin before us, we can still see Latinisms sticking out. Jonson's first impulse was towards a literal translation, and as a literal translator Jonson is a bore, as we know from his version of Horace's *Ars Poetica*, which is simply not *there* in Jonson's English. When the Classics are his commanders, Jonson is a pedant: when they serve as guides, Jonson is capable of surpassing them.

We can, in one example, see Jonson overcoming his innate tendency to pedantry and thus provide ourselves with a parallel to the contrasting versions of Petrarch by Wyatt: the bald and literal and the personal recreations. To set the example in the proper light, we need the scholarly crib (which I have taken from the Loeb edition) of the seventy-seventh epigram of Martial's eighth book: the question to be asked being, in what sense has anything been translated here?

'Liber, of thy friends the care most sweet, Liber, worthy to live amid deathless roses, if thou art wise, let thy locks glisten alway with Assyrian balm and chaplets of flowers encircle thy head; let thy clear crystal darken with old Falernian, and thy soft couch warm with love's endearments. Whoever has so lived, to him, even did the end come in middle age, life has been made longer than was appointed.'

Here, I suppose it will be granted, all that made Martial's poem a fine poem has vanished save the skeleton of a thought. It is, of course, strictly speaking, an absurd performance to offer to translate poems that are all form unless you can supply a form to replace the verse form. But this crib is not only formless, it is pointless, and an epigram exists chiefly to make points. The whole point of this epigram is summed up in the last line, where Martial contrasts life as nature gives it with life as man shapes it. The crib, however, is not only formless and pointless, it is writ in no language: it has no style whatever, neither that suited to verse nor that befitting prose. It has indeed the vices of both, being stupidly poetic and intolerably prosaic. If Martial's style had to be characterised in a word or two, we should have to call it hard and precise. The language of this crib —for example, 'couch warm with love's endearments'—is sloppy and vague.

Jonson's first attempt to catch the spirit of this epigram, however pedantic, is at least free of most of these faults:

> *Liber*, of all thy friends, thou sweetest care,
> Thou worthy in eternall Flower to fare,
> If thou be'st wise, with *'Syrian* Oyle let shine
> Thy locks, and rosie garlands crowne thy head;
> Darke thy cleare glasse with old *Falernian* Wine;
> And heat, with softest love, thy softer bed.
> Hee, that but living halfe his dayes, dies such,
> Makes his life longer then 'twas given him, much.

In favour of these lines, we can say that at least they move in imaginable speech, that at least some of the point of the original begins to peep through. Yet it would not strike a reader, coming upon it without external knowledge, as an eminently English poem standing on its own feet. The unassimilated parts of the original— for instance, the wine and the oil—are too prominent. No English- man could ever have found himself making his point in the awkward, would-be-clinching final couplet. True creation does not occur until the poem is stripped of merely Roman trappings and laced with Jonson's own vigour:

> When *Nature* bids vs leaue to liue, 'tis late
> Then to begin, my ROE: He makes a state
> In life, that can employ it; and takes hold
> On the true causes, ere they grow too old.
> Delay is bad, doubt worse, depending worst;
> Each best day of our life escapes vs first.
> Then, since we (more then many) these truths know;
> Though life be short, let vs not make it so.

This poem seems to have a mind behind it: it sounds like genuine talk to somebody capable of taking the points. In place of the un- realisable Liber, Jonson has put a man who stood to him as Liber did to Martial. William Roe, we know from depositions in a law-suit, reprinted in the first volume of the Oxford Jonson, and from another epigram (No. 128), was a close friend. We may, I suppose, take it that the advice given in the epigram was needed and to the point. But what gives the poem its strength is the placing of the words on which the argument turns at points in the line where the stress stresses the thought:

> He makes a state
> In life, that can employ it . . .

The pith of Martial's epigram is in that phrase. The conclusion, too, is natural and forceful.

Jonson produced this poem by his usual mosaic method.

> When Nature bids vs leaue to liue, 'tis late
> Then to begin . . .

is a translation from a sentence by the younger Seneca in his dialogue on the shortness of life. I have a strong impression that every phrase in this epigram is taken from Jonson's commonplace book, and that if we read the classics in Jonson's way it would be easy to supply proof that the poem is all translation.

> Delay is bad, doubt worse, depending worst

is also taken from Seneca, who wrote that delay is the chief means of throwing life away: depending on what the morrow may bring means losing the present day.

Each best day of our life escapes vs, first

is an awkwardly literal translation of a beautiful line in Virgil's
Georgics:

> optima quaeque dies miseris mortalibus aeui
> prima fugit: subeunt morbi tristisque senectus
> et labor et durae rapit inclementia mortis.

> (Poor mortals that we are, our brightest days
> Are ever the first to fly: on creeps disease,
> The gloom of middle age, and suffering.
> And soon the ruthless cruelty of Death
> Sweeps us away.)[1]

These specimens will, I hope, serve to establish a *prima facie* case
for the argument that Jonson was carrying out the Humanists' programme. The second leg of the argument: that Jonson's example
proves that the programme was a worthy, central, activity remains to
be given. What is needed is to show that when Jonson carried
through the process of translation to the end, what we have is entire
re-creation in which the Englishman is more himself than he could
have become in any other way. We need therefore a sample of the
essential Jonson, the great Jonson, who is at one and the same time
a translator and an original. We have seen that Vives advised him to
select from the classics what was relevant to the features of modern
life he wished to express, and to use his model both to find the right
distance from his contemporary topic and to penetrate to its heart.
But to complete the programme, we must see, as the result of this
process, Jonson surpassing his models, resetting them in such a way
that the originals look inferior. To provide a test by which to judge
the best of Wyatt, we need to show Jonson doing for his age what
Wyatt failed to do for the early sixteenth century. We need to see
Jonson drawing on the strength and quality of the civilisation he
inherited by his labours. For one of the great services Jonson performed for his juniors was that, in showing them how to make use
of the classics, he was at the same time showing them where the
strength of England lay and how to draw on it to create poems which
stand outside time and place.

We can find what we need in *To Penshurst*. It is clear that what
Jonson is doing here is, broadly speaking, to bring out the sanctions
upon which admiration for a noble family must rest. It is equally

---

[1] Cf. 'Soon flies the little joy to man allow'd/ And tears before him travel like
a cloud./ For come Diseases on, and Penury's rage,/ Labour, and Pain, and
Grief, and joyless Age'—Wordsworth, *Descriptive Sketches*.

clear that Jonson is here especially concerned with landed nobility and the succession of the title from holder to holder while the property each is steward of remains the same. The effect of Jonson's powerful imagination is to turn the material basis, as the Marxists would say, into a spiritual idea, an image of the good life. Jonson's imagination is that of the enlightened social historian, the critic of life as a whole. Yet, since repeated experience has shown me that this poem does not make itself felt to-day, it may be as well to approach it by a modern *détour* and to look first at an attempt by a poet of our own day to resolve Jonson's problem: how to throw the imagination round the modern evidence of persistence through the generation of a family and a home.

To call 1929 our own day is in this context a paradox, for to modern eyes every big house is a future ruin, at best only two series of death-duties away from the demolition squad, or, if preserved from that fate, doomed in at most two generations to become a national monument or another home for inebriates or a hostel for students. But twenty-five years ago it was still possible to think of a family living on a noble scale as a symbol of permanence or as something around which the ideals of the good life might crystallise. Indeed, in those years, the idea gained in intensity, as all ideals do just before they are doomed. At any rate, *Yeats'* poems on these themes may serve as a spring-board for our imagination if we are unable to see society in the days of James I as if it were contemporary.

The three poems I have in mind might fairly be called the product of thinking about what would make Ireland a great nation, and of doing the thinking in the surroundings of Coole Park; the house, the grounds, the estate, with its lake and woods. The poems could not have been written about a museum or a ruin. When Yeats wrote, he was thinking of Coole Park as a symbol of the outward activity of a family, a family he knew well and a family with a history to which the modern members were seeking to add a not unworthy chapter. The characteristic work of the imagination may be seen from the following snippets. In the poem called *Ancestral Houses* we find this passage:

> Surely among a rich man's flowering lawns
> Amid the rustle of his planted hills
> Life overflows without ambitious pains
> And rains down life until the basin spills. . . .

And in *Coole Park 1929*:

> I meditate upon a swallow's flight
> Upon an aged woman and her house
> A sycamore and lime-tree lost in night

> Although that western cloud is luminous:
> Great works constructed there in nature's spite
> For scholars and for poets after us,
> Thoughts long knitted into a single thought,
> A dance-like glory that those walls begot . . .

And this, from *Coole Park and Ballylee 1931*:

> A spot whereon the founders lived and died
> Seemed once more dear than life; ancestral trees
> Or gardens rich in memory glorified
> Marriages, alliances and families
> And every bride's ambition satisfied.

If we pick out for the moment the ancestral trees as a symbol of the persistence of a noble way of life beyond the span of a single generation, we can say that what Yeats was doing with the trees in Coole Park Jonson did with, for instance, the tree that in the family tradition was said to have been planted by Sir Philip Sidney. That Jonson's poem may have flowered from this seed is rendered probable by the fact that Jonson turned to a poem by Martial on this very subject. Martial wished to compliment a family to whom he doubtless had obligations by glorifying a huge tree which, according to family tradition, had been planted in an earlier generation by Julius Caesar. It is not a poem that would have struck an average reader of Martial. Unless he had a contemporary feeling about ancestral trees, a poet would not have seen an opportunity here for creative translation.

Since I shall be arguing that Jonson here surpasses Martial, reference to the original would be desirable. (Ep. IX, 61.) As a *pis aller* I offer a paraphrase of the part used by Jonson:

'In the central court, embracing in dense leafage all the protecting spirits of the house, stands Caesar's tree, a plane the conquering general, the man with the lucky hand, planted while on a visit here. The young tree seemed to grow the straighter from the touch of his green fingers. It flourished from the first and shot at the stars with its top branches. Beneath it, the country harvest gods, wet-mouthed Fauns, have often drunk and made midnight music, the pipe note cutting into the silence, frightening the sleepers round the court. And under these branches the tree-girl often found a place to hide after running through the empty fields all night with Pan at her heels. The whole court smelt of wine when Bacchus came in and the grape-gathering celebration culminated in baptising the tree, which seemed to grow richer and thicker for the wetting. And at the foot of the tree lie the red flowers the celebrants had put in their hair: this morning none of last night's drunks could identify his own roses.

'You are a tree that need not fear lest the axe be laid to you, nor that sacrilege may be committed by fire. The gods care for you: you are Caesar's tree: your leaves can legitimately aspire to become perennial—it was not unlucky Pompey who planted you.'

Here Martial's *conceits* are happier than Jonson's because they rest on facts. At least I take it that in the sensuality of the grape-gathering celebrations the participants were in some sense conscious of the presence of the god. They themselves for the duration of the celebrations were in some sense filled with the god, even if they were plain drunks the morning after. At least it will be granted that there was a world of religion and superstition for Martial to draw on and that the transmutation of it into literary fancy still has power. I do not mean that there was no superstition and religion for Jonson to draw on in the Kentish harvest festivals, but that Jonson cut himself off from his sources of power by retaining the Mediterranean divinities. There is something more than faintly fatuous about the lines:

> Thy *Mount*, to which the *Dryads* doe resort,
> Where PAN, and BACCHVS their high feasts haue made,
> Beneath the broad beech, and the chest-nut shade;
> That taller tree, which of a nut was set,
> At his great birth, where all the *Muses* met.
> There, in the writhed barke, are cut the names
> Of many a SYLVANE, taken with his flames.
> And thence, the ruddy *Satyres* oft prouoke
> The lighter *Faunes*, to reach thy *Ladies oke*.

This fatuity is not the result of being soaked in the Classics, but of not reading them with a powerful imagination, of not bringing to them a strong sense of the realities the Classics are referring to, of not grasping the heart of the modern reality, that which is to be seen powerfully as for the first time by linking it with the past. The point may be brought home—and since the distinction is crucial for my argument it must be brought home—by reference to a modern instance of this *weak fancy*, this failure to translate the classics in living terms. Mr E. M. Forster comes to mind in such a passage as this:

'It is uncertain how the Faun came to be in Wiltshire. Perhaps he came over with the Roman legionaries to live with his friends in camp, talking to them of Lucretilis, or Garganus or of the slopes of Etna; they in the joy of their recall forgot to take him on board, and he wept in exile; but at last he found that our hills also understood his sorrows, and rejoiced when he was happy. Or, perhaps he came to be there because he had been there always. There is nothing particularly classical about a faun: it is only that the Greeks and Italians have ever had the sharpest eyes. You will find him in "The Tempest" and the "Benedicite"; and any country which has beech clumps and sloping grass and very clear streams may reasonably produce him.'

In such conditions a faun is made to encounter a clergyman:

'Now the Faun is of the kind who capers upon the Neo-Attic reliefs, and if you do not notice his ears or see his tail, you take him for a man and are horrified.'

The clergyman was startled, but the Faun proves reassuring:

' "No one else has seen me," he said, smiling idly. "The women have tight boots and the man has long hair. Those kinds never see. For years I have spoken only to children, and they lose sight of me as soon as they grow up. But you will not be able to lose sight of me, and until you die you will be my friend. Now I begin to make you happy: lie upon your back or run races, or climb trees, or shall I get you blackberries, or harebells, or wives——" '

The first step in making the clergyman happy was to rid him of an unsuitable fiancée. The second step occurs when the curate says a word beginning with 'D'.

'He gave a joyful cry, "Oh, now you really belong to us. To the end of your life you will swear when you are cross and laugh when you are happy. Now laugh!"
'There was a great silence. All nature stood waiting. . . .
'That evening, for the first time, I heard the chalk downs singing to each other across the valleys, as they often do when the air is quiet and they have had a comfortable day. From my study window I could see the sunlit figure of the Faun, sitting before the beech copse as a man sits before his house.' [1]

Jonson steadies *his* flight of mere fancy with a straightforward factual evocation stressing the material aspect of the park, the side that would appeal to a prospective buyer or a tax assessor. But Jonson sees the sanction of this material wealth in the opportunities it affords for liberal hospitality. What throws a colouring over the fat

[1] From 'The Curate's Friend' in the collection *The Celestial Omnibus*, 1911, pp. 129–42.

stock, the arable land and forestation is the suggestion that here nature is being put to the purpose it was meant for:

> 'Tis Use alone that sanctifies Expence,
> And Splendour borrows all her rays from Sense.

Although more than a hundred years divide Jonson from Pope, and we feel the vast changes between Jonson's view of Penshurst and Pope's survey of the great houses of his day, yet the two poets have in common this solid appreciation of the bases on which the good life can be erected.

Jonson moves from the material fact to the spiritual significance by way of another conceit, and once again he goes to Martial to fetch it. The epigram in which it occurs is a lyrical advertisement for a holiday resort, and the particular passage Jonson borrowed runs more or less as follows:

'Here you don't have to put out to sea and *look* for fish: just lean out of bed and the fish will pull on your line. When the wind works on the waves, your landlady laughs at the storm: she has her private fishpond and rears her own turbot and bass. The lamprey swims up when she calls. When the butler announces his name, the gurnard comes forward to kiss hands, and when properly invited the elderly mullets put in an appearance.' [1]

In re-setting this conceit Jonson has made it weightier:

> Thou hast thy ponds, that pay thee tribute fish,
> Fat, aged carps, that runne into thy net.
> And pikes, now weary their owne kinde to eat,
> As loth, the second draught, or cast to stay,
> Officiously, at first, themselues betray.

Jonson, however, rises to the height of his theme when he sees the country house as performing an integrating service in society, as the focus of a culture based on the countryside. Here Jonson clearly surpasses Martial, for Martial had no such subject matter as Jonson had. Martial could only point to the self-contained farm with its home-born slaves and a backward peasantry, in short, to a more primitive form of civilisation than Jonson was born into. Consequently, Jonson's translation informs the Latin with a glow of power gained from real factors of civilisation, as we may see by putting the passages alongside:

'Nor when the peasants come to pay their respects do they come

[1] Martial, Lib. X, Ep. 30, lines 16–24.

278

empty-handed: one brings pale honey in the honey-comb: one, a cone-shaped local cheese: one offers sleepy dormice: another, the kid crying for his bearded mother: another, capons deprived of their love-life, and strapping daughters of the better sort of peasant bring their mother's offerings in wicker baskets.' [1]

> But all come in, the farmer, and the clowne:
> And no one empty-handed, to salute
> Thy lord, and lady, though they haue no sute.
> Some bring a capon, some a rurall cake,
> Some nuts, some apples; some that thinke they make
> The better cheeses, bring 'hem; or else send
> By their ripe daughters, whom they would commend
> This way to husbands; and whose baskets beare
> An embleme of themselues in plum, or peare.

Because Jonson here had his eye on the realities of the country life, he was able to make a real translation: by comparison Martial seems merely pretty.

The next theme of the poem was one deeply felt by Jonson. In the conversation with Drummond we find:

He made Much of that Epistle of Plinius, wher ad prandium non ad notam is:

In this letter Pliny writes about a gross habit of Roman society, that of inviting intimate friends to good food and wine and at the same time serving inferior food and drink to inferior friends. Pliny claimed that he served the same to all his guests: 'I invite people to a common meal not to a public insult.' How familiar a part of Jonson's thought this had become we may judge from another remark in the conversation with Drummond:

'being at ye end of my Lord Salisburie's table with Inigo Jones & demaunded by my Lord, why he was not glad My Lord said he yow promised I should dine with yow, bot I doe not . . .'

This is a quip from Martial, who refers to the treatment he received as a poor literary man when dining with the rich. The depth of Jonson's feeling is to be explained by the strength with which he felt the positive ideal, the true banquet and the importance of genuine hospitality.

Since it is here that the chain linking together Horace, More, Erasmus, Wyatt and Jonson is most obvious, I make no apology for

---

[1] Lib. III, Ep. 68, lines 33–40.

breaking off the commentary to explore further what hospitality meant in Jonson's scheme of things. To focus the discussion we need to have before us Jonson's 101st Epigramme: *Inviting a Friend to Supper.*

Every civilisation is organised round a few central ideas. The Renaissance ideal of the good life finds, as we have seen, its truest expression in the *alfresco* meal at the point where town and country touch. Here Man and Nature meet on the most advantageous ground, for man was thought to be most civilised where he had thrown over the artificial extravagance of the City and the Court. The ideal had to fight for its existence against its two enemies: unmeaning expense on outward display, and unmeaning elaboration of ceremonial, the bugbears of life at court. The ideal meal is always a simple meal and ceremony is reduced to a minimum. As we have seen, the mealtime provides the framework in which philosophy is brought down to the human scale; for, while the meal exists to produce

The Feast of Reason and the Flow of Soul,

the simple necessities surrounding it command the tone of the discourse. There is room for wit and mirth, for the display of real ease in human intercourse, neither too familiar nor too stiff. There is no room for logic-chopping or for rhetorical display.

Here, then, we have two things: first, a social fact, the actual practice of compensating for the formality and unreality of public life by the informal, yet regulated genuine relations of private life: secondly, the crystallisation of these ideals in a literary form. The form is two-fold: satire against the vulgar and extravagant meal in which the ideals are desecrated, and the verse epistle, the letter of invitation setting out the prospect of the ideal meal.

In order to see what dignity Jonson was conferring on contemporary life by adopting this form, we need a formal analysis of his archetype, the Fifth Epistle of Horace's First Book. Here we have an invitation to a grave person, such as Jonson's Camden, and the point of the letter is to invite him to release his mind from his grave cares by drinking wine. There is no pretence that these cares can be permanently forgotten, but a strong plea to allow for one evening other standards of living to prevail, and to try to relieve for a short time the permanent, as it were, atmospheric weight of the cares of life. Secondly, it is an invitation to an elegant meal, not to a debauch; an invitation to clean napkins and polished silver. These, however, are only the outward signs of the spirit of the party, for, thirdly, and most important, it is an invitation to free yet measured conversation, in which no word that is said will go beyond the walls of the room or the garden. The point of this letter is to keep close to actualities: in tone, for the speaker is both joking and serious as he would be in a real, spoken invitation; and in precision about the food and drink: it is a real and appetising menu card. The poem can afford to insist on the particulars because it rests on other poems setting out the ideal justification of the meal.

Now it is a surprising fact that, though Jonson had this model before him, he preferred to make his invitation by weaving together three such poems by Martial. For though Martial retains the outward forms of the invitation, he has none of the spirit, or rather, while he has a keen appreciation of the pleasures of agreeable conversation and a clear understanding both of the conditions which further it and of those which mar it, he does not see the evening party as the ideal centre from which to view Man and Nature. He is not imbued with the philosophy which makes a meal among friends almost a religious symbol.

The first epigram used by Jonson is the seventy-eighth in Martial's fifth book. It is an invitation to a friend to share a modest meal and includes the menu: various appetisers to 'rectify the stomach', a light main dish with home-grown and freshly-gathered broccoli, and fruit as dessert. Olives, he says, will be served to whet the appetite for wine. A very slight meal, by the standards of the day, but—and here comes the part that impressed itself on Jonson:

'Though the meal is undoubtedly on a modest scale, you don't have to put on false airs there and you won't meet with false airs and manners. You can lie back and relax, drop the public mask and be yourself—and be at ease, for your host won't bring out a fat volume to read through at the meal, nor will there be the kind of floor show a man cannot sit through without undergoing a direct attack on his feelings.[1] The only musical entertainment will be provided by my little servant, who will oblige with something neither boring nor in poor taste.'

The invitation is cast in a courtly form, and Jonson may have taken one of his compliments from it:

> It is the faire acceptance, Sir, creates
> The entertaynment perfect: not the cates,

which is in the spirit of Martial's: *uinum tu facies bonum bibendo*.

That this invitation was a fixed form may be seen by noting the

---

[1] Martial is more specific.

similarity of another invitation, the forty-eighth poem in the tenth book. Here again the menu is set out in the same divisions. Once again Martial stresses the preliminary course designed to whet the appetite and secure good digestion. Here, too, Jonson has seized on the moral aspect: *accedent sine felle ioci*. What this meant we may learn from Drayton's *The Sacrifice to Apollo*:

> Let your Jests flye at large; yet therewithall
> See they be Salt, but yet not mix'd with Gall:
> Not tending to disgrace,
> But fayrely given,
> Becoming well the place,
> Modest, and even;
> That they with tickling Pleasure may prouoke
> Laughter in him, on whom the Jest is broke.

Martial continues:

'We shall speak our minds freely and not wake up the next morning terrified to think what we might have blabbed out and wishing we had never opened our mouths . . . nothing said over our drinks will get us into court.'

Jonson brings this alive by referring to the two notorious informers who tried to trap him.[1]

From Martial's third invitation, the fifty-second poem in the eleventh book, Jonson has borrowed the part where it deviates from the norm: after giving the familiar menu, Martial adds:

'If that menu won't fetch you, I'll invent one and tell you a lie: you shall have fish, mussels, sow's paps and fat birds of the poultry-yard and the marsh. (The latter are the birds we find in Jonson. With the draining of our marshes they have ceased to visit us and their names are no longer household words.) In short, I'll promise to out-do all Stella serves when she is giving a special dinner. More, I'll promise to read you nothing of my own, even if you read out your own epic from cover to cover, or your bucolic poem which rivals that of immortal Virgil.'

So once again we see that Jonson has made a poem from his commonplace book. Yet though Jonson has drawn on the great tradition, he has made it his own. This is not an exclusively *literary* poem: it rests on facts, even if it heightens them. It presupposes that

---

[1] Cf. R.E.S., xiii, pp. 386–7.

there was a select public capable of realising in the social form the ideal of the good life in so far as that ideal could be expressed through the form. That this was so we may see by referring to the rules Jonson drew up and which were set on the wall of the Apollo room at The Sign of the Devil. Here Jonson presided, here his 'sons' were nominated.

The very existence of these rules, however, proves that as in Horace's day so in Jonson's the ideal had also to be asserted in the teeth of the actual. The need to assert it so often only arose because it was so often flouted. Hence we get the other literary form, satire on the abuse of hospitality. Here the archetype for Jonson was the Fifth Satire of Juvenal, in which the comparatively poor man, Trebius, describes the treatment he received when invited to dine by a richer man who enjoyed tormenting his poorer guests. Since Jonson has so freely re-imagined the situation in English terms in *To Penshurst*, a mere summary of the events will serve to show that here the model was guide, not commander.

The first indignity Trebius has to suffer is to drink execrable wine, though before that the poor man is expected to provide a little horseplay: a mock fight is staged with real wounds. The host meanwhile drinks good wine and keeps it to himself. While Trebius drinks, a servant is on guard to see that he does not steal the precious goblet. The host is served by a minion fit to pour wine for the gods, but the poor man is waited on by a blackamoor who looks like a convict. The haughty servant is deaf to the poor man's requests and finds it intolerable that he must stand while the poor guest reclines. Trebius is served with a mouldy black crust and is punished if he stretches out a hand towards the basket where the host keeps his snow-white bread. And so it goes on throughout the meal: delicacies for the host, abominations for the poor guest.

We may now grasp what lies in and behind Jonson's praise of the master of Penshurst:

> whose liberall boord doth flow,
> With all, that hospitalitie doth know!
> Where comes no guest, but is allow'd to eate,
> Without his feare, and of thy lords owne meate:
> Where the same beere, and bread, and selfe-same wine,
> That is his Lordships, shall be also mine.
> And I not faine to sit (as some, this day,
> At great mens tables) and yet dine away.
> Here no man tells my cups; nor standing by,
> A waiter, doth my gluttony enuy:
> But giues me what I call, and lets me eate . . .

283

The next part of *To Penshurst* has been so well handled by Professor L. C. Knights that I reproduce his own words:

'This is an idealized but not, I think, a misleading picture, and it gives a fair impression of what 'housekeeping' meant for many great families of the time. It meant hospitality, and it meant sharing in the community life of the village in a fairly intimate fashion. It meant something altogether different from a condescending interest in "the villagers". In the same poem Jonson tells how King James paid a surprise visit to Penshurst when the mistress of the house was away:

> What (great, I will not say, but) sodayne cheare
> Did'st thou, then, make 'hem! and what praise was heap'd
> On thy good lady, then! who, therein, reap'd
> The iust reward of her high huswifery;
> To haue her linnen, plate, and all things nigh,
> When shee was farre: and not a roome, but drest,
> As if it had expected such a guest!

The 'good lady' who is praised for her 'high huswifery' is Lady Lisle, and it is significant that Jonson can use these homely terms in her praise.

I do not want to idealize the life of the aristocratic households in town and country in which the poets and men of letters had a footing. But it does seem true to say that they were places where a variety of living interests were taken for granted, and where men of different bents and occupations could find some common ground. And since the country houses were still functional units in the rural economy of the time, I think they helped to foster that intimate feeling for natural growth and the natural order—something so very different from the modern 'appreciation of nature'—that almost disappears from English poetry after Marvell.' [1]

After this the best commentary on this part of the poem and particularly on the lines

> and not a roome, but drest,
> As if it had expected such a guest!

is the following contemporary poem:

> Yet if his majesty, our Soveraign lord,
> Should of his owne accord
> Friendly himselfe invite,
> And say I'll be your guest tomorrowe night,

[1] *Scrutiny*, vol. XIII, No. 1, pp. 48–9.

How should we stir ourselves, call and command
All hands to worke! 'Let no man idle stand,
Set me fine Spanish tables in the hall,
See they be fitted all:
Let there be roome to eate,
And order taken that there want no meate,
See every sconce and candlestick made bright,
That without tapers they may give a light:
Looke to the presence: are the carpets spred,
The dazie o'er the head,
The cushions in the chayre,
And all the candles lighted on the staire?
Perfume the chambers, and in any case
Let each man give attendance in his place.'
Thus if the king were coming would we do;
And 'twere good reason too;
For 'tis a duteous thing
To show all honor to an earthly king;
And, after all our travayle and our cost,
So he be pleas'd, to think no labour lost.
But at the coming of the King of heaven
All's set at six and seven,
We wallow in our sin,
Christ cannot finde a chamber in the inn.
We entertain him always like a stranger,
And, as at first, still lodge him in the manger.

I have given the poem to the end, for, after all, Jonson's poem, too, ends on a religious note:

These, PENSHVRST, are thy praise, and yet not all.
Thy lady's noble, fruitfull, chaste withall.
His children thy great lord may call his owne:
A fortune, in this age, but rarely knowne.
They are, and haue beene taught religion: Thence
Their gentler spirits haue suck'd innocence.
Each morne, and euen, they are taught to pray,
With the whole houshold. . . .

The weight of the poem is left there, reminding us that if Jonson has borrowed heavily from the pagan Martial, he is nevertheless a Christian Humanist. But in Jonson's case as in Marvell's, where they succeed in being fully classical, their Christianity is no longer the Christianity of, say, Herbert. To ask how Jonson differs as a *Christian* Humanist from Wyatt is to begin the story of the transformation of the Humanist heritage, whereas my theme here is its completion only in Jonson. All I can allow myself to say is that Jonson rounds his poem off with a quip from a poem of Martial's (Ep. XII, 50) of which this is a witty adaptation:

> See, sir, here's the grand approach,
> This way is for his Grace's coach:
> There lies the bridge, and here's the clock,
> Observe the lion and the cock,
> The spacious court, the colonnade,
> And mark how wide the hall is made!
> The chimneys are so well design'd,
> They never smoke in any wind.
> This gallery's contriv'd for walking,
> The windows to retire and talk in,
> The council chamber for debate,
> And all the rest are rooms of state.
>   Thanks, sir, cried I, 'tis very fine,
> But where d'ye sleep, or where d'ye dine?
> I find, by all you have been telling
> That 'tis a house, but not a dwelling.

Jonson's ending is much more dignified:

> Now, PENSHVRST, they that will proportion thee
>   With other edifices, when they see
> Those proud ambitious heaps, and nothing else,
>   May say, their lords haue built, but thy lord dwells.

To Penshurst is, and always has been for me, a sufficient testimony, and I am reluctant to add to it, yet, having met with so many people who give this poem at best a grudging reception, I will add that, if the reader feels that my commentary has consisted largely of putting into the poem what I wanted to find there, by turning to the next poem in *The Forrest,* he can find for himself all the evidence he needs to show that Jonson's *feelings for the countryside of England were the place where above all the classical and modern meet.* Furthermore, by a brief glance at a few passages we can justify the claim that when Jonson is happiest in recreating from the Classics he most resembles Shakespeare, who uses the Classics in exactly the same spirit.

Here is an example to make the point clear that Jonson and Shakespeare succeed in translating from the Classics when they penetrate into the things referred to in their originals by bringing to their reading a powerful impression from the life around them. The framework of the part of Jonson's poem I wish to quote from comes again from Martial. Wishing to pay a compliment to Sir Robert Wroth, and in this part of the poem to compliment the country sportsman, Jonson turned to a poem by Martial which had the same theme. 'There', says Martial, in the words of the Loeb crib, 'will you slay does enmeshed in yielding toils and home-bred boars, and with your stout steed ride down the cunning hare' (Ep. I, 49). Jonson bridges past and present as follows:

> And, in the winter hunt'st the flying hare,
>   More for thy exercise, then fare;
> While all, that follow, their glad eares apply
>   To the full greatnesse of the cry . . .

Shakespeare gives reality to a classical scene by the same method:

> I was with *Hercules* and *Cadmus* once
> When in a wood of Creete they bayed the Beare
> With hounds of *Sparta:* neuer did I heare
> Such gallant chiding. For besides the groues,
> The skies, the mountaines, every region neere,
> Seem'd all one mutuall cry. I never heard
> So musicall a discord, such sweet thunder.
> —My hounds are bred out of the *Spartan* kinde,
> So flew'd, so sanded, and their heads are hung
> With eares that sweepe away the morning dew,
> Crook-kneed, and dew-lapt, like Thessalian Buls,
> Slow in pursuit, but match'd in mouth like bels,
> Each vnder each. A cry more tuneable
> Was neuer hallowed to, nor cheer'd with horne,
> In *Creet*, in *Sparta*, nor in *Thessaly*:

Surely it is clear that here the classical stuff has been made real by grafting it on to the modern reality, and though the practice Shakespeare refers to was not classical, in the end the impression of a classical hunt is more vivid than at the beginning?

Similarly in this poem Jonson overcomes the weakness I noted in his retaining of the classical figures in *To Penshurst* by assimilating them to the actualities of English country life:

> Thus PAN, and SYLVANE, hauing had their rites,
>   COMVS puts in, for new delights;
> And fills thy open hall with mirth, and cheere;
>   As if in SATVRNES raigne it were;
> APOLLO's harpe, and HERMES lyre resound,
>   Nor are the *Muses* strangers found.
> The rout of rurall folke come thronging in,
>   (Their rudenesse then is thought no sinne)
> Thy noblest spouse affords them welcome grace
>   And the great *Heroes*, of her race,
> Sit mixt with losse of state, or reuerence.
>   Freedome doth with degree dispense.
> The iolly wassall walkes the often round. . . .

287

Jonson is doing here what he claimed to be doing for Mary Sidney in the hundred and fifth poem in his *Epigrammes*:

> Madame, had all antiquitie beene lost,
>   All historie seal'd vp, and fables crost;
> That we had left vs, nor by time, nor place,
>   Least mention of a *Nymph*, a *Muse*, a *Grace*,
> But euen their names were to be made a-new,
>   Who could not but create them all, from you?
> He, that but saw you weare the wheaten hat
>   Would call you more then CERES, if not that:
> And, drest in shepheards tyre, who would not say:
>   You were the bright OENONE, FLORA, or *May*?

Does not this, together with the reference in our poem to 'feasts that either shearers keepe', waft us irresistibly towards *The Winter's Tale*?

> These your vnvsual weeds to each part of you
> Do giue a life: no Shepherdesse, but *Flora*
> Peering in April's front. This your sheepe-shearing
> Is as a meeting of the petty Gods,
> And you the Queene on't.

This is followed by the enactment of a Whitsun festival, which in turn gives back to us moderns as no other method could the reality behind the classical words when Perdita distributes the flowers:

> O *Proserpina*,
> For the Flowres now, that (frighted) thou let'st fall
> From *Dysses* Waggon! Daffadils
> That come before the Swallow dares and take
> The windes of March with beauty: Violets dim,
> But sweeter then the lids of *Iunos* eyes
> Or *Cytherea's* breath: pale Prime-roses,
> That dye vnmarried ere they can behold
> Bright Phoebus in his strength . . .

Surely we may say that Shakespeare is here doing for Ovid what Jonson was doing for his classical models, and turning mythology into reality? Here is Shakespeare's raw material in Golding's translation:

> While in this garden *Proserpine* was taking her pastime,
> In gathering eyther Violets blew, or Lillies white as Lime,
> Dis spied her: loude hir: caught her vp . . .
> The Ladie with a wailing voyce afright did often call . . .
> And as she from the vpper part hir garment would haue rent,
> By chance she let hir lap slip downe, and out her flowers went.

This poem will also support the contention that Jonson's Christianity is the bridge between two worlds. The simplicity and pathos of

God wisheth, none should wracke on a strange shelfe

look back to the Humanists with their love of aphorism and proverb,
but the lightness and economy of the whole passage raise Jonson
into a timeless centrality:

> God wisheth, none should wracke on a strange shelfe:
>   To him, man's dearer then t'himselfe,
> And, howsoeuer we may thinke things sweet,
>   He alwayes giues what he knowes meet;
> Which who can vse is happy. Such be thou:
>   Thy morning's, and thy euening's vow
> Be thankes to him, and earnest prayer, to finde
>   A body sound, with sounder minde . . .

Our sense that this is firmly central is not shaken by comparison with
Jonson's great Christian namesake in the eighteenth century (where
both are making a Christian comment on Juvenal):

> Still raise for good the supplicating voice,
> But leave to heav'n the measure and the choice,
> Safe in his pow'r, whose eyes discern afar
> The secret ambush of a specious pray'r.
> Implore his aid, in his decisions rest,
> Secure whate'er he gives, he gives the best.
> Yet when the sense of sacred presence fires,
> And strong devotion to the skies aspires,
> Pour forth thy fervours for a healthful mind,
> Obedient passions, and a will resign'd. . . .

Thus Jonson provides the key to and the measure for understanding the central activity of those capable of 'making it new' in the
early years of the sixteenth century. To judge the Humanists we
needed an answer to the question: what is the proper use of the
Classics, proper, that is, for the profit of English life and literature?
Jonson, I believe, and no other Englishman before him, gives us the
answer. The Classics are properly used when they enable an Englishman to become fully aware, that is, in his own idiom, of the aspirations to conceive life in ideal terms which are found in all attempts
to make life civilised. This answer enables us to distinguish the mere
Humanist, who, as it were, has the Classics in his head, from the
true Humanist who has *translated* the Classics into the only form
in which they can still live.

INDEX

Alamanni, Luigi, *Opere Toscane*, 203, 207, 211, 222, 223, 224

Allen, J. W., *A History of Political Thought in the Sixteenth Century*, 49, 111

Allen, P. S., *The Age of Erasmus*, 30 *Opus Epistolarum Des. Erasmi Roterodami*, 47, 128

Ames, Russell, *Citizen Thomas More and His Utopia*, 48

Andrew of St. Victor, 262

Apuleius, Lucius, *Apologia* tr. H. E. Butler, 269–70

Aretino, Pietro, *I Sette Salmi*, 203, 206, 208, 209, 212, 213, 215

Arnold, Matthew, *The Study of Poetry*, 5, 6, 9, 12, 14, 32, 261

Askew, Anne, 244

Atkins, J. W. H., *English Literary Criticism: The Renascence*, 66

Bale, John, *The lattre examinacion of Anne Askewe*, 244

Bannatyne Manuscript, 52

Bateson, F. W., 4–5, 19

Belles-lettres, cult of Style in, 28, 33–5, 39, 49

Bennett, H. S., *Chaucer and the Fifteenth Century*, 14–15

Berdan, J. M., *Early Tudor Poetry*, 10

Boccaccio, G., *Decamerone*, 173

Boleyn, Ann, 166, 172, 178, 182, 189, 198, 232

Bradner, Leicester, *The Latin Epigrams of Thomas More*, 44, 50–1

Brampton, Thomas, 208

Brian, Francis, Sir, 203–4, 231, 232, 234

Brinklow, Henry, *Complaynt of Roderyck Mors*, 113–16

Burckhardt, Jacob, *The Civilization of the Renaissance in Italy*, 20

Burnet, Gilbert, *Utopia*, 132–3

Campensis, Johannes, *Enchiridion Psalmorum*, 206–7, 209, 212, 241, 242, 243, 245, 246

Catholic Reform, 87, 101

Caxton, William, *Golden Legend*, 208, 209

Ceremony, 135–40

Chaloner, Thomas, *The Praise of Folie*, 84

Chambers, R. W., *Thomas More*, 37, 38, 39, 59, 72, 73–4, 96, 103, 104, 106, 123, 124, 126, 127, 128, 139

Charles d'Orléans, 164–5

Chaucer, G., amateur poets borrowed from, 165, 167

combines levity with seriousness, 75

courtly love in, 157–8, 159, 160, 163

Douglas borrows from, 249, 251

grant translateur, 23–4

Humanists' cult of, 228

Leland thought Surrey as good as, 236

nature, insight into, 15

observaunce of May, 165, 166

Petrarch translated, 194–5

popular material reworked, 161

simple and direct speech, 177

superiority over contemporaries, 12

Surrey linked to 'popular' poetry through, 239

Surrey prefers Wyatt to, 181

transcends mere literature, 16

Wyatt borrows from, 165, 166, 198, 213, 224

Wyatt saw Horace through, 201, 229, 230

Wyatt differs from, 233, 234

290